THE CAMPAIGN IN BOHEMIA
1866

SPECIAL CAMPAIGN SERIES. No. 6

THE CAMPAIGN IN BOHEMIA
1866

By
LT.-COL. G. J. R. GLÜNICKE

WITH MAPS AND PLANS

The Naval & Military Press Ltd

Published by

The Naval & Military Press Ltd
Unit 5 Riverside, Brambleside
Bellbrook Industrial Estate
Uckfield, East Sussex
TN22 1QQ England

Tel: +44 (0)1825 749494

www.naval-military-press.com
www.nmarchive.com

Cover illustration:
Cavalry engagement at the Battle of Königgrätz (Alexander von Bensa, 1866)

In reprinting in facsimile from the original, any imperfections are inevitably reproduced and the quality may fall short of modern type and cartographic standards.

Print and page size has been increased over the original publications to accommodate the oversized maps.

PREFACE

ALTHOUGH the war which is the subject of this volume had the most far-reaching consequences in the re-establishment of the German empire and the altered equilibrium of the European powers, it seems never to have attracted great attention in England; indeed, the author has been surprised to find, in military circles as well as in general society, how little the history of this war is known. And yet within a few years after its conclusion many books and pamphlets were written in Austria, Prussia and France, sharply criticising or eagerly defending the strategy and tactics of that memorable four weeks' campaign.

The narrative is based on the histories of the war written by the Prussian and the Austrian general staffs, and the plans of the battlefields are reproductions of those drawn by Prussian officers detailed for their survey during the time of the armistice and the simultaneous occupation of Bohemia that preceded the conclusion of peace. A map of Germany showing her subdivisions before the war has been added. This will appeal to students more readily and more effectively than an ordinary chapter on the geography of the country.

The author hopes that this historical essay will be found capable of interesting as well as instructing those whom he has had the privilege of reckoning among his pupils, and that it will also be found useful by those students of military history who have so far looked in vain for an account at once accurate and concise of the events of this particular campaign.

G. J. R. GLÜNICKE

Mostyn Hall,
May, 1907.

WORKS CONSULTED :

Der Feldzug von 1866 *in Deutschland.* Redigirt von der Kriegsgeschichtlichen Abterlung des Grossen Generalstabs.

Österreichs Kämpfe im Jahre 1866. Nach Feldacten bearbeitet durch das K.K. Generalstabs-Bureau für Kriegsgeschichte.

CONTENTS

CHAP.		PAGE
I	THE CAUSES OF THE WAR	1
II	THE OPPOSING POWERS	17
III	MOBILISATION AND INITIAL MOVEMENTS	35
IV	COMMENTS ON THE PRUSSIAN PLAN OF CAMPAIGN	57
V	INVASION OF BOHEMIA	75
VI	EVENTS ON JUNE 28 AND 29	99
VII	AUSTRIAN RETREAT	125
VIII	THE BATTLE OF KÖNIGGRÄTZ	149
IX	THE RETREAT AND PURSUIT	173
X	THE END—THE COMBAT OF BLUMENAU	199
	APPENDIX I	209
	,, II	211
	,, III	217
	,, IV	218

LIST OF MAPS AND PLANS

                                                         FACES PAGE

I. SKETCH OF THE PROJECTED MARCH OF THE 2ND PRUSSIAN ARMY 70

II. SKETCH OF THE POSITIONS OF THE UNITS OF THE 1ST PRUSSIAN ARMY ON THE 24TH AND 25TH OF JUNE 78

III. SKETCH OF THE POSITIONS OF THE OPPOSITE FORCES ON THE EVENING OF THE 26TH OF JUNE . . 84

IV. MAP OF GERMANY IN 1866

V. MAP OF THEATRE OF OPERATIONS

VI. PLAN OF PODOL-MÜNCHENGRÄTZ

VII. PLAN OF TRANTENAU AND SOOR

VIII. PLAN OF NACHOD, SKALITZ AND SCHWEINSCHÄDEL

IX. PLAN OF PODKOST

X. PLAN OF GITSCHIN

XI. PLAN OF KÖNIGINHOF

XII. POSITION OF FORCES ON THE EVENING OF THE 2ND OF JULY

XIII. PLAN OF KÖNIGGRÄTZ

XIV. PLAN OF BLUMENAU

In pocket at end of the book.

THE CAUSES OF THE WAR

CHAPTER I

The Causes of the War

For any student of Military History who is not satisfied with merely following the events of the great war of 1866 and learning the lessons conveyed by the first battles fought under new conditions of fire tactics, but who also wishes to glean and understand the interesting circumstances which brought about that momentous struggle, it is necessary to submit with patience to the perusal of a concise narrative of the political events which took place in the Germanic body after 1848.

In that year, ever memorable on account of the wave of revolution which swept through Europe and made even the time-honoured throne of the Hapsburgs shake in its very foundations, the fervent wishes of thousands of enlightened German patriots were raised in hopeful expectation of a better and worthier political existence than that afforded by the rotten conditions of the old "Bund," which after the wars against Napoleon had been patched up again in its obsolete and anti-national form by princes who disregarded, when smiled on by victory, the promises of constitutional institutions which they had proffered to their subjects in the hour of deep distress and slavish misery under the foreign yoke. The clamour of the whole nation for a political renovation rang out so loud and unmistakable that the governments were obliged to allow the election of the first

May, 1848 National Assembly which met at Frankfurt-on-the-Main, and was composed of delegates from all states and provinces of Germany. This assembly was much divided between monarchical and republican

May, 1849 principles, but after long labours it produced the completed proposal of a German constitution based on the following institutions. There was to be a "Reichstag" consisting of two bodies: (1) a "Staatenhaus," composed of members nominated in equal numbers by the governments and by the people's representatives of the various states; (2) a "Volkshaus," composed of deputies elected by the whole nation: a monarchical imperial power was to be invested with the prerogative of a merely suspensive veto.

During the debates on these subjects two parties gradually formed themselves: the Great-Germanics (Pan-Germans), who wanted to retain in the German empire the German provinces of Austria, and the Little-Germanics, who wanted to exclude Austria from the new empire, and wished for a closer amalgamation under the hegemony of Prussia, which, in 1813, had certainly led the van in the great national rising against Napoleon's dictatorship and had made the greatest sacrifices in the battles which drove the foreign legions from the German soil.

April, 1849 In April 1849 a deputation of the National Assembly offered to King Frederick William IV. of Prussia the dignity of *Emperor of the Germans*, but he refused it on the ground that he could only accept the imperial dignity with the consent of all the German governments, and at the personal request of all the princes of the Bund. A number of deputies were recalled by their governments after this demonstration and the passing of the draft of the new German constitution, or seceded voluntarily from the Frankfurt National Assembly, and a so-called Rump Parliament, formed at Darmstadt by democratic members only, was dissolved.

February, 1850

In February 1850 the King of Prussia and the two Prussian houses of deputies took the oath on a revised constitution, and the Prussian government now endeavoured to create a new German confederation with the exclusion of Austria : this object was actively supported by a party in favour of a hereditary imperial throne. A so-called "Three Kings' League" was formed between Prussia, Hanover and Saxony, and was at once joined by the princes of most of the small German states; but it was soon practically dissolved again by the secession of Hanover and Saxony, who feared the grasping imperious supremacy of Prussia. Nevertheless, a parliament was opened at Erfurt, and

April, 1850

within a month completed the task of producing the constitution for a new German League.

Austria had in the meantime been endangered in her very existence by the rebellions in Vienna and Prague, and still more so (chiefly) by the nearly successful struggle of the Hungarians for national independence, and by the rising of her North Italian provinces; but when her government had at length been relieved from its dangerous position—mainly by the armed assistance of Russia—it had at once protested against the attempt of the King of Prussia to establish any new form of union in Germany : it declared that the resolutions of the Erfurt Parliament were invalid, that the old relations of all the German states amongst each other under the ascendency of Austria remained in full strength, and that at the most it would consent to some modifications of the old constitutions. Accordingly, it invited all the German governments to a congress at Frankfurt to enter upon discussions on such points, but, in reply, Prussia denied the existence of the old Federal Constitution, and the princes of the numerous petty states which had formed the new League assembled at Berlin. Although at this " Congress of Princes " the Elector of Hesse-Kassel declared his withdrawal from the League, the other princes accepted the Prussian proposal of a permanent " Princes' Conference."

May, 1850

Austria opposed and counteracted these aspirations of Prussia by the reopening of the Frankfurt Bundestag on September 2 : the controversy between the old and a new Germany was to be decided by force of will or by force of arms, the struggle was to be between Austria and Prussia, and the " man of blood and iron " who had then already set his mind on the solution of that question, was soon to appear on the political arena of Germany.

In consequence of a rising of the people of Hesse-Kassel in defence of their constitution against their prince, the Elector, the latter left his country and appealed for help to the Bundestag, which granted armed assistance, and appointed the Austrian General

Haynau, as military dictator of the principality. Prussia protested, and nearly all the Hessian officers resigned their commissions. In consequence there was a rupture between Prussia and Austria, and the Emperor Nicholas of Russia was appealed to by both sides : he was closely related to the King of Prussia, but, being intent on continuing to play the part of protector of Austria, whose monarchical constitution he had saved by the defeat of the Hungarian national armies, he decided in favour of the claims of the reactionary Austrian Government, who also obtained the support of the Kings of Bavaria and Würtemberg. The Bundestag now decided upon military proceedings against Hesse, i.e. to suppress the popular rebellion by force of arms, and ordered Austrian and Bavarian troops to enter the principality for that purpose. The Prussian Government now also sent troops into Hesse, and seemed, at the time, determined to oppose the execution of the mandate of the Bundestag : it remained for the King to decide between armed resistance to Austria and the humiliation of the complete abandonment of Prussia's claim to leadership in any German union. For some time conflicting influences made the King hesitate, but his army was not then in a condition to fight with any prospect of success against the Austrian forces, which were returning victorious from the fighting in Italy, and he was also intimidated by the decided position taken up by the Czar in favour of Austria. In consequence he had to consent to the disastrous and humiliating *Convention of Olmütz*,[1] in which he submitted to Austria's

October, 1850

November, 1850

[1] The Prussian envoy Count Brandenburg felt the National dis-

categorical demands for the dissolution of the Prussian League, the recognition of the Federal Diet (the old Bund) of 1815 as still existing, and the evacuation of Hesse by the Prussian troops; he also had to accept the settlement of affairs in Hesse and in Schleswig-Holstein by the Federal Diet. The Austrian Prime Minister had even desired to obtain, in addition, the concession that the entire Austrian empire should form part of the German Federation, but this proposal of a Central European power of seventy millions of inhabitants controlled by the Cabinet of Vienna did not suit the views of foreign powers: England protested that such an amalgamation of forces would upset the balance of power in Europe, and France expressed the same opinion in threatening language, so that the project had to be dropped.

The sacrifice of her political dignity and importance to which Prussia had thus been forced by Austria was bitterly resented by the educated classes of the great Frederick's proud nation, and was felt, with great disappointment and deep humiliation, by all true German patriots as the deathblow to their hopes and aspirations. In Prussia this unfortunate event was followed by the introduction of a reactionary system of government marked by subservience and hypocrisy, by petty persecution and mean oppression; her best, most intellectual and enlightened citizens suffered under a hateful police régime,[1] their highest and noblest political aims were

grace so keenly that he committed suicide after having presented his official report.

[1] The author's mathematical professor at school had undergone twelve years imprisonment in a fortress because as student he had indulged in expressing too liberal ideas in speeches and in drafts of pamphlets seized by the police.

the objects of suspicion and vague apprehension to the *sbirri* of a degraded government: no more could be hoped for Prussia's or Germany's liberty under existing circumstances, all hope had to be deferred to a future period.

January 2, 1861

King Frederick William IV. died and was succeeded by his brother *William*, the Prince Regent, who, in 1850, had been strongly opposed to Prussia's submission to the Convention of Olmütz, and who had the firm conviction that his country was entitled to hold a higher place in Germany and in Europe than she had enjoyed in his brother's reign. He was certainly a firm believer in the divine right of kings, but did not object to a certain amount of liberalism, and when, as Regent, he dismissed his brother's narrow-minded, reactionary, Austrophobe ministry, he raised hopes anew which had been given up in 1850. But soon there arose a conflict between him, when King, and his parliament on account of heavy extra grants of money demanded for the reorganisation of the army, the reason for which was not evident to the representatives of the people, and which met with very strong opposition. In his difficult position the King, wishing to strengthen himself, appointed as Foreign Minister and President of the Cabinet *Otto von Bismarck*, who had been a member of the United Prussian Parliament in 1848, and from 1851 Prussia's representative at the Frankfurt Bundestag, where, in constant contact with his overbearing Austrian colleague, he had formed the conclusion that nothing but the military overthrow of Austria could give to Germany any tolerable system of national government, or secure to Prussia even her legitimate share of influence in the concert of the great powers. In 1858 he had been sent as Ambassador to St. Petersburg, where he managed to establish those friendly relations between Russia and Prussia which in later years were so eminently useful, so indispensable to his policy; and in May, 1862, he had occupied the same post at the French Court, when he had his first opportunity of forming his opinion of Napoleon as a politician. As Prime Minister he met the refusal of the Prussian Lower House to pass the military budget by a dissolution, and, aided by the War Minister, General von Roon, influenced the King in cynical disregard of all constitutional rights to rule without parliament, being determined to carry out, against and in spite of all opposition,

August, 1863

his plans, which could not even be hinted at to the people without the chance of raising Austria's suspicions. When a congress of German princes was assembled at Frankfurt by the Emperor Francis Joseph with the object of remodelling the constitution of the Federation, King William was induced by Bismarck to refuse the most pressing and flattering invitations to attend, so that the meeting dissolved without any result.

November 15, 1863

Frederick VIII, King of Denmark, died. In accordance with the London Protocol of 1852—not recognised by the German Bundestag—he was succeeded as king of the whole monarchy by Christian IX, who accepted the recently passed new Danish constitution, by which the duchy of Schleswig was incorporated as an integral part of the kingdom. This step produced great excitement all over Germany, where public opinion was strongly in favour of the complete separation of Schleswig-Holstein from Denmark to be independent duchies under Prince Frederick of Augustenburg, and to be attached to the German Federation as it then existed. But Bismarck intended that Schleswig and Holstein should be incorporated more or less directly with Prussia, and should be made the means of the destruction of the existing Federal system and of the expulsion of Austria from Germany. That another petty state should be added to the number of those which acted as Austria's vassals and instruments, would in his eyes have been detrimental to the interests of Prussia, and he determined to prevent this calamity in spite of all the short-sighted opposition of her unsuspecting people.

Austria and Prussia, as signatories of the London Protocol, were obliged to recognise the succession of Christian IX, but the public opinion of Germany demanded from the Federal Diet the at least temporary occupation of the two duchies. Under the influence of Prussia and Austria, the Diet determined on the occupation of Holstein only as belonging to Germany, for which purpose Hanoverian and Saxon troops were designated and despatched. Now Prussia and Austria demanded of Denmark to renounce the constitution of November as opposed to former stipulations (1852), by which she had promised to respect the ancient rights and claims of the two duchies, and when this demand met with refusal from the Danish Government, Prussian and Austrian troops entered Schleswig. The war thus commenced was naturally disastrous to Denmark, and was concluded by the peace of Vienna (October 30), by which she was obliged

February, 1864

to give up Schleswig and Holstein in favour of the Allies, and undertook to recognise the validity of the arrangements which would be made by them for the government of the two provinces.

After the Federal troops originally charged by the Bund with the ejection of the Danes had been recalled on the motion of Prussia and Austria, these two powers settled on a joint government for the two duchies. But whilst the question of the succession was being eagerly discussed at the Federal Diet, in diplomatic negotiations and in the press, the Austrian and Prussian joint-commissaries soon found themselves in regrettable conflict. In order to terminate this unsuitable arrangement and to avoid further recurrence of friction, the final decision on the status of the two duchies was adjourned *sine die*, and the *Convention of Gastein* was concluded between Prussia and Austria, by which it was stipulated that the two powers reserved for themselves the joint sovereignty over the two duchies; that Austria was to undertake provisionally the administration of Holstein, Prussia that of Schleswig; that Kiel was to be a Federal port under the command of Prussia, who was also to have a line of communication and of postal and telegraphic connection through Holstein. In execution of this treaty Prussia occupied Schleswig, whilst Holstein received an Austrian governor and garrison. This arrangement averted the immediate outbreak of war, peace was made possible for a few months longer, and thus Bismarck gained time to persuade his hesitating king to the adoption of extreme measures and to carry out some arrangement with Austria's enemy outside Germany.

August, 1865

Italy having been constituted as one kingdom a few years previously, mainly by the intervention and assistance of Napoleon, was longing for the possession of the province of Venetia which still remained in the hands of Austria, and the prospect of attaining that coveted object might well tempt Italian statesmen into an alliance with Prussia. But Bismarck, knowing that they could not act without Napoleon's permission, paid a visit to this sovereign, who thought himself a master in the arts of policy, and induced him in private interviews—no doubt by verbal promises of an indemnification in the shape of territories on the French north-east frontier—to put no obstacle in Italy's way, if her statesmen should be willing to join Prussia. Napoleon evidently thought that Austria would prove a match for both powers allied, and that in case of an undecided struggle he would be able to act as mediator at the price of German territory west of the Rhine. After long negotiations a treaty of defensive and offensive alliance was concluded between Prussia and Italy. As soon as this act was notified by Napoleon to the Austrian Government, the latter offered to Italy the province of Venetia as price for her neutrality, hoping to compensate themselves by taking Silesia from Prussia. The offer was declined.

April 8, 1866

In the meantime Austria had not ceased to advocate the recognition of the Prince of Augustenburg as Duke of Schleswig-Holstein and his reception as a sovereign within the German Federation, but Prussia had stipulated her conditions, if this were to happen, as follows: The military forces of the two duchies would form an integral part of the Prussian army and navy, the administration of the post and telegraph was to be under the Prussian ministerial department, and a few important military posts on the northern frontier were to be handed over to Prussia for protection against Danish aggression. The Austrian Government had permitted the inhabitants of Holstein to agitate in favour of the pretender, and at public meetings a demand was made for the convocation of the provincial estates. Bismarck thereupon had taxed Austria with abetting revolution and had demanded explanations, which were refused by the Emperor, and on March 16 the Austrian Government announced that they should refer the affairs of Schleswig-Holstein to the Federal Diet. As this step was a clear breach of the Convention of Gastein, King William was greatly offended by it, and now fell in more willingly with the warlike policy of his minister, although the party at Court in favour of peace was still very strong. In fact, public opinion in Germany generally and even in Prussia was greatly incensed against Bismarck, who was denounced as the criminal instigator of fratricidal war of Germans against Germans: the word *Bruderkrieg* was the chief topic of the man in the street. He had aroused general hatred and indignation, and even the King had become exceedingly unpopular, especially in his own capital, as the author can well remember; the parliament had fought obstinately against the still more obstinate minister, until it was prorogued once more. An attempt on his life was made in the streets of Berlin.

May 28   Warlike preparations had begun on both sides, when invitations to a Congress were issued jointly by France, England and Russia; but the intended mediation of the powers was frustrated by the demand of Austria, that no proposal should be discussed which might involve an increase of power or territory to one of the states invited. At the same time Austria proposed to the Federal Diet to proceed to the settlement of the affairs of Schleswig-Holstein, and convoked the Holstein Estates by the governor of that province. Bismarck now declared the treaty of Gastein to be broken, and ordered the Prussian troops in Schleswig to enter Holstein, whereupon General von Gablenz withdrew the Austrian force into Hanoverian territory. Diplomatic relations were broken off between Austria and Prussia on June 12, and Austria declared in the Federal Diet the step taken by Prussia as a breach of the internal peace of the Federation; she then demanded and obtained by a large majority of votes the mobilisation of the entire army of the Federation, exclusive of the Prussian army corps. Thereupon the representative of Prussia declared that this act was equivalent to the dissolution of the Federal Union and left Frankfurt. On the following day Prussia demanded of Saxony, Hanover and Hesse-Kassel to withdraw from the decision of the Federal Diet, to keep their troops on the peace footing and to join a new League under the leadership of Prussia. As this demand was refused, Prussian troops marched into these territories and the war had begun.

June 14

THE OPPOSING POWERS

CHAPTER II

A. THE PRUSSIAN MILITARY SYSTEM

Its History AFTER the Prussian army and nation had been laid prostrate in 1806 by the defeats at Jena and Auerstädt, and after the ignominious treaty of Tilsit had been concluded, which reduced Prussia to comparative insignificance, General Scharnhorst proffered the idea to replace the hitherto professional army, which had stood quite outside the people and apart from it, by a national army; in fact, to create a nation in arms by making every citizen consider it not only his first duty, but his great privilege to give his personal service for the defence of his country and its institutions. In execution of this principle every citizen was declared liable to military service from his 17th to his 45th year of age, and this system has remained in force ever since. By virtue of this law every man pronounced physically fit had to serve for two years with the colours, whilst during the remaining years of his liability he passed through various classes of reserves. The actual term of service in the line and the reserves had originally been fixed at twenty years, but had by 1860 been reduced to twelve years; the yearly contingent of recruits, originally fixed at 40,000 from the number of troops which Prussia had been permitted to maintain by the treaty of Tilsit, had been adhered to, although the population had doubled under careful administration. This number had been chosen as representing ½ per cent. of the population in 1807, but at the same percentage the yearly contingent of recruits in 1860 should have been 80,000.

The King after his succession to the throne desired to obtain this higher establishment, but met with strong opposition. Of course, a system of general liability to military service should be worked in such a way that the industrial and commercial life and work of the nation are disturbed by its requirements in as small a degree as possible, but the military interests demand that all men be trained, whilst with the colours, so thoroughly that they can be employed again at any moment with the certainty of proving themselves efficient. In Germany two years are considered sufficient for such training, and this period has recently been adopted again by the Government instead of the term of three years favoured by King William, who thought this length of time indispensable and insisted on its introduction in spite of the strong opposition of his parliament, and even against the advice of his war minister, who did not consider the difference worth the conflict which it caused between the crown and the people : the yearly contingent of recruits was raised from 40,000 to 63,000.

Personnel As stated above, every male subject of the state was legally liable to service if pronounced physically fit, but there were various cases of exemption. Those young men who had attained a certain educational standard, and who were able and willing to clothe, equip and maintain themselves during their service with the colours, were only liable to one year's service, were called volunteers, and could choose the branch of the service and the regiment in which they liked to serve. If smart in drill and all other matters military, they were appointed and admitted as officers of the reserve of the regiment after duly passing an examination in military subjects, serving a term of probation during manœuvres and being elected by the officers of the regiment. This part of the system provided and still provides a very strong and efficient reserve of officers, at present well above 50,000.

The officers of the standing army are obtained from the pupils of the higher cadet schools, which give a partly literary, partly military education—free to sons of officers—and by volunteers of a high educational standard and certain means, who, after a year's practical training in the unit, are sent as under officers for another year to one of the *Fähnrichsschulen*, the course at which is similar to that at our Royal Military College. As the number of officers required in the large standing army is exceedingly great and the pay of the lower grades is extremely small, the supply is never excessive, so that entrance does not depend on a competitive examination, but the colonel of any regiment has it in his power to refuse admission to a would-be candidate for a commission : they are called *avantageurs* or officer aspirants.

Organisation   The army was essentially territorial, as the men of each army corps were recruited from only one province, whilst the Guards were recruited from the whole kingdom ; there were thus eight army corps besides the Corps of Guards, each consisting of two divisions of infantry and additional corps troops. Each division consisted of two brigades of two regiments each, and the regiment was divided into three battalions of four companies; to each division was attached one regiment of cavalry and one *Abteilung* of field artillery, four batteries of six guns each. The corps troops belonging to each army corps consisted of one Abteilung of horse artillery of three batteries and one Abteilung of field artillery of four batteries (thus there were fifteen batteries or ninety guns in each army corps), one battalion of jäger (sharpshooters—men drawn mostly from the Royal Forest service), one battalion of pioneers (engineers), one battalion of train (Army Service Corps), besides a cavalry brigade of three regiments. Each army corps also had nine ammunition columns, one pontoon column and three or four field hospitals.

The strength of an infantry battalion on the peace footing was about 600 men, which on mobilisation was raised to 1,000 by the addition of the youngest class of reserves; the other classes were formed into reserve battalions, the cadres of which were maintained in peace time in the regimental reserve (Landwehr) districts, where all reservists, including reserve officers, of any regiment residing in the locality had to report themselves once a year on a certain date.

Armament When mobilised the whole army totalled 660,000 men with 1,000 guns. The infantry were armed with the new needle-gun, the first breechloader used in Europe, introduced since 1858 and tried in action for the first time in 1864 in the Danish war. It had an efficient range of only 600 to 700 paces, and in ballistical properties it was inferior to the Austrian rifle ; in consequence it had attracted so little notice, and so many doubts were entertained as to its value, that within the eight years since its introduction in the Prussian army no other great power had taken into consideration the advisability of providing its battalions with a rifle of the same description. The new weapon was certainly still very primitive, for firing at more than 300 paces was considered a waste of ammunition, and only picked men were allowed to use a greater range at special objects. But in spite of these undoubted initial shortcomings the needle-gun afforded the immense advantage that it could be loaded not only rapidly, but also when the man was prostrate, and this superiority showed itself in a very striking manner in the disproportion of the losses of the opposing forces on the field of battle. The possibility of its misuse in the shape of extravagance in the expenditure of ammunition and consequent bad shooting was counteracted by a severe fire discipline and the careful individual training of the men, which was testified to by the fact that only two millions of cartridges were used in this campaign by the Prussian infantry : a comparison of this number with the lists of Austrian casualties shows that the figure is equivalent to an expenditure of fifty bullets for every man put *hors de combat*. This is a very low average when compared with the number of bullets used by the British army in the Crimean War, viz. 740 for each casualty.

The Prussian artillery were armed with 4-pounder, 6-pounder and 12-pounder bronze guns, of which 40 per cent. only were rifled ; their effective range did not exceed 1,500 paces, and on the whole they did not do good service; they were also badly handled tactically, being generally kept behind the infantry columns, so that they often came into action too late.

B. THE AUSTRIAN MILITARY SYSTEM

Conscription The system by which the Austrian army was recruited, maintained and completed to war strength was that of conscription on the French model, which implied that every individual unwilling to render military service had the liberty of purchasing a substitute from amongst those who had drawn a lucky number at the recruit lottery. The total length of service amounted to eight years in the line and two years in the reserve, but as a rule men were kept only three years with the colours.

Military history has shown that this system, besides providing only a small number of reserves to fill up the cadres on mobilization, produces a lower intellectual and moral standard in the mass of an army than is provided by the system of universal service such as had obtained in the Prussian monarchy, and the truth of this conclusion has been acknowledged by the fact that all the continental countries of Europe and Japan have since adopted the Prussian system. But there was another factor which came into consideration, the great difference between the homogeneous nature of the Prussian units and the composite character of the Austrian forces; for the latter consisted of men of various nationalities not at all friendly towards each other, some of which had in fact not many years before fought obstinately against their own war-lord. In consequence of the political differences and quarrels between the component parts of the vast empire, Italian regiments were garrisoned in Bohemia, Hungarian regiments in Venice, so that the calling in and the joining of the reserves presented great difficulties in the case of mobilisation, which was thereby much complicated and delayed. Again, the war organisation of the Austrian army was not necessarily the same as the peace distribution and composition of the forces, but the *ordre de bataille* was fortuitous and arbitrary. The consequence was that at the outbreak of war some large units might find themselves under generals who did not know their subordinate commanding officers nor the standard of training they had attained in their regiments : this fact would naturally be felt as a serious defect and drawback in the mechanism of the conduct of operations.

Strength and Organisation of Forces
In absolute and still more in relative strength the Austrian military forces were inferior to those of Prussia, for with a population of 35 millions the total strength of the army could only be raised to 600,000 men, whilst 660,000 was the strength of the Prussian forces produced by a population of only 18 millions. In fact, the military organisation of Austria might have sufficed for ordinary cases of war, especially when the armed assistance of all the other German states could be secured, and therefore her statesmen ought to have prevented political situations such as placed her then in opposition to Prussia allied with Italy, which latter power, though still in its infancy, could place in the field more than 300,000 men.

On the peace establishment the army was organised in seven army corps, each consisting of four brigades of two regiments of infantry and one jäger battalion, each with one battery of eight guns attached to it. The infantry regiment had four battalions, but only three of them were included in the brigades, whilst the fourth battalions were used for garrison purposes; thus each brigade in the field army had seven battalions, and an army corps had twenty-eight battalions and thirty-two guns to which were added the following corps troops: one cavalry regiment, six batteries called the reserve artillery, one company of engineers and one field ambulance. The order for mobilisation arranged the field army in ten army corps, of which seven were formed as northern army to act against Prussia, with a cavalry complement of four divisions of six regiments each.

Armament
The infantry were armed with the rifled muzzle-loader, model Lorenz, which had a longer range and a less elevated trajectory than the Prussian needle-gun: it fired an expansive bullet, model Podewils. But since the Italian campaign in 1859, when the French infantry had been most successful in their attacks with the bayonet, the Austrian infantry had been trained and taught to rely entirely on this mode of fighting, and the Government, in its craze for economy, had only made a yearly allowance of twenty rounds per man for musketry training, so that the men could neither shoot straight nor the officers judge distances. If this had not been the case, the natural tactics for the Austrians, with their greater range rifle and greater number of rifled guns—they had no smoothbore weapons—would have been to avoid close combat as much as possible, to engage the enemy's artillery at 2,000 paces, to make their infantry advance to about

600 paces from the enemy outside their effective range of fire, to overwhelm them with a steady, well-aimed fire from that distance, and thus to prepare the final attack. Instead of proceeding in this rational way, the Austrian infantry almost invariably tried the attack without previous preparation by fire : their generals perhaps were influenced by the opinion of Colonel Schönfeld who had been military attaché at the Prussian headquarters in the Danish war, and who had reported that a Prussian corps was such a rabble of reservists that they would not be able to resist the attack of an Austrian corps for twenty minutes.

Artillery fire at 2,000 paces against the Prussian artillery would have been most advantageous to them, for as the shells from their guns had not a flat trajectory, they were not well suited for use against infantry advancing from a greater distance. Their artillery nevertheless established a reputation for their fire efficiency, but this was really only due to the fact that they frequently had fixed objects for targets, such as woods and farms. They kept up fire very constantly, but did not inflict considerable losses, nor did they succeed in checking the forward movement of the Prussian lines.

Summary Such were the organisation, strength and some of the properties of the forces which were to oppose each other on battlefields where the main power of decision in the infantry combat was, for the first time, shifted from the columns to the skirmishers' lines, thus marking a most important tactical progress. For the new infantry fire by breach-loaders demanded very quick deployment of columns into skirmishing lines, and as this movement took a long time with battalion columns, the employment of company columns now became a case of necessity, and the company became the fighting unit: the company officer at last found his proper position as one of the strongest elements and props of the modern conduct of combat.

C. Military Condition of Austria's Allies

Composition of Forces The following German states had declared in favour of Austria: the kingdoms of Bavaria, Saxony, Hanover and Würtemberg, the grand-duchies of Baden and Hesse-Darmstadt, the duchy of Nassau and the electorate of Hesse-Kassel. The armed forces of all the southern states composed the VII and VIII Bundes Corps under the command of Prince Karl of Bavaria, and contained the following contingents:—

52,000 Bavarians, 16,250 Würtembergers—10,850 Badish, 9,400 Hessians (Darmstadt), 5,400 Nassovians: total 94,000.

The Saxon army, about 24,000 strong, was intended to join the Austrian army in Bohemia: they had always enjoyed a high reputation for efficiency. The army of Hanover, also of good quality, was 18,000 strong, and endeavoured to join the southern forces; the contingent of Hesse-Kassel 7,000 strong, joined the composite VIII Corps under Prince Alexander of Hesse.

Thus the total strength of the armed forces provided by Austria's allies was 143,000, but the fighting value of the majority of them was not equal to the numerical strength.

D. Possible Results of Hostilities.

That the war against Prussia was expected by the Austrian generals to be full of danger and difficulty was proved by the conduct of Archduke Albrecht, the son of the famous Archduke Charles, who defeated Napoleon at Aspern. He did not wish to have the chief command in Germany, but claimed that same position in Italy; Benedek was to make room for him there, and also to let him have his well experienced chief of the staff, the Archduke John. After a short resistance Benedik, vain and weak as he was, allowed himself to be persuaded by the Emperor to accept the more important command, but without insisting on having the full power of directive indispensable in such a position : it is true, it was hinted to him that probably all the existing differences would be settled by the campaign in Italy and thus actual fighting be avoided in the north. He also allowed General Krizmanic to be imposed upon him as his chief of the staff: this officer was in the confidence of Archduke Albrecht, who therefore had an interest in having him attached to Benedek. Krizmanic had been present at the battle of Solferino as sub-chief of the staff of the first army, and had shown himself so totally incompetent that any government in its proper senses would have been very careful not to have employed him again, but as favourite of the Archduke Albrecht he represented the small but powerful war party. Being a clever, cunning, astute Croatian, he had known how to get into favour with

His Imperial Highness by ostentatious adoration of the late Archduke Charles.

There were decided pessimistic feelings amongst the higher Austrian military authorities; they were well-founded and foreboding omens of the worst calamities: for man can only conquer when he has self-confidence and cheerful courage unclouded by doubt, such as was possessed by the triumvirate in Berlin, who enjoyed the unshaken confidence of their king in spite of all intrigues in the royal family and court circles.

E. Political Conditions in Europe.

It was very fortunate for Germany that in 1866 neither France nor Russia were ready to take action, the former through the difficulties created by the ill-fated Mexican expedition,[1] the latter through the after effects of the last Polish revolution in 1863; for if these two states, as in the seven years' war, had joined Austria, which her government might have attained by holding out to them the possiblity of acquiring respect-

---

[1] In October, 1861, England, France and Spain had joined to force the republican government of Mexico to fulfil its obligations towards subjects of the three nations. After the occupation of La Vera Cruz and resultless negotiations with the President Juarez, England and Spain withdrew from the operations; the French, after severe fighting, took Puebla in May, 1863, and entered Mexico. An assembly of notables then proclaimed a monarchy, and Maximilian, a brother of the Austrian Emperor, accepted the imperial crown offered to him by Napoleon. In spite of the continued presence of French troops, the republican forces rendered successful resistance to the establishment of the imperial authority, and when, after the conclusion of the war of secession, 1865, the Government of the United States demanded the withdrawal of the French forces, the fate of the new monarchy was sealed. Maximilian refused to leave together with them, was besieged at Queretaro, taken prisoner, put before a court-martial and shot (June, 1867).

ively the frontier of the Rhine and the boundary line of the lower Vistula, Prussia might have been crushed and almost annihilated, as had been the wish and the object of the Cabinet of Vienna in 1850. If Austria had then annexed Silesia, if Saxony had regained the territory given to her by Napoleon in 1807 and restored to Prussia by the Congress of Vienna in 1815, if Hanover had been extended to the Rhine by the acquisition of Westphalia, the remnants of Prussia would once again—as in 1807—have become the focus of resistance to reactionary government, and the supremacy of Austria would hardly have lasted; for the princes and the people of the German states objected even more strongly to the latter than to the hegemony of Prussia. The final result of these combinations would probably have been the resuscitation of Prussia with the help of Russia, as in 1813, which then would have meant to Austria the loss of Silesia, Galicia and Hungary, and would have opened for Russia the door to the Balkan peninsula and Constantinople, even if Prussia had obtained complete possession of a badly clipped Germany. The destruction of Austria would have been the natural consequence of her obstinate desire for aggrandisement, for she cannot protect herself under normal conditions against Russia by her own forces, unaided by the power of Germany.

F. Prussia's Aims, Difficulties and Possibilities

The object of Prussia's policy was, as shown in the introduction, the acquisition of Holstein and Schleswig and the military hegemony in North Germany: proposals embodying these demands were made to Austria up to the last moment. This deliberate statement of a definite object marked a great progress in Prussian policy, for since the death of Frederick the Great clear aims had been wanting or they had been stupidly chosen, as in the period from 1786 to 1806, when the Prussian policy started without a definite plan and ended with a deplorable disaster. Likewise there was no independent policy between 1806 and 1850 : it was dictated alternately from Vienna or St. Petersburg, and when it was devised in Berlin up to 1862, it was pusillanimous, therefore hurtful rather than resultless. This lack of independent, energetic action during fifty years had reduced Prussia to a condition of universal low estimation, and it was found very difficult to conduct a strong foreign policy by the minister who wanted to carry out a cool and practical system of policy without dynastic sentimentality and submission to court influences. Intrigues and rivalries were so powerful that when the war broke out in spite of their machinations and counter efforts, even the most necessary matters had not been considered, the most indispensable measures had not been prepared. Thus the court had hoped up to the last moment that Hesse and Hanover would concede the demanded neutrality of their contingents, and in consequence the Government had omitted to provide for the eventually necessary administration of these territories and to form a decision about the fate of their armed forces. It would also seem that it would have been correct and natural to have exploited the political conditions of the South German states : Bavaria wanted to take the leadership amongst them, but this claim was refuted by the others. These states, formed by Napoleon in 1806 as members of the Rheinbund, and exploited by him with an iron hand till 1813 to the advantage of France, were quite unfitted for independence, and thus had to fall under Austrian, French or Prussian supremacy: they were the certain prey of the power which acted rapidly, boldly, powerfully. Under these circumstances it would appear to have been advisable to have occupied Frankfurt at once, to have forced Baden [1] and Hesse-Darmstadt to hand over their contingents, and to have invaded Würtemberg, with the alternative proposal of alliance or absorption. The road to Munich would then have been open, and Austria being then powerless to help Bavaria, a Prussian army corps with South German auxiliaries could have been on the Bavarian frontier of Austria on the Danube by July 22, the day on which the armistice was concluded. Such energetic procedure would have made any intervention on the part of France quite impossible and illusory, but it would have been useless to propose such projects to King William, who, imbibed with legitimistic ideas, would have considered such a *modus agendi* as much too forcible and unjustifiable. We do not meet in the actual political combinations the boldness of ideas and resolution, the rapidity of execution and the formidable intensity of action of a Frederick the Great: everything remained w thin the limits of mediocrity. But then one must make the allowance that Prussia was only awaking from a long sleep of peace and from her political lethargy, which had been the result of exhaustion caused by the French occupation and

[1] The Government of Baden was not disinclined to act on the side of Prussia, and its grand-duke was the son-in-law of King William.

extortions from 1806 to 1813. The state recovered during that period of political stagnation from the fearful material misery produced by the Napoleonic wars, the population gradually regained something of the former comfort and prosperity, and thus became once again more active and more hopeful, and enterprising enough to throw off the dangerous system of passive endurance and inactive indifference.

MOBILISATION AND INITIAL MOVEMENTS

CHAPTER III

A. Mobilisation and Concentration of Forces

In Prussia THE first order for mobilisation had been given in the beginning of May, and the army corps affected by it were ordered to assemble as follows: the 6th Corps at Neisse, the 5th at Schweidnitz, the 3rd and 4th between Cottbus and Torgau, but the 8th Division (half of the 4th Corps) was to remain at first at Erfurt. The 8th Corps was to concentrate at Koblenz with the exception of the 32nd Brigade, which was to assemble at Wetzlar. The Guards Corps was to assemble in Berlin, and of the 7th Corps the 13th Division at Minden and Bielefeld, the 14th at Münster and Hamm.

On the whole such concentrations of large bodies of troops are not advisable before the beginning of their transport towards the frontier, but in this case the nature of the strategical deployment (*der Aufmarsch*) could not be fixed upon until it was known whether Bavaria and the other German states would be hostile or neutral.

When in the course of the month of May it became probable that Prussia would practically stand by herself, her Government knew that they would have to encounter the following forces: 36,000 men in North Germany,

100,000 men in South Germany, 260,000 Austrians and Saxons.

The main task was to oppose the latter with a force sufficiently strong to ensure decisive victory over them, as such an event would easily paralyse the badly prepared and organised South German contingents, and as the seven army corps, including the Guards, in the eastern part of the monarchy did not seem sufficient for that purpose, the 7th and 8th Army Corps also were ordered to take part in the campaign against the Austrians, with the exception of the 13th Division, which was to be the nucleus of a special army intended for the eventual defence of the Rhine-lands or for offensive movements against the contingents of the smaller states.

On the eastern theatre of operations it would have been desirable to have massed the whole army in one position which would equally well cover Berlin and Breslau, and the most suitable point for that object would have been the neighbourhood of Görlitz. But the concentration of a quarter of a million of men at one point by means of only two or three lines of railway would have taken a few weeks, therefore nothing remained but to assemble two separate armies for the protection of Brandenburg and Silesia. It was evident that a concentrated Austrian army might fall with full force upon one of the two halves, but the geographical formation of the theatre of war could not be altered, nor the fact that an enemy in Bohemia stands between Silesia and Lusatia.

The territory of Saxony could not be used for the movement of troops before the declaration of war, so that the lines of railway available for this purpose practically ended at Zeitz, Halle, Herzberg, Görlitz, Schweidnitz, and Neisse; the troops had to be detrained at these places, which formed a curved line of a length of about 280 miles; whether the concentration of the separate corps in two armies would have to be done by marches along the frontier or by means of operations towards a common centre depended on the final decision with regard to the choice between the offensive and the defensive.

On May 14 General Moltke, head of the Prussian General Staff, reported to the King that on June 4th 270,000 men would be ready to march into Saxony and Bohemia; he advised to declare war on that day and to begin the invasion on the 5th: the King emphatically refused to do this. In consequence the troops, after detraining, had to be placed in cantonments near the terminus stations of the various lines along the frontier. This procedure was in a way a compromise between the military requirements and the reluctance of the King to begin the war.

On May 16 orders were issued to bring the 2nd Army Corps from Pomerania into cantonments at Herzberg, the Guards were to march into quarters between Baruth and Luckau; the 3rd and 4th Corps were still between Torgau and Luckau, and a special corps of cavalry was formed of the cavalry regiments of these four corps, which now were constituted as the 1st Army under the command of General Prince Frederick Charles.[1]

On May 24 orders were given that the 6th Army

---

[1] The so-called "red prince," father of H.R.H. the Duchess of Connaught.

Corps should occupy cantonments about Waldenburg, the 5th round Landshut, their corps cavalry in one division round Striegau : these troops were to be the 2nd or Silesian Army under the command of the Crown Prince of Prussia, who as Frederick III succeeded his father William as Emperor of Germany in 1888. For the protection of the frontier of Upper Silesia, the southeastern portion of the province, two small separate detachments were formed near Oderberg, one under General Knobelsdorf, the other under General Count Stolberg.

The 1st Army Corps, located in East Prussia, received orders to get ready for gradual transport to Görlitz, where it was to form a link between the 1st and the 2nd Army, and to be ultimately apportioned to the one or the other according to circumstances.

Previous orders given to the 8th Army Corps were now altered ; its two divisions, after assembling at Köln and Koblenz respectively, were to be transported by rail via Hanover to Halle, where they were to go into cantonments. The 14th Division of the 7th Corps was to be carried by rail to Zeitz, and to form, together with the two divisions of the 8th Corps, a third army, the Army of the Elbe, under General Herwarth von Bittenfeld.

The brigade Beyer of the 8th Corps, detached at Wetzlar, was reinforced till it became a strong division of eighteen battalions with some artillery and cavalry. The division Göben was at Minden, and the division Manteufel entered Holstein from Schleswig on June 7.

The division Beyer should have been ordered to march at once on the outbreak of hostilities for Frankfurt and

Hanau so as to isolate the Hessians. But the Court in Berlin entertained to the last, as before mentioned, the hope of inducing the King of Hanover and the Elector of Hesse-Kassel to conclude a treaty of neutrality, and the opinion prevailed that in such a case the divisions Goebel and Beyer were sufficiently strong to contain and neutralise the South German forces. But as the division Manteufel would, under any conditions, have been in a better position at Eisenach or Erfurt than in Holstein, it ought to have been sent and arrived there as early as June 10, which might have caused the Hanoverians to forego their attempt of breaking through to the south.

A reserve corps was formed at Berlin composed of twenty-four battalions of infantry, twenty-four squadrons and one reserve artillery regiment of eight batteries: they were intended to occupy the line of communication but were capable of employment in the field army.

During these moves the railway lines transported in twenty-one days, 197,000 men, 55,000 horses, and 5,300 vehicles, including guns, over distances varying from 140 to 420 miles without any accident or serious irregularity.

Between May 30 and June 8 the 2nd, 3rd and 4th Corps closed in to the left to get nearer to the 2nd Army, and during the same days the three divisions of the Army of the Elbe were brought to this river from Zeitz and Halle, and went into cantonments on both its banks, between the Mulde and the Elster. The last parts of the 1st Army Corps had arrived at Görlitz on June 6, and on the following day the corps started to march on Hirschberg. The original extent of the armies had now been shortened by nearly one half.

Concentration of Austrian Forces

In the beginning of June the bulk of the Austrian North Army was assembled in Moravia, where Field-Marshal[1] Benedek had his headquarters at Olmütz, whilst the I Army Corps only was in the north of Bohemia. There were four army corps on the direct line Vienna-Neisse, near Brünn and Zittau, the II Corps to the west of this line near Zwittau, the VI to the east of it at Prerau. These two corps, with the IV between them on the direct line, were probably meant to form the first line of the *ordre de bataille* for the advance into Silesia with the III, X, and VIII Corps as reserves, the latter as far south as Auspitz and Austerlitz; three large cavalry divisions were in cantonments between these groups: it would have been more appropriate to have had them pushed forward to Pardubitz and Hohenmauth in order to establish in that way a connection with the I Corps stationed on the river Iser, where it was waiting for the arrival of the Saxon Corps. Benedek had written to the Crown Prince of Saxony, who was in command of the latter, that he intended to commence his march to Josephstadt on about June 10, to effect a junction there with his own and the I Corps under General Count Clam Gallas, but at that date many units had not yet arrived, and the arrangements for transport and supplies were far from complete. Then again the Austrian War Office had informed the Bavarian Government that the North Army would by the end of June be concentrated in the north-east of Bohemia between the Elbe and the Iser, and had asked for the early assembly

---

[1] Feldzeugmeister is the Austrian title.

of the Bavarian troops and additional forces from the VIIIth Bundescorps (Würtemberg, Baden, etc.), in the neighbourhood of Baireuth-Schweinfurt, so as to be in a position ready to join the Austrians. But on June 18 Benedek was informed that the Bavarian Government had no intention of sending their troops into Bohemia, a decision which might have been foreseen; for it was at least unreasonable to expect that Bavaria and the other South German states would send their forces to swell the Austrian army, and thus leave their own provinces undefended and open to the unhindered incursion of the Prussian Western Army. The mere suggestion of such a step tends to show how the Austrian Government were used to treat the interests of the smaller German states.

The first reliable news about the disposition of the Austrian forces was received at Berlin on June 11, when it became known that the main force, viz. six army corps, was still in Moravia, whilst only one was in Bohemia: the Austrian military journal later on made the following statement on this point: "The army though completely assembled was not strong enough numerically for an aggressive advance, but the concentration at Olmütz had kept Prussia in uncertainty, and had thus obliged her to separate her forces." But as a matter of fact, all doubts about the possible movements of the Austrians vanished as soon as this news was received, for an invasion of Prussian territory could now only take place in Silesia.

It has just been stated that the hope of the Austrian War Office about the co-operation of the Bavarians had been disappointed by their refusal to come to Bohemia;

the Saxons also would have liked a junction with the Bavarians for the defence of their own small country, which now they had to give up without striking a blow for it, to go and fight as auxiliary troops in Bohemia, a lamentable position for a brave army fond and proud of their own country.

New Positions for Prussians Necessary As the only line of advance into Silesia possible for the Austrians now lay in the direction of Neisse, a position taken up behind the river of that name would defend the whole of Silesia, as they could not advance on Breslau by going round this position without giving up their communications. The position was good, as its left rested on the fortress Neisse, and if the Austrians tried to attack the right, they would have the fortress Glatz and the mountain chain on the frontier behind them. The Crown Prince Frederick, opposed as he was to the main strength of the Austrian army, fully appreciated his danger, and selected the position behind the Neisse, which he thought strong enough to enable him to oppose the force of an attack even by overwhelming numbers. He therefore asked for and received permission to occupy that position, but as his two army corps might be attacked by five or even six, his army was strengthened by the 1st Army Corps, which at Hirschberg and Warmbrunn had to watch the roads leading across the mountains from Friedland, Reichenbach and Trautenau. The Guards Corps was now also allotted to the 2nd Army and was to occupy the left flank of the new position. But at that time it was still in Berlin, and the 1st Reserve Army Corps was then only forming in the neighbourhood of that capital.

INITIAL MOVEMENTS

Thus the army was not yet by any means complete, and all its operative dispositions were only pointing to a purely defensive protection of their own country, certainly not to offensive operations.

We have noted already that about June 10 the Austrian North Army had arrived nearly complete in Moravia near Olmütz and Brünn, and might have been assembled—with but little altered arrangements—just as well in Bohemia for the offensive against the Prussian army, then still engaged, as we have seen, in moving to places of assembly and new positions. The Austrians then enjoyed a further advantage inasmuch as their forces were all close together, whereas the different component parts of the Prussian army could then scarcely support each other under the difficulties presented by the geographical features of the country. The Prussians therefore were not ready before the Austrians, but unfortunately the latter had assumed the certainty of being forestalled so strongly, that the opinion prevailed amongst their generals that their army could only be safely assembled in a fortified camp many marches distant from the frontier. This first assembly of the Austrian army was a mistake productive of the most serious consequences, which they could only have mended, if they had boldly crossed the frontier against the army of the Crown Prince, as soon as the details of its disposition became known to them.

New Positions Occupied In consequence of the resolution to have the position behind the Neisse occupied by the Silesian army, the following movements had to be made:—

The 6th Corps to Steinau via Reichenbach, Frankenstein and Ottmachau; the 5th Corps to Grottkau via Schweidnitz and Lauterbach; the 1st Corps to Münsterberg via Kupperberg, Schweidnitz and Nimptsch; the Cavalry Corps moved to Strehlen via Melkau. A detachment of the 1st Corps of six battalions, four batteries and two cavalry regiments was left at Waldenburg to watch the passes between Landshut and Charlottenbrunn. All these movements were completed by June 18, by which day the greatest part of the Guards also had arrived at Brieg, and all preparations were made for a rapid concentration, if it should suddenly become necessary.

The following movements were made in the 1st Army: the 3rd Corps marched into the district Löwenberg, Friedeberg; the 4th Corps to Lauban and Greiffenberg; the 2nd Corps took up quarters between Reichenbach, Görlitz and Seidenberg; the Cavalry Corps on both banks of the Bober about Löwenberg; the roads across the mountains via Löbau, Zittau, Friedland and Reichenberg were occupied, and a separate detachment was pushed forward to Warmbrunn. These moves also were finished by June 18.

The Army of the Elbe of course had not been able to move on account of Saxony blocking its nearer approach to Bohemia. Now, if the Saxon corps should retire into Bohemia to join the Austrian army, the Army of the Elbe could follow them, but if the I Austrian Corps, now near the Saxon frontier, should join the Saxon troops and together with them occupy one of the many naturally strong positions near Dresden, their united strength of about fifty battalions, with ten cavalry regiments and twenty-four batteries, would paralyse the

Army of the Elbe; therefore, to provide for this case, orders were given for the new reserve corps forming near Berlin to be moved towards Torgau without delay: this move would raise the strength of the Prussian forces on the Elbe to sixty-two battalions with nine cavalry regiments and forty-four batteries.

Thus the whole Prussian army was posted in three groups near Torgau, Görlitz and Neisse respectively, which places were 93 and 115 miles distant from each other. The forward march into Saxony therefore now became a necessity, not only from political causes, but also because it made possible the strategical deployment, that is in this case the co-operation of the 1st Army and the Army of the Elbe on the line Bautzen-Dresden in but few marches, by numerous and converging roads. After that junction had been effected, there were only two armies to be manœuvred, so that they could co-operate for the final decision, a task not easy but capable of accomplishment.

B. Movements in Hanover and Hesse-Kassel

It has been stated at the end of the first chapter that the war actually began with the march of Prussian troops into Hanover, Hesse-Cassel and Saxony on June 16, and it seems advisable to narrate in short outlines the minor preliminary events in the north-west of Germany, before beginning the detailed account of our main subject, the Campaign in Bohemia.

Occupation of Hanover — General Vogel von Falkenstein had been appointed to the command of the small Army of the West, which consisted of the divisions Beyer, Göben and Manteufel, with orders not only to occupy all places of importance in Hanover, but also to bring about the surrender or the destruction of the Hanoverian army.

The division Göben occupied the town of Hanover on June 17, after the Hanoverian army—12,800 men with 18 guns—had already withdrawn to Göttingen on its march towards the south to join the Bavarian troops who were expected to have advanced to Meiningen: they had destroyed the railway behind them. The division Manteufel left Holstein on the 16th, crossing the Elbe at Harburg, and then marched on Hanover. The division Göben could have reached Göttingen complete by the 20th, but their advance was slow. On the 21st the Hanoverian corps started from Göttingen for Eisenach via Mühlhausen, but instead of hurrying on across the railway line to Erfurt, the Staff wasted time with requests for help being sent to the VIIIth Bundescorps at Frankfurt and to Prince Karl of Bavaria, the Commander-in-Chief of the Bavarian forces.

On the 22nd General Falkenstein and the division Göben arrived at Göttingen, the division Manteufel at Nordheim and Nörten. Göben should have been ordered to send at once all his artillery and cavalry after the Hanoverians to retard their march, and then to hurry forward his infantry to attack them wherever they were met with: their strength, condition and position were known. At the same time General Falkenstein ought to have wired orders to General Beyer to leave one battalion at Kassel and march with the remainder of the division via Fulda to Hanau and Frankfurt. Manteufel, on the other hand, should have been ordered to hurry to Mülhhausen as quickly as possible, so as to support Göben if needed, and to join him to encounter the Bavarians at Meiningen.

Falkenstein, thinking that the Hanoverian corps could not be stopped, prevaricated and attempted to make for the second part of his task, viz. the occupation of Frankfurt, which he had been ordered to carry out after dealing with the Hanoverian force. Much valuable time was lost in exchange of telegrams with the Headquarters Staff at Berlin, and Falkenstein disregarded or misconstrued several instructions sent by Moltke ; but on the 24th, in obedience to the King's emphatic orders, he at last sent General Fliess with six battalions and one battery to Gotha, and General Göben with six battalions, two squadrons and two batteries from Kassel by rail to Eisenach, so that 11,000 men were assembled there by the morning of the 25th, whilst in the meantime Bavarian cavalry had reached Meiningen.

Langensalza After a confused succession of negotiations and misunderstandings the Hanoverian Staff decided to retire on the 27th behind the river Unstrut at Merxleben, and General Fliess advanced with about 9,000 men to Langensalza, where he thought he had to deal with only the rearguard making a stand to oppose him : a serious fight ensued, which ended with the retreat of the Prussian force, after they had lost 41 officers and 772 men killed and wounded ; the Hanoverians, with about 16,000 men in action, had lost 102 officers and 1,327 men. During the following night General Fliess was asked by the Hanoverian Staff to grant an armistice on the condition of free departure of their forces to the south in return for a promise not to fight against Prussia for two months. This request was refused, and on the next morning General Fliess was already reinforced by seven battalions and two batteries from Eisenach; in the afternoon eleven additional battalions and four batteries were advancing on Langensalza, and by the evening the Hanoverian army was already surrounded by nearly 40,000 men.

Surrender of the Hanoverians
In consequence the King of Hanover, to avoid further useless fighting, consented to capitulate. The King of Prussia allowed special honourable conditions in appreciation of the brave resistance shown in the battle, and in order to remove the possibility of a future bitter remembrance of dishonourable treatment; as a matter of fact, 456 out of a total of 751 officers entered the Prussian service and were received with the utmost cordiality and heartiness. The troops were sent to Celle and Hildesheim on June 30 and July 1: then they were dismissed to their homes.

Comment
When General Falkenstein, on his arrival at Hanover, learnt that the Hanoverian army was already at Göttingen, he ought to have followed them with the utmost energy, without giving his troops any rest: he ought to have repaired the strategical contretemps by a tactical *coup de force*; he ought to have sacrificed the last man and have attacked, beaten, scattered and pursued the enemy at all costs, an enemy—above all—who retreated from their own country unwilling to leave it, with hesitating step. He had received orders to render the Hanoverians and Hessians harmless by attack or by capture, therefore it was his duty to carry out these orders rapidly,

even if a junction with the Bavarians had been already effected, and it was utterly incorrect and inexcusable to desist from and neglect this primary obligation, because he thought he could not overtake the fugitives. Self-willing and self-opinionated, he answered Moltke's suggestions by rude, evasive assertions, and hardly obeyed the King's direct orders.

Occupation of Kassel

In the meantime the electorate (*Kurfürstentum*) Hesse had also been occupied. General Beyer, who was quartered about Wetzlar with his division of 19,000 men, had been directed to prevent the assembly of troops in the principality and, in case this had already been effected, to attack, disarm and disperse them, before they could effect a junction with other hostile contingents. On June 15 he received telegraphic orders to commence the march on Kassel on the next day : there were at that time at Wiesbaden a Nassau contingent of 5,000 men, 12,000 Hessians at Darmstadt, one Hessian regiment at Hanau, another at Fulda, and the other 4,000 near Kassel. General Beyer marched on the 16th through Giessen to Bettenhausen, and then on towards Fritzlar and Kassel ;

Comment

but he would have done better, if at Giessen he had seized the station and the rolling stock, and then sent a few battalions to Kassel by rail; with his main body he should have hurried to and secured Frankfurt, have fallen upon the regiment at Hanau, and contained the Nassau and Darmstadt troops. One brigade advancing from Hanau via Fulda would have sufficed to make Hesse-Kassel acknowledge and accept the Prussian command, whilst eleven battalions with two batteries could hold Frankfurt. The verbal text of his instructions empowered the general to act in this way, and he might thus have occupied Kassel already on the 16th or 17th. If he had held Frankfurt and driven the Hessians smartly out of Darmstadt, the VIIIth Bundes Corps would hardly have been formed, for Baden would have readily joined Prussia, and this would have made Würtemberg hesitate and retain its contingent for home defence. However, General Beyer reached Kassel on the 19th and was then placed under the orders of General Falkenstein, so that he got implicated in the general confusion, which lasted till the capitulation of the Hanoverian army.

C. Positions and Movements on Both Sides on the Bohemian Frontier

Positions The Austrians were in Bohemia and Moravia 247,000 men strong, of whom the I Army Corps, reinforced up to 36,000, was concentrated at Jung Bunzlau, and was to be joined by the Saxon corps of about 24,000 men. The other Austrian corps were in Moravia, the II at Wildenschwerdt and Zittau, the IV at Troppau, Teschen and Sternberg, the VI in and round Olmütz, the III in and around Brünn, the X in Brünn and Meseritsch, the VIII farthest back near Auspitz and Austerlitz.

The Prussians were along the frontier 254,000 strong: the 1st Army, consisting of the 2nd, 3rd and 4th Army Corps and one cavalry corps, around Görlitz with 93,000 men; the Army of the Elbe, composed of the 8th Army Corps and the 14th Division, 46,000 strong, near Torgau; the 2nd Army, containing the Guards, the 1st, 5th and

6th Army Corps with one cavalry division, on the Neisse between Brieg and Patschkau, with a total of 115,000 men.

Occupation of Dresden
On the morning of June 16 the Army of the Elbe crossed the Saxon frontier and reached Dresden on the 18th; two days later a division of landwehr of the Guards arrived there with orders to remain in Saxony. The Saxon army had left Dresden for Bohemia on the 17th, and was to take up quarters about Chlumetz.

The Austrians Move
On the 17th General-in-Chief Benedek received information from Vienna that the bulk of the Prussian army was still on the Elbe; in consequence he determined to march off into Bohemia to take up the position Josephstadt-Miletin, and this movement was to be covered on the right flank against the fortress Glatz by the II Light Cavalry Division. The information, if accepted as true, ought to have determined him to march into Silesia; for, if it was correct, it was possible for him to reach the neighbourhood of Schweidnitz before the enemy's main forces, and to attack them with concentrated strength.

The X Army Corps with one cavalry division was to march on the right of the first line, the III Corps in the centre, another cavalry division on the left. In the second line were the VI Corps from Olmütz on the right, the VIII Corps in the centre, and the II Corps with the army artillery reserve on the left: one brigade of this corps with a regiment of lancers was left at Wildenschwerdt for the protection of the railway; the IV Corps and the III Cavalry Division followed in the third line: it was hardly possible from the start, that the intended rendezvous of the whole army on the Upper Elbe could be reached before July 2.

On June 21 General Clam Gallas, commanding the I Army Corps, who had posted the Saxon troops in the neighbourhood of Chlumetz-Pardubitz, received from the Commander-in-Chief the order to keep both corps in position at Jung Bunzlau and not to concentrate to the rear, which makes it appear that Benedek still hoped to get to the river Iser before Prince Frederick Charles. But on the 20th he had learnt that four Prussian army corps and one cavalry division were on the Neisse, and that some of these troops were on the move against the nearest passes in the giant mountains (Riesengebirge) leading into Bohemia. As

The Prussians Advance

a matter of fact, orders had been sent from Berlin directly after the occupation of Saxony that the different armies were to concentrate on the Bohemian frontier, and that the declaration of war was to be handed to the Austrian outposts on crossing the frontier. On June 22 the additional order was received that the ultimate junction of the armies was to be effected at or near Gitschin (Jicin), but that the 6th Corps was to remain near Neisse until further orders. On the 23rd the main bodies of the 1st Army and the Army of the Elbe crossed the frontier, but the corps composing the 2nd Army were still a few marches distant from it. It was then known at the Headquarters of the General Staff that the Austrian army was also on the march towards the same locality; if they managed to arrive in great strength at the passes out of which the troops of the Crown Prince had to debouch, his success was certainly doubtful. The 6th Corps left behind at Neisse had orders to make feint movements via Neustadt and Ziegenhals, but was on the 24th directed to march into the district of Glatz to take up a position fronting south, so as to secure the rear and the flank of the 2nd Army: a rumour had spread that the Austrians intended to break through in that direction. On the 25th the 1st Army Corps reached Libau on the road to Trautenau, the Guards were at Neurode and Wünschelberg, the 5th Corps at Glatz, all ready for the great movement into Bohemia.

This juncture appears to us as the proper time to insert a short chapter dealing with the discussions on the various points on which Moltke's plan of campaign has been criticised, attacked and condemned by various writers, French, Austrians and Germans.

COMMENTS ON THE PRUSSIAN PLAN OF CAMPAIGN

CHAPTER IV

Comments on the Prussian Plan of Campaign

To obtain a solid starting point for criticism, we ought to take into first consideration the fact that, by the initial arrangements and preliminary disposition of troops, Brandenburg and Silesia had to be covered, and that any crossing of the frontier by the enemy had to be prevented, as this was an absolute necessity from the political and therefore also from the military point of view, not only with reference to Austria, but also with regard to Saxony and the other hostile or uncertain German states. But these considerations were well known and appreciated at the time. The armies which had to advance separately from Silesia and Lusatia, were in the beginning certainly not in a very favourable condition to give mutual support to each other, but near the Elbe or on the Iser each of them might, in case of necessity, take the risk of being attacked by considerably superior forces; for Moltke was fully conscious of the advantages accruing from the possession of the needle-gun and of the superior fire tactics of his Prussians; he could take these into full account, when important political considerations demanded the most determined military offensive.

There were three ways in which the invasion could be

carried out : (1) The way in which it was done ; (2) by advancing with the main forces through Lusatia, whilst Silesia was covered by only a small force ; (3) by advancing the main armies through Silesia whilst covering Lusatia by a small force. Moltke selected the first of the three, because it afforded the armies more freedom of movement, better chances of obtaining fair quarters and ample provisions; the plan adopted was also likely to facilitate the deployment after the passage of the mountain passes, as troops can more easily debouch into the plain by six than by three roads, and certainly it was sure to shorten the time required for the passage through the mountains. There are also strategical advantages in starting armies on a broad front instead of bringing them up in formations of great depth, for the manœuvring and co-operating are much facilitated by an extensive general front of advance. In making his choice in favour of advancing on two lines, Moltke may have been influenced by these reasons drawn from the principles of the science of war, and also by his opinion of the opposing general, who had to act according to them. He had to expect that his advance thus arranged would lead to operations on exterior lines against an enemy occupying the interior line, and he was probably well aware of the warning which Napoleon expressed against such operations, when he said : " To operate from directions wide apart, and between which there is no direct communication, is a fault which generally leads to others." It was surely also probable that Benedek would take advantage of his favourable position. Moltke's task then would be to encircle his opponent with all his forces and thus to throttle him,

Benedek's task would be to prevent such a blow and to singly defeat the separate armies which were acting on the principle of converging and concentrating on the interior line, which is the same as Napoleon's strategic method to " divide the army for movement and subsistence and to unite it for battle."

Benedek failed to take the advantage offered by his position, but he need not be specially blamed on that account, and Moltke was justified by events in the history of war in greatly doubting the success of the operations from the interior line. If the guarantee of victory lay in the timely adoption of that line, then the Austrians in the Danube campaign of 1809 ought to have signally beaten Napoleon. Not many generals have known, how to use the advantages of the inner line, and the great emperor himself, although he professed to condemn the exterior lines, preferred adopting them, when he knew, he was the stronger. In the days of Leipzig he lost the campaign on the interior line, and in spite of all his successes in the first months of 1814 he could not save his cause. Acting on the interior line requires a leader of rare qualities; it makes very great demands on his readiness of decision and on the marching power of his troops, and has therefore also great disadvantages. Above all, the general must have the power of making his troops move about regardless of fatigue and privations. Napoleon did this in 1814, and he could do it, because he was monarch as well as general-in-chief, and his corps were then not numerous; but even he had failed to do so in 1813, owing to the greatly larger forces to be handled in that campaign and to the poor quality of many of his regiments.

Moltke in 1866 did not foresee everything, but he certainly knew that Benedek was not a Napoleon, and, considering that the latter had succumbed in the Leipzig campaign when acting on the interior line, he could hope that Benedek would not fare much better in the same position with still larger forces than Napoleon had had to move. In 1809 the Austrian Archduke Charles tried to operate on the interior line in the campaign of Ratisbon, but he split up his large forces, and, in spite of the great advantages of a superior position up to the 17th and even 18th of April, he was by the 21st at the mercy of Napoleon, who had crushed his isolated left wing and driven it out of the field.

Benedek then was not likely to show himself more capable than Charles had been in the execution of this most difficult rôle of commanding armies acting on the interior line, and besides, he had shown at Solferino, under smaller conditions and within the scope of tactics, that he did not know what to do and how to act on the interior line; otherwise he would, after defeating the Piedmontese, have thrown round three-fourths of his forces and made them play their part in the decisive stage of the battle. In fact, Benedek was deficient in the very qualities needed for such a part—ready conception of ideas, independence of decision and initiative.

The principles of strategy should of course not be despised, but the preceding examples show that tactical considerations point more to the realities of action and to the manipulation of principles than to the obedience to mere theory. Moltke never stuck timidly to principles except one to which all others had to give way, viz. to push forward to the junction of armies, which he always effected at the decisive hour.

Benedek had his forces assembled according to all the rules of the art of war and of its principles *before* the decisive time, but *at* the decisive time, June 27–30 they were scattered and out of hand.

To have drawn together in Silesia the bulk of the Prussian forces, after the Austrian line of operation had become known, would have taken very much time with the railway system such as it was then, and it would have been the worst step which Moltke could have taken; for during that time the Austrians would have had the finest opportunity for threatening Berlin, for which purpose the Saxon army corps was standing ready, like an advanced guard, at a distance of only six days' march. The hostility of Saxony and the proximity of her forces demanded from the outset the direct protection of Berlin in that direction, for the possibility of their reinforcement by Bavarian troops could not be excluded. This fear for the safety of the Prussian capital of course vanished as soon as the evacuation of Saxony by her troops became known at the Prussian Headquarters, but this was not before the middle of June. If at that time the assembly of the bulk of the forces in Silesia combined with a secondary force in Saxony and Lusatia had been decided upon (or vice versa), the translocation of troops necessitated thereby would—with the railway system of that period—have taken eight to ten days, a loss of time which was of great consideration, as there was the fear of having to meet at any point the united Austro-Saxon army, who, in the salient angle between Saxony and Silesia, had everywhere shorter roads and better conditions for operations. If Moltke's plan was adhered to, the two Prussian armies would within those eight or ten days most probably be on Bohemian soil, and ready to seek a decision, and this did happen almost within that time.

Prussia had known very early that Austria was arming, but at the time when Moltke fixed on the plan of operations he did not know where Austria would assemble her main army. The circumstance that Prussia from political reasons had first to wait for the vote of the " Bund "—i.e. June 15—was for Austria and her allies of advantage : by that date the Austrian forces were already assembled at Olmütz. Without taking into consideration these political combinations and the actual geographical configuration of the hostile states, nobody can understand and judge Moltke's dispositions From these reasons the Prussians had to take into consideration the following three points : (1). The Austrians might direct their main operations against Silesia or Lusatia ; (2) it was not impossible that the Austrians might anticipate a Prussian attack in both directions ; (3) Prussia had not only to reckon with the Saxon army threatening Berlin, as it were like an advanced guard, but also with the possibility that Bavarian reinforcements could arrive by rail within twenty-four to forty-eight hours. Therefore the dispositions to be taken had to provide for the protection of Silesia *and* Lusatia, which had to be maintained till the actual commencement of hostilities : then, of course, it was too late for a change of positions. It may be casually mentioned that as early as June 10 rumours were current in the Army of the Elbe that Bavarian troops had been detrained at Wurzen (*circa* twenty miles east of Leipzig). These rumours were repeated during the next days, and on the 16th and 17th reports even were brought to the vanguard, that strong Bavarian forces had arrived in Saxony; in consequence cavalry was sent forward to get reliable information. Whilst the Prussians took up their assembly positions at Torgau, Görlitz and Waldenburg up to June 10, they heard of the assembly of the Austrian North Army at Olmütz, which was completed by the 14th. This arrangement could not but rouse the suspicion that Benedek intended an offensive movement against Breslau via Glatz; but at the same time the Austrians assembled also considerable forces in the very north of Bohemia. Originally Moltke had distributed his forces so that five army corps were to advance through Saxony from Lusatia, three from Silesia, whilst he kept the Guards Corps at his disposal to be used according to circumstances.

Up to June 16 it could not be seen, whether the Austrians would turn from Olmütz against Silesia or towards Lusatia, or whether they would operate in such a manner as to be able to turn from the interior line against both sides. The safest plan therefore for the Prussians was to take the offensive at once to make the enemy's choice more difficult, and thus they started operations on that day; the Austrians likewise on the next day marched off from Olmütz in three columns—not towards Silesia, but to the north of Bohemia. As the Prussians had no reliable news as to this movement, the safest plan for them in their uncertainty was to paralyse it by an energetic offensive. However, it was possible that the 2nd Army in Silesia would have to meet the first shock, and therefore the Guards Corps was allotted to it. It certainly was not advisable to remain inactive till the Austrians had shown their final intentions of attack, for a sudden and rapid interchange of main bases was not to be thought of on account of the deficient railway system. Therefore the only chance of success at this stage lay in the capacity of manœuvring most rapidly and with all precaution as to security. The Austrian operations against Regensburg in 1809 have already been mentioned, and Moltke had made a special study of them, so he was not likely to commit the same mistake as was then made by Archduke Charles, especially as there was neither spare time nor superiority of forces available.

After the movements had once started, the main question was as to which of the two opponents would be ready first to strike with assembled forces. The Austrians wanted to be on the safe side on this point, and therefore marched in massed armies from Moravia into Bohemia; the Prussians preferred the more comfortable way of advancing in separate bodies with the initial general direction on Gitschin. Although it was not known that the assembly of the Austrian forces at Olmütz was based on the idea of defensive action, it could be calculated that even if they intended taking the offensive, the Prussians could be on the line of the river Iser a day or two before them; for the distance from Torgau, Görlitz and Waldenburg was about nine days' march, that from Olmütz a march of eleven days. But if once five Prussian army corps were standing on the Iser before the Austrians, it could be expected that the latter would turn their main forces against this Prussian army which otherwise would threaten their left flank in any other movement.

In the worst case the Prussians would have had to fight—in this strategically and tactically favourable position—a defensive battle, which they could well risk against superior numbers on account of their better firearms. The Austrians would have had to put at least six army corps against the Prussian force so as to obtain a superiority of strength, but it was certainly doubtful, whether then their other two corps could have repelled the attacks of the four corps from Silesia. One must not play one's hand therefore with only strategical principles, but strategy has to take into calculation what can be performed from a tactical point of view; the consideration of the two together only can show, whether the plan for a campaign is correct or not. Since 1864 the Prussians were fully convinced of the superiority of their arms and tactics, and against such an enemy it is doubly dangerous to operate on interior lines; for superiority of numbers and of strategical leading can utterly fail against superior tactics. Moltke always affirmed that strategy accepts with thanks any success of tactics, even if it had not been intended or expected.

On the day (June 23) on which the Prussian armies entered Bohemia the Austrians were on the line of Landskron; the point to be marched on was fixed at Gitschin, five days' march for each of the two Prussian armies: the Austrians were seven days' march from it; besides, as the former were marching on two lines, their operations could be expected to be more rapid than those of the enemy. Although all this was not known before the drawing up of the plan of campaign, an approximate calculation was justifiable, as it could be modified on the arrival of detailed information. As far as events could be foreseen or guessed at, the order given for the advance on the 22nd was therefore well-founded, and the operations could well be based on even the approximate certainty that from their two starting points they would be sooner at the goal than the enemy could reach it.

Although the plan of marching into Bohemia had been settled upon before the 22nd, yet that day is the one of the great decision for the operations. As the Austrians till then had marched from Olmütz to Landskron, it was to be assumed that their main army would not turn towards Glatz-Breslau nor send off large forces in that direction. The continuation on the line of march chosen would bring the Austrians first of all to the Elbe between Königgrätz and Josephstadt; what they would undertake then, whether they would continue the march towards Lusatia with flank protection against Silesia or vice versa, could not be made out before the 22nd, but the two alternatives had to be taken into consideration; however, it was then certain that they could not develop superior forces against the 2nd Army (Silesian) by the 27th, nor against the 1st Army by the 29th.

In consequence the following steps were necessary: The 1st Army and that of the Elbe had to operate with energy towards the Iser in order to gain the advantage of time over the enemy, if they also should be marching for the same line; the 2nd Army had to start at such time that they could have the mountains behind them by the 27th, and to provide for the possibility that fighting should begin in the last days of the month, both armies had to be given a preliminary or temporary aim of operations, which implied for both only the common direction, and perhaps could later on serve as point of junction. The actual circumstances being well considered, Gitschin would seem the most appropriate point.

The 1st Army and the Army of the Elbe could be joined together any day after their advance into Bohemia, as they were moving (on one line) abreast almost in contact of each other.

But there were difficulties with regards to the 2nd Army, for it was possible that its different corps might be attacked separately, and the movements towards the necessary later co-operation with the other two armies could not be foreseen or prearranged. It was necessary to make the best assignment of the different roads to the four army corps, and to time their several marches so that they could be in a position for mutual support.

The most difficult point was the fixture of time for the start, for it depended partly on the news received about the enemy's march, partly on the localities reached by the other two armies. For if the 2nd Army crossed too soon, it might get into a dangerous position, in so far as no pressure from the other two armies would as yet have been felt by the Austrians; if they crossed too late, the latter could unmolested move nearly their whole force against the 1st and the Elbe Armies. Making the right choice of the objective point of advance and fixing the right time for the start of the various units are looked upon as the marks of a good general: genius as well as carefully studied calculation are required for this difficult task.

The right time for starting the march of the 2nd Army occurred when the 1st Army arrived near Reichenberg. For this calculation the positions of the most distant

Prussian corps (5th, 6th and Guards at Glatz, Rückerts and Neurode) were decisive. The 1st Army was about Reichenberg on the evening of the 24th : in four days it could be well beyond Gitschin, but by that time the 2nd Army could stand on the Elbe. Therefore the 5th and the Guards Corps were ordered to start on the 26th, the 1st Corps at Liebau on the following day.

The plan for the march into Bohemia of the 2nd Army could thus be settled in advance, but the time of actual execution depended on eventual later considerations. According to the plan, the 1st Army Corps was to reach the Aupa at Trautenau on the 27th, the Elbe at Arnau on the 28th ; the 1st Division Guards was to be at Ditersbach on the 26th, at Eipel on the Aupa on the 27th, at Königinhof on the Elbe on the 28th ; the 2nd Division Guards was to reach Politz on the 26th, Kosteletz on the 27th, Königinhof on the 28th ; the 5th Army Corps at Reinerz on the 26th, at Nachod on the 27th, at Gradlitz on the 28th ; the 5th Corps followed by the 6th. If the direction towards the line Landskron-Josephstadt was followed, the 2nd Army in the execution of its movements would probably meet with considerable hostile forces, especially the most southern column (5th and 6th Corps), which seemed most exposed to danger. Care had to be taken therefore, that the different corps could support each other as early as possible during the operations, and the most southern column was made the strongest. Thus careful arrangements had been made for all details, but some faults were committed in the execution. On account of a mere rumour, the Commander-in-Chief of the 2nd Army posted the 6th Corps at Habelschwerdt on the 27th, so

Sketch 1.

PROJECTED MARCH OF THE 2ND ARMY FROM THE
25TH TO THE 28TH JUNE.

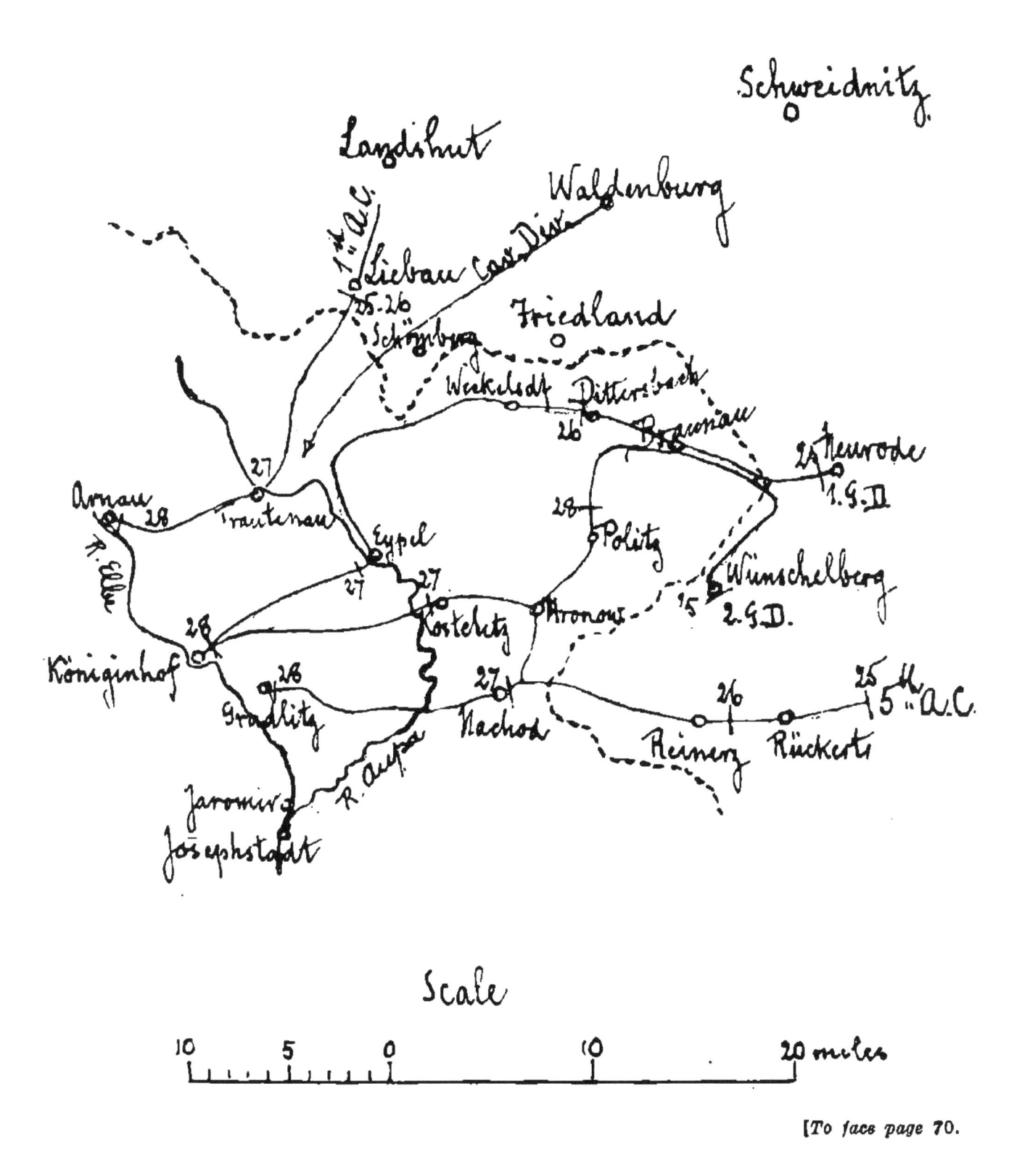

[To face page 70.

that it was one day's march behind at the critical time; similarly, the 1st Corps lost one day's march on the 27th by going—unnecessarily—back to the starting point after the unlucky engagement at Trautenau. In consequence of these two contretemps the position of the 2nd Army was not very enviable on the 28th, and on that day Benedek might have scored a considerable success in that direction.

With regard to the mutual support between the columns on the march, this order did not refer to the army corps of the 2nd Army on the 26th, because on that day they were in three parallel valleys without transversal communications; but *if* the enemy had made his appearance, he would have been in the same unfavourable circumstances. If no hindrance had occurred, the 2nd Army would have reached the Aupa on the 27th after a hard day's frontal march, and the Elbe on the 28th after a short day's march in the same order. The chief danger could then have been considered as surpassed; the lines of march of the two Guards Divisions were so arranged that already on the 27th one of them could have supported the 5th Army Corps over Hronow, both could have done so on the 28th. And they were also able to lend support to the north, which they actually did at Trautenau. This ought to satisfy a critical observer, that everything possible had been done by the Chief Command to assure complete cohesion, exact co-operation and mutual support; and if in two instances the instructions on these three points were neglected, the fault cannot be ascribed to the Chief Command.

Now it has been stated by critics that not only Moltke's

original plan was faulty, but also his operations, because he contradicted himself and his orders of June 22 by the later determination to keep the armies longer separated, when he stated that it seemed advantageous to keep up even after June 30 the separation which at first had been unavoidable. The idea and the order to get all the forces joined at Gitschin had been based on the assumption and calculation that the decisive action might take place in that neighbourhood; when the expectation of meeting the collected Austrian forces there had proved incorrect, it was the right thing to keep the armies separate, and wait for the moment, when their junction would become necessary. Again, in originally assuming that Gitschin might become the point of rendezvous for the forces, Moltke was not very far out in his calculation, for the war was decided only two days' march from that place.

The question has also been asked, whether it was part of the secret of Moltke's strategical combinations that during the crisis from the 25th to the 29th he and the General Staff were not with the army but in Berlin, so that the generals in command were managing matters according to their own fancies: for instance, one of them concentrated his army at Münchengrätz instead of pushing it forward to Gitschin, and thereby separating the I Austrian and the Saxon Corps from the rest of their forces, and endeavouring to effect a junction with the 2nd Army; whilst another detached the 6th Army Corps into the southern part of the county of Glatz on the mere rumour of an Austrian invasion in that direction, thereby extending his front line to a length of fifty miles.

The answer to these criticisms is the following : There was no factor of danger or inconvenience in the stay of Moltke and the General Staff at Berlin, which was in constant telegraphic connection with the three armies and not far away by rail, until the moment arrived for the tactical co-operation of all the forces, i.e. June 29. On the contrary, this procedure was very appropriate, because Prussia was, at the same time, carrying on another campaign in North-Western Germany, the events of which in those days had come to a critical point, and which was also directed by the General Staff. Therefore Berlin was decidedly the most convenient place for the King and Moltke. The " managing after their own fancies " on the part of generals in command did hardly go beyond the degree of independent action generally allowed to such leaders of separate armies. Now everybody knows that mistakes were made, but the defaulters were not aware of their errors at the time. And have not the most fatal mistakes been committed on the Austrian side during those very days, in spite of the presence of their Headquarters ?

Another question has been asked, viz. how events would have been shaped, if the Prussian Staff had from the outset renounced the idea of concentrating the three armies, and if the 2nd Army had been ordered to observe what was going on from the position Nachod-Neustadt. With an effective of 115,000 men and 342 guns it would have been opposed to 167,000 Austrians with 632 guns, and this disparity of numbers would have made a general battle unadvisable for the 2nd Army, unless previous engagements had furnished undoubted data on the relative fighting efficiency of the opposed forces, and given to the Prussian troops the feeling of superiority. For if this has once been established on one side, accompanied by a feeling of incompetence or inferiority on the other side, this unequality increases rapidly; for as Napoleon has often maintained, moral impressions in war have a more decisive influence than mere numbers. The fact would soon have been established that the Austrian losses in fighting were fourfold those suffered by the Prussians, and that therefore the 2nd Army was superior in fighting value to the opposing Austrian main force. It seems impossible that under these circumstances Benedek could have turned against the 1st Army; he would have endeavoured to secure his line of retreat to Vienna, and would probably have directed the Crown Prince of Saxony to approach the Northern Army by way of Kollin and Czaslau. Evidently the 2nd Army would then have been in a position to endanger Benedek's retreat to Brünn, and to force him to make rapid marches, generally accompanied by confusion and disorder. If decisive engagements had taken place about June 26–28, the 2nd Army could have reached Brünn by July 3, and the 1st Army have gained Iglau by the same date.

All this might have happened, and the success under these circumstances would have been much greater than that actually achieved, but the question is: Would it have happened? The concentration of the three armies was planned and executed according to the rules of a correct system, and it is idle to say that rules are crutches good for lame people, but not made for those who can run.

INVASION OF BOHEMIA

CHAPTER V

A. Advance of the 1st Army and the Army of the Elbe into Bohemia

Austrian Movements — On June 23, when the leading columns of the Austrian army had reached Opocno, Wildenschwerdt and Kunstadt, the I Corps was assembling on the Iser, and the Saxon Corps, 24,000 strong, arrived there on the 25th; both had been advanced from their first assembly position at Jung-Bunzlau.

Prussians Move — The 1st Prussian Army was marching on Reichenberg, the Army of the Elbe on Rumburg; detachments of Austrian cavalry were retiring before them towards the Iser. On the 24th the Austrian advanced posts were pushed back to Turnau, and the Crown Prince of Saxony, who was now in command of the two corps, received the following telegram from the Austrian Headquarters in the afternoon: " Your troops are intended to oppose the enemy advancing from Reichenberg or from Gabel. In this task you will be either supported by troops arriving successively, or you will have to retire on the main army, in case of being attacked by greatly superior forces." On the 24th the 3rd and 4th Divisions of the 1st Prussian Army got to Kratzau, the 5th and 6th Divisions to Reichenberg, the 7th to Gablonz, the 8th to Eibicht, the 14th Division (of the Elbe Army) advanced to Zwickau, the 15th and 16th to Haida. On the 25th the 15th Division reached Gabel, the 16th Brims, the 14th Kunersdorf, and General Herwarth, in command of these divisions, received orders from Prince Frederick Charles, who had been appointed Commander-in-Chief of both armies, to advance to Niemes and Oschotz on the following day. The Prince intended the 8th Division to carry out at the same time an extensive reconnaissance beyond Liebenau, whilst the other divisions of the 1st Army were to mark time in order to await the moving up into line of the right wing.

Herwarth in consequence ordered his advanced guard to march beyond Niemes as far as Plauschnitz, and to push detachments forward to Hühnerwasser and Hirschberg; the 15th and 16th Divisions were to follow as far as Niemes, the 14th was to advance on the left to Oschotz.

Action at Hühnerwasser The advanced guard—five battalions, five squadrons and two batteries—after passing through Niemes came upon some Austrian cavalry patrols, who retired into the wood in front of Hühnerwasser. A slight cavalry skirmish was followed by a short engagement, in the course of which an Austrian battalion was driven out of the place and pursued into a wood beyond it. Herwarth ordered a halt, and outposts were placed towards Münchengrätz, Weisswasser and Gablonz. In the evening there was an outpost engagement caused by the reconnaissance of an Austrian jäger battalion from Münchengrätz, who

Sketch II.

POSITIONS OF THE DIVISIONS OF THE 1ST ARMY
ON THE 22ND, 23RD, AND 24TH JUNE.

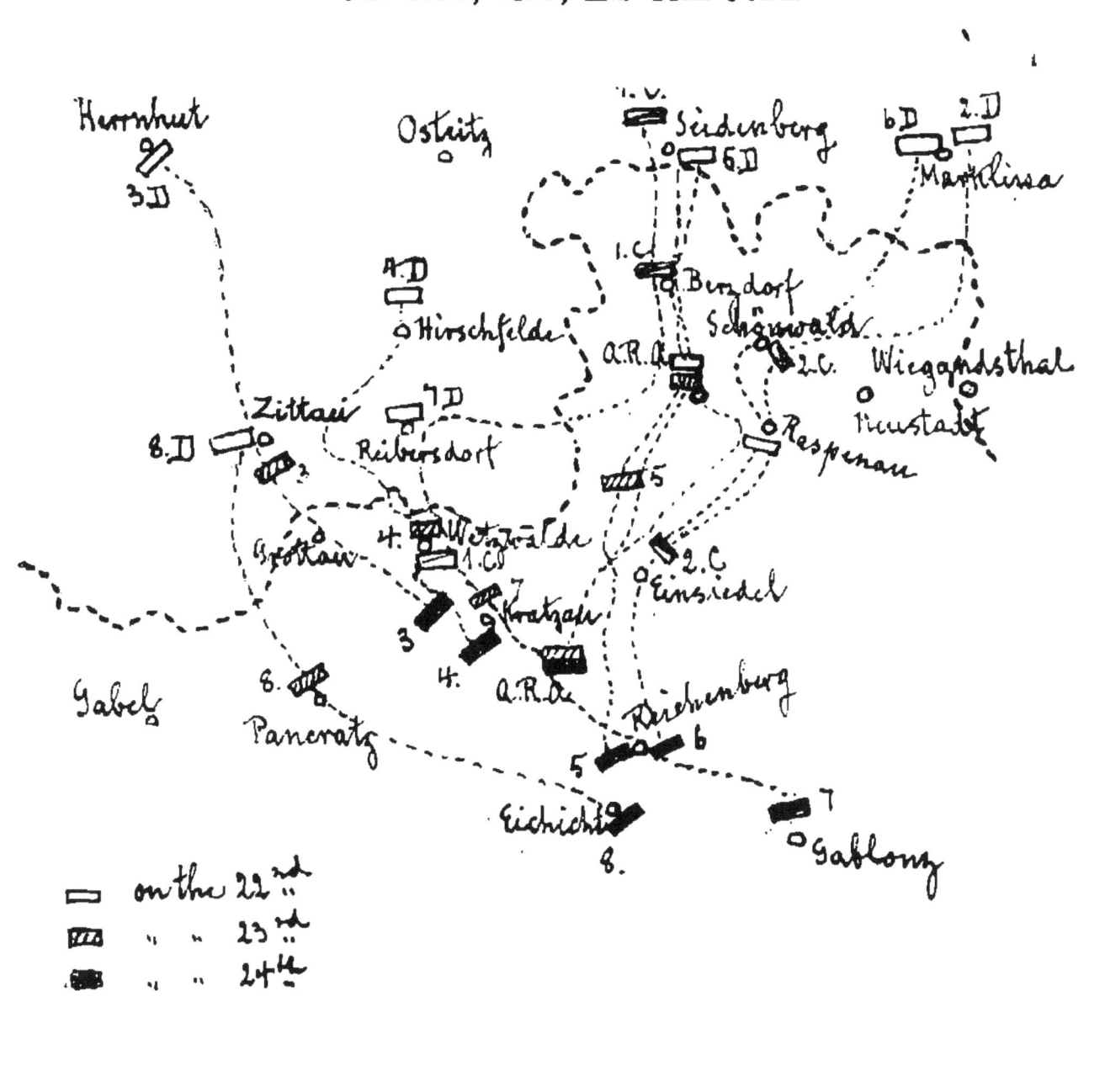

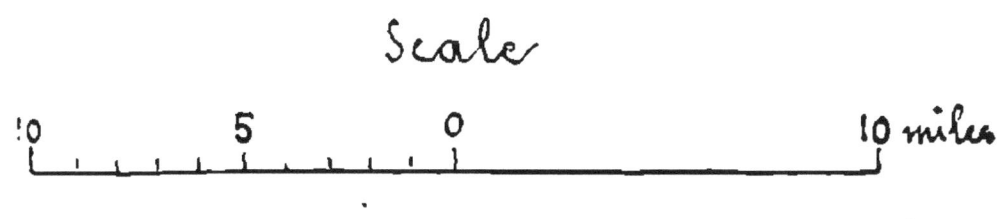

[To face page 78.

were driven back with some loss by superior numbers : the fall of night only put an end to desultory firing. The total loss of the Prussians during the day was 50 killed and wounded, whilst the Austrians had 277 killed, wounded and missing.

Advance to Turnau
When the advanced guard of the 8th Division, detailed for a reconnaissance in force, issued from Liebenau, they were met by some advanced Austrian cavalry with one battery, who retired on Turnau after an eventless artillery duel. The Prince had then already sent orders to the 7th Division to advance to Turnau and to occupy the important defile at that place, whilst the 8th was to advance to Preper and push forward outposts towards Podol.

When the 7th Division reached Turnau, General Fransecky found it unoccupied, and was told that an Austrian cavalry division had left the place in the morning for Münchengrätz. The bridge across the Iser, which was partly destroyed, was at once repaired, and a pontoon bridge also thrown across the river.

Austrian Orders
In the Saxo-Austrian Headquarters a telegram from the Commander-in-Chief had arrived at 2 p.m.: it contained the order to hold Münchengrätz and Turnau at all costs. The Saxon Crown Prince and General Count Clam Gallas came to the conclusion that the best way in which the object of this order could be obtained was to occupy, on the next morning, a certain position north of Sichrow, and when the news arrived that Turnau had already been occupied by the Prussians, it was arranged to commence the execution of this operation that very evening by retaking Turnau by a surprise attack, and by occupy-

ing the height of Swigau opposite Podol, so as to secure the advance to Sichrow on the morrow.

Comment From the circumstances narrated it can easily be seen that the time for the execution of this plan had been allowed to pass, for even in possession of the defiles at Swigau and Sichrow, their troops in the farther advance would have had the 1st Army in front, the Elbe Army on their flank and the Iser behind them.

The advanced guard of the 8th Division reached Preper at 6 p.m., and a reconnoitring patrol reported that Podol was occupied by the enemy. The order was given to take the place and secure the passages across the river.

Action of Podol One company of the 4th jäger Battalion took the barricades in the village, another cleared the Swigau heights of the enemy and also entered the village; the small Austrian garrison retired, and the riflemen, following them, crossed all four bridges over the Iser. Reinforced by two companies of infantry, they took up a position on the other side, and the engagement seemed finished. But at 9.30 these advanced companies were attacked by troops of the Austrian brigade Poschacher, which had been detailed to occupy the heights of Swigau (which commanded the passage of the Iser), and which had only then arrived. The Prussians were driven back across the bridges, and when another Austrian battalion was reported to advance against the village from the west, the officer in command decided at 11 p.m. to retire from the place. But the Brigadier-General Bose, who in the bivouac at Preper had heard the increasing rifle fire at 10 o'clock was now coming up with two battalions of infantry, and although he was told of the superior numbers of the Austrians, he determined to attack at once, considering rightly that this important passage had to be taken at all costs, and that, if put off, it would probably demand much greater sacrifice. The Austrians made several counter-attacks in column formation, which were repeatedly repulsed by volleys delivered four deep at thirty paces distance. When two more battalions arrived, they were led forward to attack the bridges, but at sixty paces were met by frontal and enfilading fire, which checked the advance. The brigadier himself seizing a rifle led them forward to the attack with the bayonet, drove the Austrians across the chief bridge, beyond which three companies took up a position. By this time the Austrian General Count Clam had brought up details of two more brigades, and several attempts were made to retake the bridges, which had all been lost, but in vain. The fighting ceased after 1 o'clock in the morning.

Comment
General Bose had correctly recognised the full importance of the passage over the Iser. Its possession opened the shortest route to Gitschin and threatened the junction of the Saxo-Austrian Corps with the great army, and it was now impossible for Count Clam to carry out his projected offensive movement against Turnau.

The material result of this engagement was as satisfactory as the strategical advantage gained by it, for the loss on the Prussian side was only 12 officers and 118 men killed and wounded, whilst the Austrians had lost 6 officers and 537 men killed and wounded, besides 5 officers and 504 men prisoners.

B. Movement of the 2nd Prussian Army.

2nd Prussian Army on the Frontier   Whilst the Elbe Army had thus gained the road to Münchengrätz by the combat at Hühnerwasser, and the 1st Army had taken the defile of Podol and occupied that of Turnau, the Silesian Army also had taken a step farther forward towards the intended general junction. On the evening of the 26th the 1st Army Corps was at Liebau and Schömberg, the cavalry division at Waldenburg, the Guard Corps at Dittersbach and Pickan, the 5th Corps at Reinerz and Jörker, the 6th Corps at Glatz, and the Headquarters of the Crown Prince at Braunau. Thus the Guards were in the centre between the two points where the 1st and the 5th Corps had to cross the mountains on the frontier, and fourteen miles distant from each of them, and could therefore support either of them when debouching on Austrian territory.

During the day some small cavalry skirmishes had taken place, and Nachod had been occupied by two battalions of the advanced brigade of the 5th Corps, after the small Austrian detachment holding the town had retired from the place on being shelled. The various Austrian advanced cavalry detachments reported correctly to Josephstadt early in the afternoon that the Prussian army was advancing in three widely separated columns.

Comment on the Austrian Dispositions   To oppose their deployment and advance on Austrian soil three corps could be used at once on the 27th, viz. the VI, X and IV, and could be reinforced by the evening by the III and VIII Corps. But the Chief of

INVASION OF BOHEMIA

the Staff had already, on the start of the march from Moravia, made it his fixed object to lead the army into a position on the right bank of the Elbe between Josephstadt and Königinhof, with a flank covering line Horitz-Miletin, to accept battle there, just as Daun would have done 100 years before. The march into Bohemia was not part of a well-considered, obstinate defensive, nor of a bold, self-confident offensive, which would point the way into the enemy's country, but it was a middle course, which leads but too often to an abyss.

Benedek had indeed replied to the imperial order of the 16th to begin operations with the assurance that he would direct the army to Josephstadt, to offer battle in that neighbourhood, or, under favourable circumstances, to take the offensive, and, in case the hoped-for junction with the Saxons and Bavarians should have been effected, to do this for certain in order to find and fight the main army of the enemy. Up to that moment the Chief of the Staff wanted to adhere to his preconceived idea of assembling the army in the position Jaromir-Miletin, and to see its salvation in the agony of passive expectancy. Merely to cover this strategical junction, the X Corps was to advance to Trautenau, the VI from Opocno to Skalitz : *all* available forces ought to have been rapidly assembled and pushed forward to drive back the invading enemy. The consequence of these half measures was a series of unsuccessful, unfortunate actions.

Not till 8 p.m. on the 26th the following orders were issued by the Austrian Staff :—

" The VI Corps will march at 3 a.m. from Opocno

to Skalitz, where a position is to be taken up; an advanced guard is to be pushed forward towards Nachod.

"The X Corps is to march at 8 a.m. to Trautenau where it takes up a position provisionally. After the troops have passed Kaile, the brigade posted there is to be drawn in. This disposition has the object to cover the not yet completed assembly of the army at Josephstadt, which, however, is not to exclude an energetic attack on the enemy, if the opportunity occurs. A pursuit, however, must be kept within the limits of this chief object. I expect early reports on the strength of the forces opposed to the VI and the X Corps."

Evidently the strategical assembly was considered to be the chief point, the enemy and his doings were deemed of secondary importance.

It was known to the Staff that Nachod had been occupied by the enemy in the afternoon; the order to the VI Corps should therefore have run: "The enemy have occupied Nachod, the VI are to find out their strength." This would have given General Ramming complete liberty of action in attaining his object.

The VIII Corps, assembled near Königgratz, also received orders to march via Josephstadt into the bivouacs abandoned by the X Corps about Schurz, but when already on the march next morning, this corps was stopped by the counter order to proceed via Jaromir to Czaslawek and Dolan, and to encamp there with the eventual destination of supporting the VI Corps.

Furthermore the IV Corps, which had already reached Lanzow after crossing the Elbe, was directed back to Jaromir, whilst the IIIrd Corps continued the march from Königgrätz towards Miletin.

Sketch III.

POSITIONS OF THE UNITS OF THE OPPOSING ARMIES
ON THE EVENING OF THE 26TH JUNE.

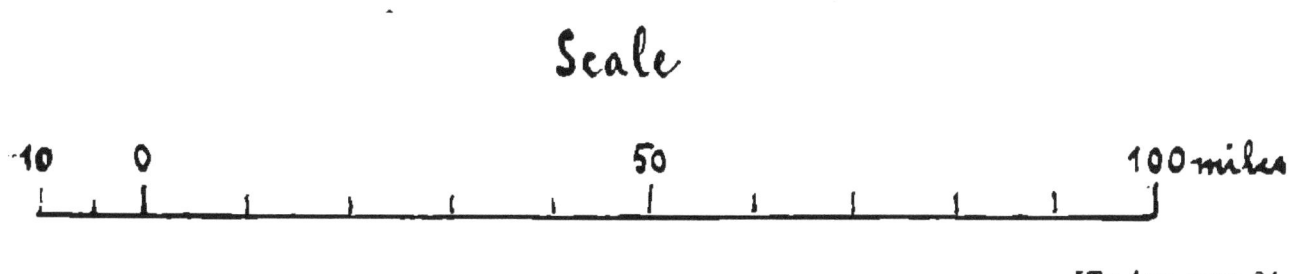

[To face page 84.

Orders for the 2nd Prussian Army

In the 2nd Prussian Army the dispositions for the 27th were as follows: The 1st Corps was to advance to Trautenau and, if possible, push its advanced guard forward to Arnau, the main body of the 5th Corps was to march on Nachod. The two divisions of the Guard Corps were to advance so that each of them could act as reserve to one of the other two corps.

No objection can be raised against these dispositions for the following day, but it seems difficult to explain why no rôle was assigned to the cavalry of the Guard. These regiments should have been pushed forward beyond Eipel to Studenz and Raatsch to observe the roads leading northward from Josephstadt. Altogether the Prussian cavalry was not made full use of, at least not in the beginning of the campaign.

The general object and guiding aim of these dispositions seems to have been to advance with three corps by way of Arnau, in order to effect a junction with the 1st Army, and to leave the 6th Corps in Glatz for the protection of that county The theoretical idea of the converging movement from exterior lines of operation put all other considerations in the background, and obscured the chances of attaining more far-reaching results by other methods; for the 1st Army could evidently be supported much more quickly if the whole 2nd Army occupied a position west of Josephstadt, and thereby interrupted the Austrian line of retreat to Vienna.

C. Events on June 27

The troops of the 1st Prussian Army and of the

Elbe Army did not meet the enemy on that day; the 5th Division of the 1st Army was moved from Gablonz to Eisenbrod; the 6th Division closed up to near the 7th and 8th, which remained on the Iser between Podol and Turnau; the 2nd Army Corps got near Liebenau. The advanced guard of the Elbe Army remained at Hühnerwasser, its three divisions came up as far as Böhmisch Aicha.

According to reports received at the headquarters of the 1st Army, Münchengrätz was still occupied by one Austrian brigade, the Saxon Army Corps and a cavalry division; it had been observed that entrenching was being done, which seemed to indicate that General Count Clam intended to hold the place and to await reinforcements, but in the course of the day he decided to retreat on the morrow.

Battle of Trautenau The 1st Prussian Army Corps, under General Bonin, started for Trautenau at 4 a.m., one division from Liebau, the other from Schönberg, whilst a separate detachment marched on the right flank via Schatzlar to Ober Altstadt, northwest of Trautenau. The two divisions had orders to join at Prauschnitz and there to rest for two hours, under protection of the advanced guard, which was to occupy Trautenau.

The left column arrived at Prauschnitz at 8 a.m., but the march of the right column had been so much delayed that the head of the advanced guard furnished by that column did not appear near the town till 10 a.m., and the cavalry of the vanguard found the bridge over the Aupa barricaded and occupied by dismounted cavalry, who, however, retired on the approach of infantry.

They retreated through the town, which was then occupied by the Prussians. But at that juncture the Austrian brigade Mondl arrived on the heights of the Galgenberg and Hopfenberg, which rise with steep slopes south and east of the town high above the banks of the river Aupa. Two battalions of the advanced guard deployed to attack this position, but, though supported by some companies of the flank detachment and the enfilading fire of two batteries, they made no progress. At 11.30 General Bonin detailed five battalions and one battery under General Buddenbrock to advance in the direction of Hohenbruck-Alt Rognitz, to attack the flank of the enemy's position. At the same time he sent urgent orders to the battalions of the advanced guard to press the attack on the heights to the utmost. As the plateau is only accessible by deep valleys with steep sides, the advance of Buddenbrock's battalions was extremely difficult, and so slow that the heights were taken by the renewed efforts of the reinforced advanced guard before the outflanking force arrived. At 1 p.m. they began to emerge from the ravines, and to attack the flank of the retreating Austrians, but only three and a half battalions continued the frontal attack, as the other three and a half battalions were withdrawn to Trautenau, evidently under the impression that the crisis had passed. By 3 p.m. the Prussian battalions occupied the position Hohenbruck-Alt Rognitz, whilst the brigade Mondl, by order of General Gablenz, commanding the X Army Corps, was falling back to a position at New Rognitz, where they were to await reinforcements.

At 1 p.m. the 1st Guard Infantry Division had arrived

at Parschnitz on their march to Eipel, but their assistance was declined by General Bonin, as he thought the fight was progressing well, and he had only one brigade opposed to him. As the fire ceased about 3 o'clock the battle seemed over, and the Guard Division continued their march.

But at 3.30, when the remaining three and a half battalions of the frontal attack had all been recalled to Trautenau by a signal given by mistake, Buddenbrock's battalions were attacked on the left by the newly arrived brigade Grivicic, and in front by the brigade Mondl; after a vigorous resistance they began to retreat at about 4 p.m., when they were in danger of being quite outflanked. The advance of the enemy was temporarily checked by four battalions, who came up into a line stretching from the heights south-east of the Kapelle to the edge of the wood north-east of Kriblitz. But the enemy was now reinforced by the brigade Wimpfen, and forty guns opened fire on these heights and the town, from which the troops were withdrawn towards Parschnitz at 4.30. For some time two battalions of the 43rd Regiment repulsed all attacks of the brigade Wimpfen, but when at 6.30 another Austrian brigade, that of Knebel, joined in the attack from Alt Rognitz, a retreat on Parschnitz was commenced and covered by two battalions, whose determined attitude prevented the Austrians from issuing from the town till 9 p.m., when they followed the general retreat. The Austrians made no attempt at pursuit, for three companies of the 41st and 43rd Regiments remained quite unmolested at the eastern end of Prauschnitz till 3.30 next morning

And yet the retreat of the whole army corps was

continued through the night, till the troops, utterly exhausted, reached the places of bivouac on the northern side of the mountains twenty-four hours after they had left them.

It seems hopeless to try to find any excuse for such senseless proceedings, which worthily crowned the follies committed during the battle.

Comment. The army corps suffered all day long from the initial mistake of not occupying the heights commanding the town, and the outlets of the two defiles directly after the arrival of the left column. Opposed for hours by only one brigade, the army corps profited in no way by its great numerical superiority. Whilst the greater portion of the corps remained inactive north of the Aupa, the actual fighting was carried on by single disconnected battalions detached from different brigades without any central control; they were indeed reinforced at times, but by driblets and in a fitful fashion. The infantry fought most obstinately, but almost without any support from the other arms, for the greatest part of the artillery remained in their initial positions, from which their fire could not reach the actual field of action. Out of twenty-five battalions only nine were seriously engaged, as can be proved by the list of losses. The withdrawal of units from the fighting line merely on the ground of a temporary cessation of fire was naturally followed by the most serious consequences, and seems quite inexcusable, not to speak of the fact that a bugle signal sounded by mistake caused three and a half battalions to retire from the firing line at a time, when their presence could not be spared. Evidently no serious attempt was made to restore the battle, when the

Austrians were enabled by their reinforcements to take the offensive, and the various units seem to have commenced and continued the retreat without any orders or attempts to stop them. And yet the retreat was carried on with the knowledge and almost under the eyes of the General, who, during the greatest part of the day, had been two and a half miles from the ground where the turn of fortune took place. If at least the two defiles had been kept guarded during the night by a position taken up on the heights between Nieder-Altstadt and Welhota, the General could have waited there without danger for the advance of the Guard Corps to disengage him, or could have repeated the attack in the morning. Neither the defeat nor the retreat were reported to the Crown Prince, who had only received news of a victory gained by 1 o'clock.

The Austrians in a force of 28 battalions and 72 guns lost 183 officers, 4,231 men killed and wounded, 8 officers and 365 men prisoners; the Prussians, 25 battalions strong with 96 guns, lost 56 officers and 1,196 men killed and wounded, 86 men missing.

Battle of Nachod It has been already mentioned that General Ramming, commanding the VI Austrian Army Corps, received at Opocno the order to advance to Skalitz on the 27th and to push one brigade forward to Nachod. This order, issued at Josephstadt at 8 p.m., did not reach Ramming till 1.30 a.m., although the distance between the two places is only about nine miles: a clear proof that the proceedings of the Austrian Staff were not very business-like, and not calculated to deal with critical situations where rapidity of execution is of the utmost importance.

The faultiness of the order itself has already been pointed out.

Ramming had 28,000 infantry, 4,000 cavalry and 88 guns; General Steinmetz, commanding the 5th Prussian Corps, 22,000 infantry, 2,000 cavalry and 90 guns.

At 2.15 a.m. Ramming issued orders that the brigade Hertweck was to march on Wysokow, the brigade Jonak via Wrchowin to Kleny, the brigade Rosenzweig to Skalitz, and the brigade Waldstädter to the same place by a different road.

The brigades were late in starting. Ramming rode at 5 a.m. from Opocno to Skalitz, then to Kleny, where he was informed that the 1st Reserve Cavalry Division had had to give up Wysokow; at 8.30 he gave orders that the brigades Rosenzweig and Jonak, the cavalry division and the artillery reserve, should be drawn up at Kleny.

Hertweck ought to have marched to Wysokow on the ridge of hills, but in the intention not to be separated from the main body of the army corps he took the direction towards Kleny, so that his brigade, at 7.30, arrived at Sonow, where they found detachments of the Prussian advanced guard, which consisted of five and a half battalions under General Löwenfeldt. Hertweck deployed his advanced troops near the church at Wenzelsberg, and formed up his brigade astride the road. After keeping up a useless musketry fire for nearly an hour, the heights held by the enemy were attacked, but without success; the brigade had to fall back across the road to Sonow.

Hertweck had requested Jonak, who had arrived at

Domkow, to come to his assistance. His brigade came into the fighting line north of Sonow at 9.30, then the brigade Rosenzweig prolonged the left wing east of Promodow, and the brigade Waldstädter also received later on the order to attack Wysokow. The artillery reserve, i.e. the corps artillery, which ought to have prepared the general attack, did not arrive at Skalitz till 11 a.m., together with a cavalry brigade.

The Prussian battalions had been driven back behind the road to Neustadt, and they maintained with difficulty the uneven fight against twenty-one Austrian battalions, whilst only two batteries kept up their fire against thirty-two guns till 12 o'clock. At that time the position of the Prussians became very critical, but momentary relief was afforded by a successful charge of a cavalry brigade on the right flank : they not only drove the cavalry brigade Solms on the Austrian left back to Kleny, but also broke several rallying squares of the infantry on the left flank.

Then, soon after 12 o'clock, the leading battalions of the 10th Prussian Division arrived on the battlefield, and attacked first the left wing of the brigade Rosenzweig. An attack of the brigade Waldstädter at 2 p.m. was repulsed, and the whole Austrian force was now steadily driven back, as more Prussian battalions were gradually joining the advance. At 3 p.m. General Ramming gave the order for the retreat to Skalitz, which was covered by a cavalry brigade of the reserve and part of the corps artillery. The Austrians had lost 227 officers and 3,419 men killed and wounded, 5 officers and 2,068 men prisoners, also 8 guns and 2 colours. The Prussians had lost 62 officers and 1,046 men killed and wounded,

14 men missing : the cavalry charge accounted for 20 out of the 62 officers.

Comment   The retreating enemy was not pressed by the Prussian troops, who went into bivouac on the battlefield. This step seems to be open to criticism, for five out of the eight regiments engaged (3,000 each) had only lost about 100 officers and men each. Strategy demanded that Ramming's corps should have been destroyed or scattered and that Skalitz should have been occupied, which should then have caused the Crown Prince to draw together the Guard Corps complete at Eipel and Kaile before the end of the day. By these two moves the two corps would have been approached to a distance of only eight miles, and would thus have formed a strong central body in the Silesian army. It has been said that this action on the part of Steinmetz shows an example of the difference between a good leader of troops and a genius: the former carries out the orders received with energy and success, the latter, not satisfied with such a result, makes it the stepping-stone to unexpected, more far-reaching actions.

The causes of the Austrian defeat are not difficult to find. The faultiness of the initial orders was followed by the slowness in their transmission, and then again by the want of prompt decision and rapid action on the part of the General. If he had started from Opocnoc at 3 a.m. with a cavalry regiment and some of his artillery, he might have been on the plateau near Wysokow as early as the Prussians. The chief mistake lay in the fact that the Austrian brigades fought without connection and unison of purpose, just as the different units of the 1st Prussian Army Corps fought at Trautenau on the same day. Here also was missing a direct, personal control, the same as on that battlefield, for Ramming was mostly near Kleny instead of being in a central position amongst his fighting troops, as Steinmetz was on his side.

If we consider the events of the day from a tactical point of view, we see that one Prussian brigade of not quite six battalions with two batteries resisted for four hours the attacks of a force which gradually increased to twenty-one battalions. The Austrian musketry fire was bad, whilst the Prussians were firing deliberately and with good result, as can be gathered from the comparatively high percentage of the Austrian losses : their officers judged distances well and the sights were properly adjusted.

With regard to the shock tactics in which the Austrians boastingly confided, the experience of this battle showed that the Prussians attacked with the bayonet as often as the Austrians, and with greater success.

The condition of the VI Austrian Corps after the battle is clearly demonstrated by the following message which General Ramming sent, at 5.30 p.m., to Field-Marshal Benedek :—

"It is my duty to report that, without assistance, I shall not be able to oppose any attack to-morrow morning; I therefore beg to be relieved by the VIII Corps before to-morrow. My cavalry are so utterly exhausted that they are not capable of any movement."

These words show plainly, what the result would have been, if Steinmetz had executed a vigorous pursuit with all those regiments which had only been under fire a short time and had suffered small losses.

Combat of Oswiecim

On the same day took place a slight engagement on the frontier of Upper Silesia, near the boundary line of Western Galicia. The various railway bridges along the frontier had been destroyed at the commencement of hostilities, but it was thought that the task of covering Upper Silesia could be most easily accomplished by an offensive movement into the enemy's territory. To carry out this idea, a detachment of four and a half battalions of infantry, two squadrons of cavalry and two guns, crossed the frontier with the intention of occupying Oswiecim. The enemy were driven out of the village, but repeated attempts to take the station buildings proved a failure, whereupon the detachment retreated and recrossed the frontier, after sustaining a loss of 6 officers, 166 men killed and wounded.

Events on the Iser

On the 27th General Count Clam had determined to retire from Münchengrätz, and to cover the northern flank during that movement he had ordered one brigade to occupy Podkost, which afforded a strong position for the defence of an important defile against the advance of hostile forces from the north. A cavalry division was to start at 4 a.m. on the 28th, to reconnoitre towards Sobotka and Gitschin, the main body of the army corps was to follow at 5 a.m., leaving the brigade Leiningen as rearguard to take up a position at Münchengrätz.

At the Headquarters of the 1st Prussian Army the disposition of the enemy's forces does not seem to have been known, for on the 25th Prince Frederick Charles had written to General Herwarth: "In consideration of the very deficient information about the strength and position of the Austrian troops at Prag and Leitmeritz, it is distinctly necessary to cover the right flank." To attain this object the Guard Landwehr Division, which was following the advance of the Elbe Army, should have been strengthened by cavalry and artillery, and directed towards Leitmeritz and Prag via Wernstadt and Raudnitz. The general situation in fact demanded such a movement, for the occupation of this city would have given to the invading army an excellent depôt and a new basis.

Combat of Münchengrätz

The Prince also presumed (entrenching had been reported) that the Austrians meant to hold Münchengrätz, and ordered the Elbe Army to advance from Niemes, so that its forces could attack the front of the position at 9 a.m. on the 28th, whilst the 1st Army was to fall upon the flank and rear of the Austrian defence. For that purpose the 5th Division, under General Tümpling, was to advance to Rowensko and to reconnoitre towards Gitschin.

The attack of the advanced guard of the Elbe Army took place as ordered: at 10 a.m. General Leiningen had to retreat across the Iser, put on fire the bridge between Kloster and Münchengrätz, and was at 11 a.m. forced to retire from the strong position on the Musky mountain east of the town, because the danger of being outflanked from the north and perhaps cut off became then imminent. He retreated on another brigade left behind for his security by the main body, and both together followed the latter to Sobotka.

In the meantime the Austrian detachment sent to reconnoitre towards Gitschin had met a small Prussian force sent forward with the same object; after a slight engagement the latter retired in the direction of Rowensko. Thus warned of the threatening approach of the 1st Prussian Army, General Clam had Gitschin occupied by one brigade the same evening.

This day's fighting had caused the Austrians the loss of 20 officers and 1,634 men, including 5 officers and 1,211 men taken prisoners, whilst the Prussians had lost 8 officers and 333 men.

In the evening the bulk of the I Austrian Corps was at Sobotka, the Saxon Corps about Brezno and Unter-Bautzen, the Elbe Army about Münchengrätz, the 1st Prussian Army east of the Iser on the roads to Gitschin.

Late at night on the 27th the telegraph had announced at Münchengrätz that the Headquarters of the Austrian army would arrive at Gitschin on the 28th, in the morning the Crown Prince of Saxony had received the order to begin with both his corps the march towards a junction with the great army. On the 28th the Austrian Headquarters evidently still expected to be at Gitschin on the 29th and 30th, as the two corps were ordered to march early on the 29th to Gitschin and Podhrad.

Podkost

In execution of General Clam's dispositions, the brigade Ringelsheim had arrived late in the evening of the 27th at Podkost; their outposts were attacked about 11 p.m. and driven back a short distance. The firing ceased at 1 a.m.; at 3 a.m. the attack began again, but was unsuccessful, as the defile was blocked by a strong castle and the heights on both sides well occupied. At 7 a.m. the castle was abandoned and the brigade withdrawn in the direction of Gitschin, which was reached at 1 p.m.; the object of covering the flank of the I Army Corps leaving Münchengrätz had been attained.

H

EVENTS ON JUNE 28 AND 29

CHAPTER VI

A. EVENTS ON JUNE 28

Battle of Burkersdorf (or Soor) At 1 a.m. on the 28th the Crown Prince of Prussia had received the news of the unsuccessful result of the battle of Trautenau. In consequence Steinmetz could not be supported by one of the divisions of the Guards, but their whole strength had to be employed to disengage the 1st Army Corps and to open the defile of Trautenau. In the supposition that this corps would renew on the 28th the attempt to debouch from the mountains, and in ignorance of the fact that it had gone back to Liebau and Schömberg, the Crown Prince at 2 a.m. issued orders to General Prince August of Würtemberg, commanding the Guards to continue the march to Kaile, and, in case of the fight continuing at Trautenau, to proceed there and give assistance. In execution of this order the 2nd Division at Kostelec paraded at 4.30 and marched off to Eipel, where it arrived at 7.45 behind the 1st Guard Brigade, when the 2nd Brigade had already passed through, and the advanced guard was approaching Ober-Raatsch.

General Gablenz had reported to Field-Marshal Benedek, at 9.15 p.m. on the 27th, the dispositions he had made after the battle at Trautenau, had expressed apprehensions about his right flank, and asked for supports to occupy Prausnitz in order to secure that side. At 6 a.m. on the 28th he received the reply that four battalions of the IV Corps would forthwith be sent to occupy Prausnitz, Kaile and Eipel; but by a mistake these battalions were directed to a place, Prausnitz, five miles west of Königinhof, and Benedek was not informed of it. Then at 7 a.m. Gablenz received orders to leave Trautenau, to hasten his retreat to Prausnitz, and there to take up a position facing east to oppose strong columns of the enemy moving in that neighbourhood.

Comments
This partial retrograde movement could be of no ultimate advantage; the corps had suffered great losses, after which it could not be supposed to be strong enough to oppose attacks from north and east by two forces each probably superior in numbers. The corps should have been—after the issue of the battle of Nachod—taken back to Königinhof or, via Pilnikau, direct behind the Elbe.

A tangible mistake was also made in the dispositions for the march of the 2nd Guard Division from Kostelec: instead of leaving the corps artillery and the heavy cavalry brigade to march behind the infantry, they ought to have been sent on to Eipel at a trot, so as to be near the plateau of Staudenz, the only spot in that locality where they could be of much use. The Crown Prince also should have hurried there to have obtained a personal insight in the conditions of the important engagement to be fought.

The Battle
Directly after receipt of his orders Gablenz had sent off his transport towards Prausnitz,

the brigades Knebel and Wimpfen were to follow with the corps artillery, the flank was to be covered by a regiment of cavalry with one battery, ordered to march via Alt-Rognitz to Staudenz, and there to take up a position. The brigade Mondl was to form the rearguard, and the brigade Grivicic was to march from the hills at Kriblitz via Alt-Rognitz to Raatsch, and take up a position there: this should have been done on the previous evening or early in the morning.

The approach of the flank-guard to Staudenz was observed and reported by the Prussian cavalry, upon which Prince Würtemberg gave the extraordinary order for his advanced guard to fall back and take a position behind the Aupa, instead of going to see himself what was happening. He sent word to the Army Headquarters that the connection with the 1st Corps was not yet established, and that he would assume a waiting position, until he could arrange further action in concert with that corps. This decision was clearly contrary to his orders, which directed him to proceed to Kaile before entering upon any farther movements.

At 9 a.m. he ordered the advance on Burkersdorf. His advanced guard passed through Staudenz at 9.30, and then came in view of the Austrian corps artillery, which took up a position at Burkersdorf, flanked on both sides by the brigade Knebel and the cavalry regiment: an artillery duel ensued. At 11.30 the Guards attacked Burkersdorf and took it; the brigade Knebel with the batteries retired to Altenbuch, where they were joined by brigades Wimpfen and Mondl: they all then retreated towards Pilnikau.

The brigade Grivicic on the march to Raatsch, left

without news or instructions, had passed Alt-Rognitz and Rüdersdorf, when it was attacked at 12 o'clock by parts of the 2nd Guard Division : the struggle was fierce and obstinate, but by 3 p.m. the Austrian brigade was so completely routed, that only 2,000 men succeeded in getting away to Pilnikau. The Guards had lost 28 officers and 685 men, 15 and 402, respectively, in the two regiments which did most of the fighting. The Austrian loss amounted to 55 officers and 1,079 men killed and wounded ; 68 officers, 2,617 men were taken prisoners.

During the fighting, simultaneously with which an engagement took place at Skalitz, the Crown Prince had been on a hill near Kostelec, and after receipt of the news that Skalitz had been taken, had hastened to Eipel, where he learnt that his 1st Corps was at Liebau on Prussian ground. He now determined to assemble his army on the following day, the 29th, on the plateau north of Königinhof.

Comment If Prince August had not retarded the advance of the 1st Guard Division by more than an hour, and if the cavalry brigade and the corps artillery had been to the front, only small parts of the Austrian X Corps would have escaped captivity.

The most profitable way of supporting Steinmetz at Skalitz would have been to occupy Staudenz ; if this had been done early, part of the Guards could have taken the Austrians in the rear, whilst they were being attacked in front by Steinmetz.

Battle of Skalitz In consequence of the report which General Ramming had sent to Benedek after the engagement fought at Nachod, the VIII

Austrian Corps had relieved the VI Corps in the positions which the troops occupied after the fighting and the retreat to Skalitz, which had not been pressed by the Prussians: the Archduke Leopold was put in command of the two corps. The IV Corps also had been brought up as further support from Josephstadt.

At 10.30 Benedek arrived at Skalitz, and saw Prussian troops at Dubno and on the Schafberg, but drew the conclusion that a direct attack on Skalitz was not intended, but rather a turning movement via Chwalkowitz. He therefore gave the order that, in case no fighting should occur by 2 p.m., the VI Corps was to move south from Trebesow, and to be followed by the VIII Corps. Directly after this order had been written out by the head of the Army Staff, Benedek gave the Archduke the verbal order to march off at once, and when on his drive back to Josephstadt he saw General Ramming, he ordered him also to begin the movement at once : a psychologist might find it hard to explain such contradiction of purpose at a most important moment. The second order was not executed.

The brigade Schulz of the VIII Corps was posted at and about Skalitz, forming the right wing ; the brigade Kreyssern was in the centre, and the brigade Fragnern on the left wing. The position had a length of only about 2,500 yards, which allowed eight men per yard ; the Aupa, with steep rocky banks, was behind it, and 500 yards in front of the left wing there was a wood !

Ramming would have acted more wisely, if, after his retreat on the previous evening, he had occupied the heights on the right bank of the Aupa, but he hoped to be soon relieved, and had evidently not taken the trouble to study the local geography; nor had the chief staff officer of the VIII Corps inspected the position. Anyhow, General Fragnern, in command of the left wing, should have occupied Zlitsch to secure the bridge over the Aupa behind that village, as it gave easy access to the line of retreat.

The Battle Directly after Benedek had on parting given the Archduke the order to retire from his position, the latter directed verbally one battalion to reconnoitre the forest of Dubno, and, if it should be occupied by hostile troops, to drive them out; this movement, as will be seen, brought on the engagement which was to have been avoided.

Steinmetz had received orders to take Skalitz. One brigade of the 6th Corps had arrived as reinforcement of the 5th Corps, and two more brigades were expected during the day; but, to judge from their watchfires at night, the Austrians seemed to be several army corps strong. In view of these conditions of comparative strength, Steinmetz determined to seize the heights at Studnitz, north of Skalitz, in order to facilitate his junction with the promised division of Guards, and to be able, in case of necessity, to fall back on the Guards towards Kostelec; but to evacuate Wysokow was dangerous, because an Austrian force coming from Neustadt (south) could then gain the plateau and wedge in between him and the approaching main body of the 6th Corps. To obtain exact information on the possibility of such a move, he sent at 5 a.m. a regiment of cavalry to reconnoitre the whole countryside towards Neustadt, and on receipt of the report that no enemies could be seen in that direction, he ordered General

Löwenfeldt, at 7 a.m., to march off to Studnitz with six battalions, to effect a junction with the expected division of Guards, and to advance together with them against Skalitz. The advanced guard of the 5th Corps, three battalions and two batteries with a regiment of cavalry, deployed at 8 a.m. between Starkosch and the railway, the 9th Division was on the Nachod road, and on the left of it the brigade Hoffmann of the 6th Corps; the 9th Division had received the general direction to advance north of the highroad behind the advanced guard.

By 11 a.m. Löwenfeldt had passed Studnitz and reached the Schafberg, where he deployed his brigade, occupying the Dubno farm with one battalion. Steinmetz, who had just then received the intimation that only the heavy cavalry of the Guard would join him, at once ordered Löwenfeldt to attack, and sent the same order to the other units.

Nine battalions rushed from various directions into the above-mentioned wood, where the one battalion of Austrians sent there by the Archduke was severely handled and nearly annihilated; the corps batteries came up at Kleny, and began a lively artillery duel with the Austrian guns posted east of Skalitz. As the brigades Fragnern and Kreyssern had not received orders to retreat, Fragnern sent supports into the wood, also towards Zlitsch to cover the left flank, and south towards the railway. They could not advance across the embankment under the fire of infantry in the ditch of the road opposite, and, as they gradually got fire also in flank and rear, were forced to retire to Skalitz: only a few detachments managed to get back to their original position. Then five battalions of the brigade Kreyssern advanced against the railway embankment with the same result. The retreat of the two brigades was covered by the fire of two battalions and the corps batteries, whilst brigade Schulz had begun its retreat at 1 p.m. by order of the Archduke. At 3 p.m. the east entrance of the town, obstinately defended by three battalions, was taken by assault, rifle companies approached Klein-Skalitz, having passed the bridge near Zlitsch. The brigade Rosenzweig of the VI Corps at Trebesow covered the farther retreat of the VIII, and finally fell back in its own turn to Schweinschädel, where the IV Corps had arrived at 1 p.m. During the night the VIII Corps reached Salney; the VI Corps got to Lanzow on the next morning.

The Austrians lost 184 officers and 3,106 men killed and wounded, 21 officers and 2,266 men taken prisoners. The Prussian fire had been very deadly: the brigade Fragnern had 824 dead, 620 wounded; the brigade Kreyssern 352 dead, 639 wounded. The Prussians lost 62 officers and 1,290 men killed and wounded; 13 men missing.

The Prussians camped near Skalitz, the Guards Cuirassier Brigade went back to Kostelec, where their presence was perfectly useless: if they had crossed the bridge at Zlitsch and occupied the plateau of Ratiboritz, they would have covered the right flank of the 5th Corps, have maintained the connection with the Guards Corps, and been in a position to watch the Chwalkowitz road.

Comment The Archduke Leopold received the order to retreat to Salney at 11 a.m., when two roads were open to him for the movement, the main road and the one via Zwol to Jaromir. He was not talented, still less good-natured, rather irritable and self-conceited, also without any war experience; but he was Chief Commandant of Marines and Director of Engineers, also senior amongst the generals commanding army corps. When therefore he by chance heard Benedek assign an independent command to General Gablenz, he believed himself passed over purposely. In this frame of mind he sent the 4th Battalion Crenneville into the forest, which provoked and brought on the battle, during which he remained passive, because he had no practice in handling troops. In consequence there was no control or direction during the action, and the brigadiers had to act each on his own idea. Fragnern preferred the wood to the narrow ridge for fighting, other troops were attracted in the same direction by the firing, and ultimately there were 14,000 men of different nationalities crowded together on a small space of ground, hindering each other even in the use of their rifles, without direction or control, an easy target to the encircling, much weaker enemy, with the result that within an hour 3,000 men were lost. Neither fire tactics nor shock tactics had anything to do with this result; it was only a case of order and firm control defeating senselessness, lack of leading and the resulting disorder. In spite of many defects, the position might have been tenable, if the brigade Fragnern had been posted behind Zlitsch on the heights near Castle Ratiboritz, if Skalitz had been occupied by the brigade Schulz, and if the ridge extending to Zlitsch and the Aupa valley had been enfiladed by a few well-covered batteries at Skalitz.

The attack by the Prussians was started sensibly and carried through with satisfactory energy: the line of the Aupa was occupied as ordered, just as the line of the Mettau on the previous day. But from the geographico-strategical point of view communications are more important than watercourses, and therefore orders should have been given to capture the heights of Trebesow-Schweinschädel in order to place the Guards Corps at Staudenz into safe communication with the 5th and 6th Corps. The retreat of the VI and VIII Austrian Corps could be watched from the hill near Klein-Skalitz, and could not but invite a vigorous pursuit in view of the condition of the Austrian troops, evidenced by the large number of prisoners. It is true that farther advance had not been ordered, but surely an independent commander must be allowed to use all opportunities to inflict losses on the enemy, and a passive restraint after a victorious fight is therefore not justified: neither at Berlin nor at the Headquarters of the 2nd Army could these local circumstances and conditions be foreseen, judged and dealt with by special orders; these belong to the province of personal observation and of the psychological instinct of what is possible and attainable at the moment.

To reap the full advantage of the victory the Guard Cavalry Brigade and the 10th Division could advance to Chwalkowitz, the other three brigades against Schweinschädel, both merely an hour's march from the Aupa. The result would have been the defeat of the three brigades of the IV Austrian Corps, which would have immensely increased the disorder and discouragement already existing. Benedek had assembled about Skalitz three army corps, not really in order to attack, but to support and relieve each other, and this presumed prudence and circumspection would then have resulted in their retreat behind the Elbe, defeated and humiliated. Even Jaromir, with its passage over the Elbe, might perhaps have been before night in the hands of the enemy.

If Steinmetz had been in Bonin's place at Trautenau, he would, without doubt, not have hesitated a moment to attack Gablenz with all his might and to drive him back behind Prausnitz, for in that case the wording of his order would not have put a limit to his energy and natural thoroughness; he was an eminent leader, but without the exceptional fruitful talent given only to nature's few favourites. The Archduke, on the other hand, would not obey, and could not command.

The Crown Prince, who in the morning had gone to the heights of Kostelec, where the reserve artillery of the Guards Corps had arrived, moved his headquarters to Eipel, but went to Trautenau himself. The three brigades of the 6th Army Corps, which had reached Rückerts, were ordered to continue the advance, to reinforce the 5th Corps and cover the left flank of the army; Steinmetz was to command the 6th Corps together with his own.

B. Events on June 29
Battle of Gitschin

Dispositions of Forces

The orders issued by Benedek seem to be founded on the surmise that he would succeed in assembling his main forces west of Josephstadt by the 30th, so as to make an offensive movement against the 1st Prussian Army : the III Corps was to march on the 29th from Miletin to Gitschin, one cavalry division to Horiz, and on the 30th three or four more corps were to follow in the direction of Lomnitz. It seems as if he had still considered one or two corps sufficient to hold the upper course of the Elbe and cover his right flank in the intended movement to the west. This communication from Benedek arrived at Gitschin on the 29th at 2 p.m., when Clam Gallas, in temporary absence of the Crown Prince of Saxony, had the command of the two army corps ; he determined to defend the position which had been chosen as follows : On the left Lochow, on the road from Münchengrätz, was held by the brigade Ringelsheim, north-east of it the heights of Prachow and Brada by the brigades Abele and Poschacher with the brigade Leiningen in reserve behind Brada ; Eisenstadtl on the right was held by the brigade Piret, and in the interval at Diletz there was a cavalry division and the reserve artillery. The Saxon Corps, which had left the neighbourhood of Unter-Bautzen at 3 a.m., had arrived near Podhrad before noon, and two ot its brigades were detailed to move to Diletz in case of an attack by the enemy.

Prince Frederick Charles was informed on the 28th, by telegram from Berlin, of the probable location and disposition of the Austrian corps, also of the advance of the Crown Prince's forces, of which the 1st Army Corps, however, were still at Liebenau and three brigades of the 6th at Lewin. Under these circumstances it seemed necessary that the 1st Army should advance beyond the originally fixed rendezvous at Gitschin, which the Prince had already resolved to do, when, at

7 a.m. on the 29th, he received a telegram from Berlin, informing him that the King expected the 1st Army to disengage by an accelerated advance the 2nd Army, then in a difficult position. At 9 a.m. the following orders were issued: The 3rd Division (Werder) marches via Sobotka to Gitschin, to be followed by the 7th Division (Fransecky). The 5th Division (Tümpling) is to start at once, take Gitschin, and push forward advanced guards beyond it, to be followed by the 4th Division (Herwarth) and the Cavalry Division (Alvensleben). The 6th Division (Manstein), the 8th Division (Horn) and the Cavalry Division (Hann) are to take up positions at Ober and Unter-Bautzen towards Jung-Bunzlau.

The Battle   The division Tümpling left Rowensko at 1.30 p.m., and its advanced guard reached Libun at 3.30. The General resolved to hold the two Austrian brigades on the steep heights of Prachow and Brada by a containing attack by three battalions of the 10th Brigade, and to take Zames and Diletz with the 9th Brigade: this was carried out. But when the 2nd Saxon Division arrived at Gitschin, they were ordered by their Crown Prince to recapture Diletz, which they did, whilst the Austrian brigade Piret advanced from Eisenstadtl against Zames. Against this attack Tümpling was obliged to bring up the last battalion of his reserve, but at that time Major Sternberg, of the Headquarters Staff, brought Benedek's order to avoid any engagement with superior hostile forces, and to effect a junction with the main army near Horiz and Miletin, as the four army corps previously promised had meanwhile received a different destination. The Saxon Crown Prince in consequence ordered a general retreat.

I

On the Münchengrätz road the brigade Ringelsheim fought with alternating success from 5.30 against the 3rd Division Werder, which succeeded in gaining Wostrushno, and forcing the cavalry brigade to retire behind Wohawee. A counter attack made by General Ringelsheim at 8.15 was well delivered, but was defeated by rapid firing: it had evidently been made to cover the general retreat. The regiment Würtemberg fell back fighting and supported by the fire of some batteries, till it arrived in a shattered condition at the gate of Gitschin, the occupation of which was now committed to the Saxon Life Brigade. In the meantime the Saxon division had fallen back from Diletz to the Zebinberg, and the brigade Piret, whose attack on Zames had failed, to the monastery of the Carthusians; the greater part of the brigades Poschacher and Abele had retired on Gitschin, leaving at Poduls, on the Brada hill and at Prachow, a few detachments, which were later on destroyed on their retreat.

By 11 p.m. most parts of the town had been evacuated by the troops crossing in all directions, but before the Saxon Life Brigade had arrived to occupy it, a Prussian battalion had entered from the west, but was again driven out by 11.30. The Saxon Brigade marched off at 12.30, and after a short engagement with its rearguard, troops of the 3rd and 5th Prussian Divisions marched into the town. This fighting in the dark had very unpleasant results, for in the confusion caused by it the Austrian brigades did not receive the dispositions made for the retreat, and in consequence the units of the main body got mixed up retreating on Horiz and on Miletin, whilst some, mixed up with the Saxons, retired towards Smirdar.

The Austrians lost 184 officers, 4,704 men; the Saxons, 26 officers, 566 men;. the Prussians, 71 officers, 1,482 men.

Comment   The total strength of the two allied corps was 66,000 nominally, but only four Austrian and two Saxon brigades, with only a portion of the cavalry, took part in the engagement, about 42,000 men, who were opposed by two divisions of a normal strength of 26,000. This statement shows that the Allies could have employed great superiority of strength in making an attack on *one* road or taking a position of defence near the junction of both roads ; but, instead of doing either, they took up with 24,000 men the position on the northern road from Eisenstadtl to Brada, which was certainly strong in physical features and favourable artillery positions, the occupation of which, however, depended on the resistance which the brigade Ringelsheim could offer on the western road against the 3rd Prussian Division ; as soon as part of the latter obtained possession of Wostruschno, the position at Diletz would have had to be given up, even if the retreat had not been ordered from headquarters.

The point has been raised that the Saxon troops should not have been inserted in the midst of Austrian units, but should have been placed separately on the left flank between Prachow and Lochow ; but in comparing times, it would appear that the 2nd Saxon Division, which was the first to arrive, did not appear till after the fight had commenced. Therefore all surmises of a better result drawn from the assumption of the possibility of that arrangement must fall to the ground.

But it seems quite legitimate to criticise the way in

which Benedek's order was interpreted and acted upon : " to avoid any fight with *superior* hostile forces and to continue the retrograde movement to the main army " does not mean to break off a combat fully engaged, which should have been successful if properly conducted ; in fact, it was less dangerous to carry on the fight than to get disengaged and retire, as nothing was foreseen and prepared for that eventuality. Besides, such orders are only to be obeyed implicitly, if the officer who issues them has complete knowledge of the actual condition of affairs, if he is present on the spot, or can be immediately informed of the impossibility or difficulty of executing his order : this was not the case here, and the Saxon Crown Prince should have taken the responsibility of acting independently. But if the order for retreat was not warranted by the circumstances of the case, the dispositions made for it by the Staff were too complicated, belated and therefore useless. In such a case a pedantic chief of the Staff, fond of writing out detailed orders, is of no good ; a few sharp words, a few clear directions given on the spot from the saddle to energetic adjutants must suffice to set the whole machinery working in the new direction.

As it was certainly the fatal order for retreat which caused the defeat of the Allies, the question arises, why the attacking force was comparatively so small, seeing that it was even apprehended that the Saxon Crown Prince might have been reinforced by the III Austrian Corps. This question implies a doubt in the correctness of the conduct of operations by the Commander-in-Chief : an important battle of doubtful issue was fought by only about 20,000 men without the presence of a superior commander, when the Prince had at his disposal a force of about 130,000 men. The two divisions employed did not belong to the same army corps, nor did those ordered to follow them: the unity of the army corps formation, so long established in the Prussian army, had been abolished at a critical period in this one army to please and satisfy the idiosyncrasies and jealousy of command of an imperious temperament.

A great mistake in the opposite direction had been made in the useless assembly of great forces for the capture of the position of Münchengrätz: the Prince had only to march rapidly with close columns from Reichenau to Gitschin to separate the Saxon Crown Prince hopelessly from the Austrian main army. Again, if one considers the fact that the large force of cavalry was systematically left behind the infantry instead of having the theatre of operations traversed and reconnoitred by them, one can understand, how the patient Moltke even lost his patience at last, and induced the King to express an urgent demand for rapid and decided advance.

The 7th Prussian Division (Fransecky) had heard at the rendezvous at Sobotka the thunder of the guns at Gitschin, had marched off in its direction at 6 p.m. and advanced as far as Wohariz.

Situation in Other Parts of the Theatre of Operations

The 2nd Prussian Army Corps was intended to reach the Elbe on the 29th. The 1st Army Corps was moved forward via Trautenau and was in bivouac round Pilnikau, the Cavalry Division *following* (!); it arrived at

Prausnitz-Kaile, to which place the Crown Prince also moved his headquarters.

The Guards Corps and the 5th Corps did not reach their points of destination without some fighting.

Benedek saw that the corps which had got into contact with the columns of the 2nd Army on the left bank of the Elbe had been driven across the river as the result of the previous day's fighting, and he had only his IV Corps still posted on the left bank, half a brigade (three battalions) occupying Königinhof, the other three brigades at Dolan (four and a half miles from Skalitz).

Now for the first time the danger of the advance of the 2nd Army seems to have been appreciated in the Austrian Headquarters. The intended forward movement towards the Iser had to be given up, and the units which had been already sent off in that direction, viz. the III Army Corps and the 3rd Reserve Cavalry Division, received counter orders whilst on the march.

We have seen already that the I and the Saxon Corps were ordered to join the main army at Horiz and Miletin, where the III Corps was now told to remain. The other units were to be concentrated in a position on the plateau of Dubenetz (five miles west of Jaromir) to face the army of the Crown Prince. The IV Corps was provisionally to stay at Dolan, but not to engage in an unequal fight, but rather retire to Salney heights (four miles north west of Jaromir), where two cavalry divisions were already posted facing east. The II Army Corps was directed to occupy the heights from Salney to Kukus (on the Elbe, six miles west of Skalitz), and to be prepared to resist attack from east as well as from north-west. Two brigades of the VIII Corps should form the reserve to the IV and II, its 3rd Brigade be on the left of the II Corps facing north, the VI Corps to extend the line to the left with the flank covered by two cavalry divisions; the X Corps was designated to be the reserve for this flank. The Army Artillery Reserve was to remain at Gross Bürglitz (seven miles west of Jaromir), the Headquarters were established at Dubenetz and the construction of battery epaulements was commenced.

As the advanced IV Army Corps came across the Elbe in the course of the day, as will be seen later on, all the troops reached the positions allotted to them during the afternoon and evening. The army was thus able to receive on the 30th the attack of the Silesian army. In a line of only six miles there were assembled five corps and four cavalry divisions. Although the ground within the area of the position was not favourable to unhindered communication, yet it contained a considerable strength of resistance on account of the Elbe and the fair height of the hills towards north and east. On the other hand, the main road from Trautenau via Königinhof to Gitschin had been given up, and it was there that the columns of the Guards and the 1st Corps were approaching.

Capture of Königinhof

In the night after the combat of Burkersdorf detachments of the X Austrian Corps had held Upper Soor occupied, but in the morning of the 29th they retired in the direction of Königinhof. The division Hiller was ordered to take this place, and was to be followed by the division Plonski with the reserve artillery, which had somehow wandered off to Trautenau, perhaps to look for the whereabouts of the missing 1st Corps.

When the vanguard of the advanced guard (commanded by Lt.-Colonel Count Waldersee, since known as Commander-in-Chief in the China Expedition) approached the northern suburbs of the little town, they received fire from the small garrison, part of which had occupied a brick-kiln, a cemetery, and some buildings outside the suburbs. The Austrians at first resisted obstinately, but when the one and a half battalions of the vanguard were reinforced by the arrival of the mainguard and two batteries, the Austrians were driven steadily into and through the town, although four batteries of the brigade Mondl had hurried up and opened fire from the hills south of the town, but at too great a distance to be effective. The upper bridge over the Elbe was occupied, before it could be used for the retreat; then the Austrians retired through the town and across the lower bridge towards Schurz (two miles south-east), leaving 421 prisoners behind them: they had also had 48 killed and 128 wounded, whilst the loss of the Prussians was 17 killed, 52 wounded.

As the Prussians had not the intention of crossing the Elbe, they went into bivouac in the town and north of it, placing the outposts along the bank of the river.

Combat of Schweinschädel

Situation in Front of Steinmetz — Opposed to the 5th Prussian Army Corps the outposts of the IV Austrian Corps were holding the line Langwasser-Trebesow. General Steinmetz was allowing a rest during the hours of forenoon to his troops tired by the fighting of the two preceding days. The march to Gradlitz—to join the other corps of the 2nd Army—was not to be commenced till about 2 p.m., and although the destruction of the enemy's forces must always be the main object in war, Steinmetz intended, if possible, to avoid any fighting. With this intention he wanted to march round the left flank of the enemy's line of outposts through Zlitsch, Ratiboritz and Wetrnik, and thus to gain the road Chwalkowitz-Gradlitz. Only the brigade Wittich, followed by a cavalry brigade, was to proceed as flank-guard on the right bank of the Aupa to cover his own flank march and to join the main body again at Miskoles.

Steinmetz began his march with the 5th Corps, brigade Hoffmann of the 6th Corps and the Guards Cavalry Brigade, when the three other brigades of the 6th Corps arrived at Skalitz from Nachod, and when he disposed of about 50,000 men in case of a serious encounter.

Comment — Under these circumstances a really good commander would have at once conceived the plan of attacking the enemy with energy in order to drive him to the Elbe between Jaromir and Kukus, gain the passages across the river together with him, ascend the heights covered, as it were, by the fugitives, and to obtain a firm footing between Salney and Schurz with seven brigades whilst using one brigade to contain Jaromir. Steinmetz had already severely shaken and disordered the VI and the VIII, and if he succeeded in doing the same with the IV Corps, then only the II Corps was left to render serious resistance; anyhow, he could safely reckon on the confusion which is caused by an unexpected event after a series of defeats and disasters, especially when the surprise blow falls on defeated and demoralised heterogeneous masses under incapable leadership. The whole corps of the Guards could reach Königinhof on the next morning and be followed closely by the 1st Corps: in that case the Austrian North Army would have had to retreat without delay into the position of Horenowes, and the junction with the Army of the Iser would have become problematic.

But Steinmetz was only bent on executing his flank march, if possible without fighting, which was tactically impossible. His left flanking column, the brigade Wittich, with three batteries and one regiment of cavalry, came upon the Austrians at 3.30 at Klein-Trzebesow, when the advanced guard of the army corps was passing the ravine at Wetrnik. The Austrian artillery fire caused this advanced guard to form up in line near Miskoles and part of it to advance against Schweinschädel. The fire of five Austrian batteries (forty guns) at last forced the general commanding the 10th Division to order the 19th Brigade, which had already proceeded beyond Wetrnik, to form up in line near Miskoles, and to order the attack on Schweinschädel; the brigade took the place and was pushing on against Dolan, but had to come back to the plateau of Miskoles in obedience to the special order of the obstinate commanding general. At 7.30 the march to Gradlitz was continued, whereupon the IV Austrian Corps retired behind the Elbe, after having lost 1,450 men including 550 prisoners; the loss of the Prussians amounted to 394 all told.

The Fight

Comment on the General Situation

The resolution of the Crown Prince to place the 2nd Army in position on the plateau of Königinhof was natural, therefore to the purpose, for thereby the connection with the 1st Army was actually established : Königinhof is only twenty-three miles distant from Gitchin, and one cavalry regiment was sufficient to keep open the communication and perform the orderly service. But it would have been more important to have watched the neighbourhood of Josephstadt, and an immediate attack seemed demanded by the situation, as explained above. One chance had been lost, but the IV Austrian Corps had anyhow retired behind the Elbe discomfited. Troops who are constantly worsted are sure to feel a steadily increasing reluctance to fight, whilst success increases the readiness to meet dangers—every new success is a cause of satisfaction : the 2nd Prussian Army might have shown more enterprise. Perhaps General Blumenthal, the Chief of its Staff, had planned an attack on the left flank of the Austrian position, and directed the march of the 1st Army Corps on Pilnikau on that account ; if so, he had given up the idea, as Moltke did not seem to wish for an attack before the junction of the two armies.

AUSTRIAN RETREAT

CHAPTER VII

A. Events on June 30

On the Prussian Side In the morning King William left Berlin for the theatre of war with General Moltke and his Staff. Shortly before the departure he had received the news that the 2nd Army had occupied the line of the Elbe; in consequence the following order was sent during the journey to the two princes commanding the armies:—

"The 2nd Army is to hold the left bank of the Upper Elbe with the right wing ready to join the 1st Army, as the latter advances without delay in the direction of Königgrätz. If hostile forces of any strength appear on the right flank of this forward movement, General Herwarth (Elbe Army) is to attack them and drive them off from their main army."

Even before the receipt of this order Prince Frederick Charles had determined to advance beyond Gitschin on the road to Königinhof in order to get nearer to the 2nd Army. Accordingly he had issued orders for his divisions to start in the afternoon and proceed sufficiently far so that the outposts of the 5th and 7th Divisions would be near Miletin and Horiz. The 14th, 15th and 16th Divisions were to reach the neighbourhood of Libau, and the Guard Landwehr Division was to march as far as Jung-Bunzlau.

As the 2nd Army had reached the line Arnau-Königinhof-Kukus, and the farther advance of the 1st Army would necessarily lay open the passages across the Elbe, the Crown Prince had ordered that serious encounters were to be avoided on the 30th, that the different army corps had to provide for their own security, that the passages across the river were to be reconnoitred and that preparations should be made for a farther advance. Having been left till then without any news from the 1st Army beyond the advance from Turnau, the Crown Prince also ordered that cavalry detachments be sent off from the 1st Army Corps to establish direct communication: these were met at Arnau by a cavalry regiment from the 1st Army sent off with the same object. During the day there was a short artillery duel across the Elbe between batteries of the II Austrian and the 5th Prussian Corps at a distance of 4,000 yards: the losses on both sides were trifling, but a building in Gradlitz, at Steinmetz's headquarters, was set on fire by shells.

On the Austrian Side

At 7.30 in the morning the brigades Piret and Abele and the reserve artillery arrived at Miletin; Archduke Ernest, commanding the III Army Corps posted there, had learned from outpost reports, received at 3.30 and 5.30 a.m., that Gitschin had been taken by the Prussians and had telegraphed to Benedek: "I Army Corps and Saxons on the march to Miletin, Gitschin occupied by the Prussians." He now sent off the further message: "Detachments of the I Corps arriving already, unfit for fighting, ammunition park empty, no supplies, will provisionally go into bivouac behind us." During the morning the Headquarters and the brigades Poschacher, Ringelsheim and Leiningen arrived at Horiz; the latter forming the rearguard had been molested on the march by a few squadrons of Prussian Guard Lancers. The Saxon Corps arrived at Smidar and with them the Austrian cavalry division Edelsheim, which had, without orders, left the I Corps after the combat at Gitschin instead of covering its retreat: even if this was partly the fault of the negligence of the corps command, the division could easily have rejoined the headquarters of the corps early in the morning, and taken up its proper place and duties with the rearguard; their presence was not wanted by the Saxons, who had sufficient cavalry with them.

At 11 a.m. Clam Gallas at Horiz gave out the order that the troops of the I Corps should be collected and reformed by brigades there and at Miletin, that the men should be provided with food, and that at 2 a.m. next morning the farther retrograde march should be commenced towards Königgrätz. When, however, soon after alarming news arrived about the appearance of the enemy's cavalry at Wostromer, four miles from Horiz, the continuance of the retreat was resolved upon, because the troops were not fully formed, were exhausted, without ammunition and not fit to fight, and Horiz was left at about 1 p.m. There was evidently an absence of characters whose courage is not broken by misfortune, whose quickness of judgment and determination increases in proportion to the danger; for otherwise some means, however drastic, should have been devised and used to restore order and confidence and to avoid the disastrous expediency of flight. For this march exhausted the troops beyond measure, and they did not find the needed rest even at Sadowa, but remained under arms till the fall of night, as the transport columns of the army going back beyond that place kept the whole neighbourhood alarmed.

Comment Thus a panic had been produced by the appearance of a few squadrons of cavalry! This shows the advantage which under certain circumstances can be derived from cavalry, for "moral impressions are decisive in war." On the other hand, it shows the absurdity of the commanding authority wishing to conduct movements from a distance, far away from the impressions of the events of the moment. If Prince Frederick Charles had been at Gitschin with only a part of his cavalry on the evening of the 29th, he would have used the last man and the last horse to have wiped the Austrian Army of the Iser out of existence. Whence has arisen this strange manner of conducting tactical movements from a distance? Was Schwarzenberg's headquarters in 1813 taken as an example worthy of imitation? The great Frederick dictated the marching orders in his tent to the regimental sergeant-majors before the night march and attack at Soor; Napoleon, on the evening before the battle of Jena, helped to give light to his gunners as they repaired the road up to the Landgrafenberg!

Retreat of the North Army The III Corps was concentrated round Miletin, and the brigades of the I Corps, which had arrived there, marched off to Königgrätz at 5.30 p.m., whilst the III Corps itself was then ordered to fall back to Gross-Bürglitz. The other corps of the army were assembled, as we have seen, on the plateau of Dubenetz, but they could not possibly remain in this position fronting chiefly north and east, as their flank and rear were threatened by the approach of the 1st Prussian Army; nor was it possible any longer to attack either of the two hostile armies without the other appearing in the rear during the fight. The army had lost above 30,000 men in the first engagements, and the troops were fatigued, exhausted and deeply discouraged. Benedek therefore determined to take the army back to Königgrätz in the night of June 30 to July 1, and he telegraphed to the Emperor: "*Débâcle* of the I and the Saxon Corps forces me to commence the retreat in the direction of Königgrätz. Headquarters to-morrow in that neighbourhood."

Comments
The retreat was to be executed in four columns, and the start was to be made at 1 a.m. as quietly and noiselessly as possible; but as the time taken by an army corps marching in column of route to pass a certain point was at the least five hours, it would have been more practicable to detail at once two army corps, two cavalry divisions and a great part of the reserve artillery to remain in the occupied position provisionally, to observe the 2nd Prussian Army and to fall back slowly and gradually on Horenowes and Smiritz. This arrangement would have given time to the first starting corps to get thoroughly reordered and take up well-chosen positions without hurry and confusion. On the other hand, it is wrong to make demoralised troops march at night, if

it can be avoided. In such condition troops always require constant control and supervision, which at night must, of course, be defective.

Prussians at Fault At the same time the Prussians also made mistakes, as they omitted to reconnoitre, scour and seize with their numerous cavalry the district on the left bank of the Elbe east of Josephstadt, which would have been of the greatest utility because the main lines of retreat to Moravia pass through that district. The various passages across the Elbe near Königgrätz would then have been in possession of the 2nd Army directly after or even before the end of the battle, and the consequences of such an occurrence can hardly be calculated. As the Guard Cavalry Brigade had been allotted to the 5th Army Corps, it should have remained already on the 29th close to the Elbe, and, together with a brigade of the 6th Corps near Jaromir, should have carried out the observation of Josephstadt and the strip of country east of the Elbe as far as Königgrätz; on the 30th the cavalry division should have been added, which on that day was perfectly useless at Kaile. It would also have been better to have left the 6th Corps at Skalitz, or to have moved it to Rychnowek, than to make it march to the plateau of Königinhof. Concentration of all forces for the decisive battle is certainly advantageous and advisable, but the results of the events in the first days of campaigning had justified the conclusion that each of the two Prussian armies contained a greater strength than the whole Austrian army united, so that nothing should have been neglected to place the surplus of strength in such a way as to deprive the enemy of the most important lines of retreat, and to force him by a rapid advance to such an acceleration of the retreat as to turn it into dissolution and dispersal.

The Crown Prince had certainly resolved to cross the Elbe on July 2, but he ought to have done so at once when, on the 1st, he should have observed the departure of the Austrians from their position at Dubenetz: correct resolutions must and can only be taken on the spot. Surely the North Army had not been withdrawn without cause, and it should not have been left out of sight for a moment. If the Crown Prince had followed up the retreat smartly, it would have been well shattered, and the capitulation of the I Army Corps would have been the probable consequence; the Saxons also would have been pushed away from the North Army: altogether greater results might have been achieved than were gained by the battle on the 3rd.

Comment on the Austrian Retreat

The question has often been discussed, whether Benedek's retreat to Königgrätz was the correct and recommendable movement, and has generally been answered in the negative with the following suggestions. The army should have abandoned the right bank of the Elbe and been taken across the river, the passage over which was secured by the two fortresses. Behind them the Austrian corps should have been posted and the Saxons behind Pardubitz, to have given them the chance of being put again into order and made fit again to give battle. For it is the rôle allotted to fortresses by strategy in the conduct of war, that they should furnish the means to re-establish the destroyed equilibrium, to seize again the initiative, to resume the offensive—in short, to gain time to give battle again under improved circumstances.

B. Events on July 1

With the Austrian Army

The retreat from the position at Dubenetz commenced at 1 a.m. and was executed, on account of defective dispositions, in great disorder, with the most various cross movements which might easily have been avoided, for time and space are elements subject to calculation. Benedek, with his staff, started from Dubenetz at 2.30 a.m. and rode via Horenowes and Chlum to Königgrätz. Now already he had lost all confidence in himself, his staff and the army in general: he could no longer deceive himself in that he was lacking the most essential attributes of a great leader; the incapacity of the chief of his staff was quite evident, and what could be expected of an army which, composed of the most various nationalities and therefore wanting in close cohesion, was deficiently armed, badly trained and even more badly commanded!

Benedek's Advice

At Königgrätz Benedek found Colonel Beck, of the Adjutant-General's Staff, sent from Vienna to take personal observations of the condition of affairs, and a telegram from the Emperor, which expressed His Majesty's confident belief that, in spite of the news that the retreat to Königgrätz had become necessary, the Commander-in-Chief's energetic command and control would preserve order and soon obtain favourable results. Benedek sent to the Emperor at once the following historical message: " Urgently request Your Majesty to conclude peace at any price; catastrophe for army unavoidable; Colonel

Beck returns at once." Benedek received the following telegram in reply: " Impossible to conclude peace. I command—if it is unavoidable—to commence retreat in the greatest order. Has a battle taken place ? "

Benedek had thought that better conditions of peace could be obtained before a great defeat, which was fairly certain, than after having sustained it; but he did not know the Court, still less all the different contending interests which were there at work. Only when, so to say, the Prussian bayonets could be seen from St. Stephen's spire, and when it became evident that with an energetic, truly military conduct of operations on the part of Prussia, Vienna and Pesth might fall almost simultaneously, which would have rendered the further existence of the dual monarchy uncertain and dependent on King William's pleasure, only then were the authorities in Vienna induced to give in.

Benedek's Unvarnished Report At 11 p.m. Benedek sent to Vienna the following telegraphic report: " The VI and the X Corps have suffered tremendously, the VIII also considerably; the I Corps, as I personally verified to-day, and the Saxon Corps partly, have suffered much, and require several days to reassume complete order; the IV Corps also has lost. Thus out of eight army corps only two are intact, and that without having fought a general battle, after mere partial engagements; these two corps, as well as the reserves of cavalry and artillery, are much fatigued. The great losses are to be attributed to the fire of the needle-gun, the murderous effect of which has made a deep impression on everybody. All these facts and considerations forced me to fall back in this direction. On the road I found the immense transport of the army, which could no longer be placed far enough back; and if under these circumstances an energetic attack had been or were to be made by the enemy, before the I and the Saxon Corps are again solidly reformed, the result could not but be a disaster. Fortunately the enemy have not been pressing to-day till this hour, so that I shall let the army rest to-morrow and send off the transport in the front of the retreat; but I cannot remain here longer, for on the following day already there would be scarcity of drinking water; therefore, on the 3rd, I shall continue the retreat on Pardubitz. If I am not overtaken and headed off, if I can count again on the troops, and if an opportunity offers for an offensive counter-stroke, I will undertake it; but otherwise I will endeavour to bring the army back to Olmütz in as good a condition as possible, and to execute Your Majesty's orders as far as it is within my power, and certainly with absolute self-sacrifice."

Comment on Prussian Staff The fact mentioned in this telegram, that the enemy had not been pressing, shows plainly the faulty inactivity of the Prussian cavalry, which could have obtained immense successes even in Benedek's opinion. In connection with these circumstances we may be allowed the following remarks.

In the history of the war written by the Military Historiographical Department of the Prussian General Staff, we find the astonishing statement that the Prussian chief command remained in ignorance of the occupation of the plateau of Dubenetz by the bulk of the Austrian army, as well as of the hurried retreat of the latter from that position. How can this pretended ignorance be reconciled with the short artillery duel across the Elbe on June 30, which surely was sufficiently realistic to have attracted attention to the Austrian forces on the right bank of the river ? If the departure of the Austrians remained a secret to the Prussian outposts, no small fault must be found with the careless way in which reconnoitring must have been done.

The account goes on to say that it was surmised that the main forces of the Austrians were in a position behind the Elbe, with the fortresses Josephstadt and Königgrätz on the flanks : the correctness or fallacy of this surmise could easily have been ascertained by a business-like, appropriate employment of the cavalry ; at almost every step in the process of these events one can see, how little the use of this arm was known and appreciated by the generals in command.

Prussian Armies In the 2nd Prussian army the 1st Army Corps was sent from Arnau to Ober-Praussnitz, on the right bank of the Elbe, only three miles to the west of it, whilst the Cavalry Division was left at Neustadt instead of being at once pushed forward to Bürglitz. Only an advanced guard was sent forward into the abandoned position at Dubenetz ; the 6th Corps was brought to Gradlitz close to the 5th. The divisions of the 1st Army marched at 3 p.m. to a line abreast of Miletin and Horiz, the Elbe Army reached Hoch-Wesely, the Landwehr Division remained at Jung-Bunzlau. All these movements were wanting in assurance and decision. Probably orders were awaited from the King's Headquarters, now transferred to Castle Sichrow, north of Münchengrätz, where the impending arrival of the French ambassador was already announced. This warning of immediate diplomatic intervention ought to have caused increased vigour and intensity of military activity.

C. Events on July 2.

With the Austrians. Changes in High Places

On Colonel Beck's return to Vienna the Emperor ordered the Generals Krizmanic, Director of Operations, Clam Gallas, commanding I Army Corps, and Henikstein, Chief of General Staff, to be relieved of their functions and to be sent back to Vienna, although Benedek had meanwhile despatched the following telegram: "As Colonel Beck has probably reported, Krizmanic is not equal to his task. Can only think of Baumgarten to replace him. Request authority to make him director of operations and to give Krizmanic command of a brigade." In reply to the Emperor's telegram, Benedek again wired as follows: "Before executing order venture following proposal: Henikstein to command I Corps, Baumgarten chief of general staff, Ringelsheim to be detached to III Corps." The affair was settled by a final message received late in the evening, repeating the order of recall of the three generals, and granting the request about Baumgarten and Ringelsheim.

Comment

From this correspondence it is evident that Benedek was without any power in the army entrusted to his command: he was a figurehead directed by the Adjutant-General Genneville, and his proposals were simply neglected and sharply refused. But Mahan says: "A government can act absolutely only through the general-in-chief; if they do not take him into account, or act over his head without removing him from his command, disaster will follow. Nothing is more damaging to the affairs of state than petty personal conflicts and paltry intrigues."

It is true the Austrian Government was in a difficult, though self-created situation. Already after June 28 it should have been evident that Benedek's capacities did not suffice for his task, after they had taken the ill-advised step of removing Archduke John from his side. Now, if they wanted to uphold him in the chief command, they ought to have sent the Archduke back to him as chief of the staff, as he could then be spared in Italy after the victory of Custozza, and invested him with absolute full power to be able to check the increasing disorder in the army. But if they wanted to replace Benedek, they ought to have telegraphed to Archduke Albrecht to hand over the command of the South Army to General Maroiciz, to come at once by special to take over the command in the north and to bring John with him. But the most unsuitable line of action was to leave Benedek in his position, and at the same time to humiliate him by the refusal of his proposals, which would show plainly to his numerous enemies, that his power was gone, and invite every donkey to give the dead lion a parting kick.

Position of Troops In accordance with the orders issued on the previous day, the troops did not leave their position on the 2nd, and in the afternoon, after receipt of the telegram ordering the suspension and removal of the three generals, Benedek reported to the Emperor: "The army remains to-morrow in the position near Königgrätz; the one day's rest and the copious good food have had a good effect; hope not to need further retreat."

This decision would lead one to surmise that Benedek had become sick of the whole business and meant to have the wished-for battle, although he foresaw that it would spell defeat.

At 4 p.m. the orders for the following day were issued, which informed the army that they would remain in their camps, and pointed out the various bridges by which the Elbe would be eventually crossed above and below Königgrätz: passing through the fortress was forbidden. The army was encamped in the north-western quadrant of a circle of seven miles radius: the Saxons on the left flank at Nechanitz, Lubno and Prim; the III Corps and the III Reserve Cavalry Division at Sadowa; behind them the X and the VI Corps with the II Reserve Cavalry Division at Lipa and Wsestar; farther to the right the VIII, IV and II Corps between Nedelist and Trotina, with advanced guards at Maslowed and Horenowes; the I Corps with the I Light Cavalry Division at Kuklena, the Reserve Artillery at Nedelist.

On the evening of the 1st the army had still been in the greatest disorder: it was hardly known, where the various corps were and in what condition. Reports had to be awaited, which, of course, only came in during the night and during the course of the morning; then, about noon, Benedek addressed a meeting of commanding generals on all kinds of general subjects, and expressed the hope that the army would have a few days to rest and to regain confidence: not a word about any decided plan! And yet, at 3.30, he had evidently made up his mind not to avoid the decisive battle, which he himself had warned against as probable catastrophe.

Orders for Battle

At 11 p.m., that is after the receipt of the Emperor's last telegram confirming his decision about the three generals, Benedek issued the following disposition for battle, which was sent to the commanding generals at 2 o'clock in the morning :—

"To judge by movements of the enemy an attack may be expected, which would in first line be directed against the Saxon Corps. To meet this eventuality, the following dispositions are herewith commanded :—

"1. The Saxon Corps occupies the heights of Popowiz and Tresowiz.

"2. To the left of it the I Light Cavalry Division.

"3. To the right of it the X Corps.

"4. The III Corps to the right of the X to occupy the heights of Lipa and Chlum.

"5. The VIII Corps will form the support to the Saxon Corps and be posted behind it.

"6. The IV Corps takes post to the right of the III on the heights between Chlum and Nedelist.

"7. The II Corps occupies the extreme right wing.

"8. The VI Corps to be concentrated on the heights near Wsestar, the I Corps at Rosniz.

"9. The General Reserve is composed of the I and VI Corps, the five Cavalry Divisions and the Army Artillery Reserve, which takes position behind the I and IV Corps; these troops are at my exclusive disposal.

"10. I shall be on the height of Chlum.

"11. Should the army be forced to retreat, the line

Holiz-Hohenmauth is to be taken without entering the fortress."

Comment   This disposition implied fighting a defensive battle without opportunity of moving and manœuvring, with a fortress in the rear which, closed and forbidden, hindered a retreat instead of helping and protecting it. Probably Benedek in his bad temper did not care what Krizmanic had drawn up, perhaps he hardly read it : Baumgarten did not know of his appointment till next morning, when he took over duties from Krizmanic on the battlefield. Besides, Benedek was not only wanting in the clear perception of strategic proportions and relations, but also in the tactical capacity of handling large bodies of troops, which requires experience besides innate talent. He might have acquired it at Verona, where for years he commanded 30,000 men; but he never ordered manœuvres, at which he should have commanded for practice, but was always satisfied with tedious reviews, at which he could indulge his love of petty fault-finding.

The disposition as detailed above was not adapted to the actual situation : both wings were liable to be outflanked, therefore the reserves should have been placed in a ready position to meet this danger. Topographically three points were eminent : Horenowes as point *d'appui* of the right wing, Chlum as connecting it with the centre, and the heights of Hradek as mainstay of the left wing, a good position to cover the road to Pardubitz.

The I Corps, with the I Light Cavalry Division was on the 2nd near Kuklena ; they should have been, as well as the VI Corps, directed to Prim and been put under the orders of the Crown Prince of Saxony. The VIII Corps should have been left at the passages across the Elbe near Lochenitz, with orders to cross with the II Reserve Cavalry Division in case detachments of the enemy were to be seen there. On the morning of the 1st, Krizmanic had ridden with Benedek over the ground at Horenowes, and yet he selected the line Chlum-Nedelist and had it strengthened by batteries, although nobody agreed with him. Being a pure theorist, he, of course, placed the reserves behind the centre, although even if the latter had to retire, they could still have maintained the line Wsestar, Problus, Hradek, and could have used the Pardubitz road together with Königgrätz for the retreat if necessitated, as long as the left wing could hold out.

Perhaps it would have been most appropriate, if the right wing of the Austrian army (two army corps, two cavalry divisions and two divisions of the artillery reserve) had been ordered to defend the line Langenhof-Chlum-Horenowes, and in case of necessity to retire behind the Elbe and to hold the line between the two fortresses. The left wing, under the orders of the Crown Prince of Saxony (two army corps and two cavalry divisions), could then have taken up a position round Nechanitz, with the line of retreat to Prelauc; the centre, consisting of four army corps, could have been posted on the heights of Problus and Hradek, with line of retreat on Pardubitz: its right wing would have been covered by Koniggrätz. To facilitate an eventual retreat, bridges could have been thrown across the river below the fortress, by which a few army corps could quickly reach the road to Holic. By means of thus placing the chief position more to the west, the distance between it and the 2nd Prussian Army was so much increased that, after taking Horenowes, the latter would probably only have taken up a position on the Elbe above Königgrätz, and the 1st Army would scarcely have taken the heights of Problus-Prim-Hradek before the evening. The Austrians would probably have been beaten all the same, but their defeat would perhaps not have been overwhelming.

The crisis of the war lay in Benedek's resolution to accept the battle on the 3rd, yet it was by no means the result of tactical or strategical considerations, but was caused by the explosion of the latent conflict between him and the Adjutant-General. In a way Benedek had been morally forced into this resolution, and the attempt to carry out a momentous and doubtful undertaking which the commanding general considers unwise, is likely to fail in most cases. Benedek had received the promise that his measures would not be interfered with, but it was not kept. The man who has to do the work, and is responsible for it, should have full power to act; thus it was in the Roman Republic, and Wellington, in the Peninsular War, held the same position as a Roman consul, being political head and master of his army. In Austria, with her inveterate system of general mistrust, only the Emperor or a favourite archduke could command the army in the field without disastrous frictions.

If Benedek's proposals to the Emperor had been accepted and authorised, he would probably have given at once the order for the different corps to begin the retreat at two o'clock in the morning, and the Prussian armies would have found the district unoccupied by troops, except a few weak rearguards: then the mistake would have become evident, which was made by the generals commanding the two armies in neglecting after June 29 to utilise and profit by the favourable situation in which they were then placed.

<small>Dispositions at the Prussian Headquarters</small> The King's Headquarters were established at Gitschin in the morning of July 2. The General Staff supposed that the Austrian army had been withdrawn behind the Elbe, and, acting upon this surmise, orders were issued that General Herwarth with his three divisions should move on Chlumetz to reconnoitre towards Prague, and to secure the passage across the Elbe at Pardubitz; that the other corps of the 1st Army should take up a line through Horiz, pushing a part of the left wing forward to Sadowa. The 1st Army Corps was to move by Miletin to Bürglitz, the other corps of the 2nd Army to remain on the left bank of the Elbe and to reconnoitre towards the Aupa and the Mettau (*sic!*). If it should be found, that a concentric attack on the supposed position of the enemy between the two fortresses would meet with excessive difficulties, or if the Austrian army should have left that neighbourhood altogether, the general advance towards Pardubitz would be continued. Both army commanders were to send every evening officers to the Headquarters to receive the orders for the following day.

The last proviso seems to show that there was no intention to act rapidly and with vigour.

However, before these orders were despatched, reports came in from the advanced guards of the 1st Army which rectified the suppositions about the position of the Austrians and justified the surmise, that at least four

Austrian corps were still behind the Bistritz, whereupon Prince Frederick Charles determined to attack them on the following day, and sent orders to General Herwarth to march on Nechanitz as early as possible with all available troops; he also ordered his own six divisions to be at 2 a.m. on the two roads leading to Königgrätz, ready to attack the position on the Bistritz. The Prince also sent a letter to the Crown Prince informing him of his intention for the next morning, and requesting him to advance from Königinhof towards Josephstadt on the right bank of the Elbe with one or more corps, so as to secure the left wing of the 1st Army. He mentioned that his request was prompted by the fact that he did not expect a timely arrival of the 1st Corps on account of the distance it had to cover, and by the firm supposition, that no strong hostile forces would be encountered on the Aupa and the Mettau.

The Crown Prince received the letter at 2 a.m., and ordered the 1st Corps to proceed via Miletin and Gross-Bürglitz to the support of the 1st Army; the other three corps were to act in accordance with the previous received royal instructions.

Prince Frederick Charles also sent the Chief of his Staff to Gitschin to obtain the King's approval of his dispositions, and to report the information received at the Prince's headquarters. The King determined at once— 11 p.m.—to attack the enemy west of the Elbe with all forces available, whether the whole Austrian army was to be encountered or only a considerable portion of it. In consequence orders were sent to the Crown Prince to advance without delay with all his forces against the right flank of the enemy. Notification was transmitted to General Bonin at the same time, warning him to hold his corps ready to move at the first intimation from the Crown Prince, or to act independently according to circumstances. The Crown Prince received the orders at 4 a.m., but owing to the distances separating the corps, some could not start before 8 a.m., so that all these forces could not be expected to give any effective assistance before noon.

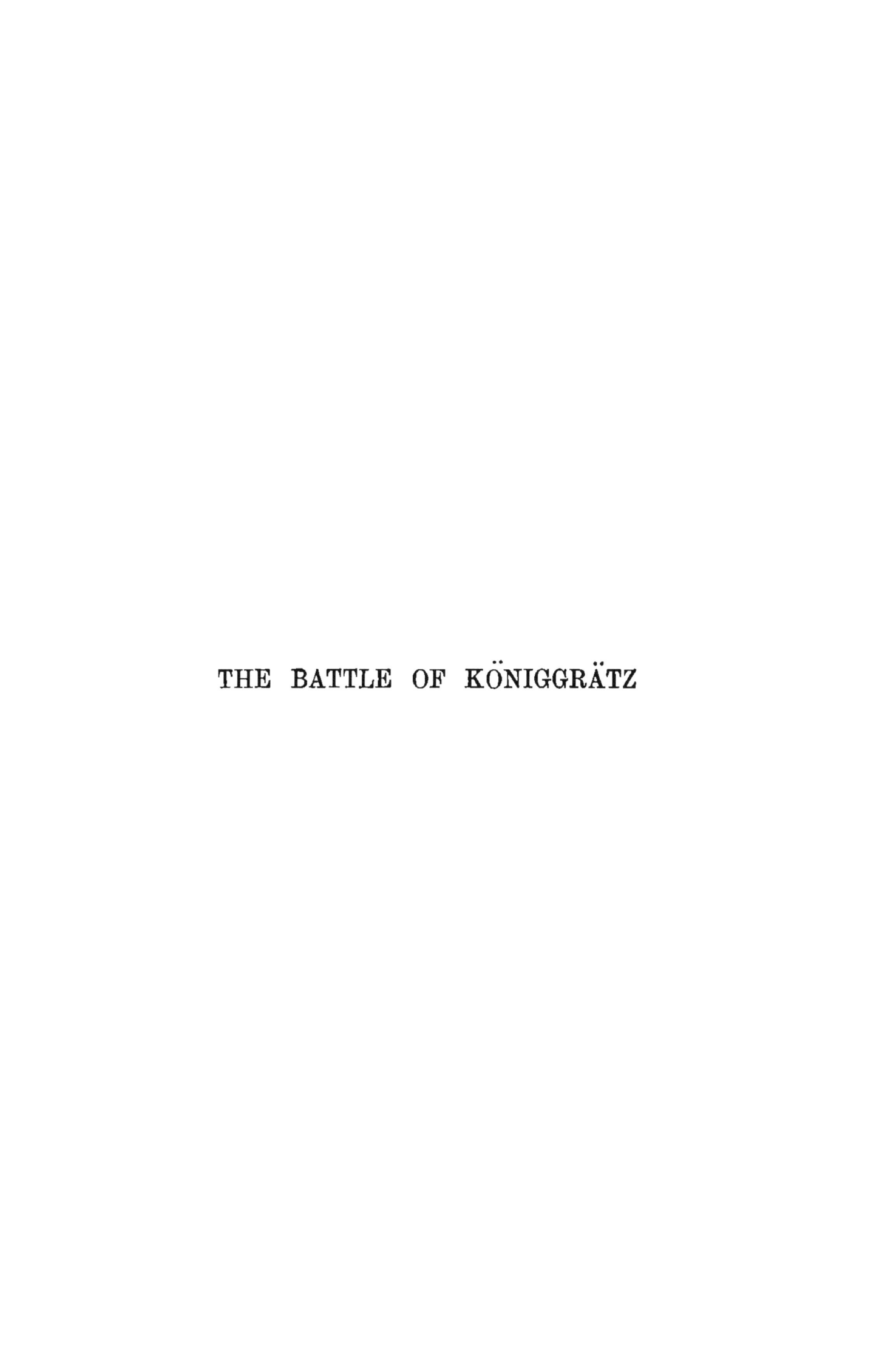

THE BATTLE OF KÖNIGGRÄTZ

CHAPTER VIII

THE BATTLE OF KÖNIGGRÄTZ—JULY 3

Prussian Dispositions — PRINCE FREDERICK CHARLES had gone at 1.30 a.m. to Milowitz, where he received at 5.45 news from General Herwarth, that he would be near Nechanitz between 7 and 9 o'clock with thirty-six battalions. Thus the co-operation of all Prussian forces was assured, for we have seen that orders to the same effect had been sent to the 2nd Army.

Under these circumstances it seemed advisable to occupy the enemy in front without waiting by the 1st Army, to draw on and contain his forces so that the double flank attack planned against him could be completely executed. Therefore, at 6 a.m., the Prince ordered a forward movement of his whole army, so as to occupy a convenient position near the Bistritz: the real attack was not to be hurried on, as the corps of the 2nd Army had to march ten to thirteen miles before they could join in the fighting. The 8th Division was to advance towards Sadowa, the 2nd Army Corps abreast with and to the right of it; the 5th and 6th Divisions were to follow the 8th as reserve by the sides of the highroad on which the artillery reserve was to follow; the Cavalry Corps was to take position behind the right wing of the 2nd Division, and was to establish connection with the Elbe Army; the 7th Division was to advance north of the 8th, as soon as fighting should begin at Sadowa, and to support it according to circumstances. Thus at 6 a.m. the columns of the Elbe Army and of the 1st Army were all advancing towards the Bistritz.

At this time the order to march had in the 2nd Army only been communicated to the Guards Corps and the 5th Corps; the 1st Corps had been ordered at 5.45 by its commanding officer, to get at once ready for an advance in the direction of Sadowa; but the 6th Corps, ready in its bivouacs east of Gradlitz to start on the first received orders for an advance on Josephstadt, had not then received the new orders which directed it to march on Welchow.

Austrian Positions — Strong detachments of the Austrian troops had been pushed forward to and beyond the Bistritz as advanced guards and outposts, and occupied the following positions:—

On the extreme left Alt-Nechanitz, Nechanitz and Hradek were held by one battalion each of the Saxon Corps; to the north of Nechanitz the outposts of the X Corps held the right bank of the Bistritz; one brigade of the III Corps was at Sadowa, and Cistowes was held by one of its battalions; the line from the Bistritz to Benatek, Horenowes and Racitz, including the wood in front of Maslowed, was held by detachments of the IV Corps, and on the right, as far as the Elbe at the village Trotina, behind the river of that name, were the troops of the II Corps, whilst one cavalry division had been left north of the river, covering with its outposts the extreme right wing.[1]

Events in the Centre
At 8 a.m. King William arrived on the height of Dub and gave the order to force the passage of the Bistritz.

To prepare the attack 100 guns gradually opened fire, which at 9 o'clock was replied to by about the same number of Austrian guns; by 9.30 more than 300 guns were engaged. The 7th Division advanced on Benatek, and about the same time the 8th Division crossed the Bistritz at Sowetitz and took the Skalka wood, whereupon the Austrian advanced detachment retired out of Sadowa, so that by 10 a.m. the whole III Corps was in position between Lipa and Chlum: the prodigious fire of its batteries forced the 8th Prussian Division to seek protection in Ober-Dohalitz and in the Hola wood. About the same time the 2nd Prussian Corps had arrived at Mzan and Zawaldica, and placed its eight batteries on the slope south-west of Mzan; the 3rd Division formed up in front of Mokrovaus, Dohalicka and Unter-Dohalitz, on the right of the 8th Division, whilst the 4th was posted behind the 8th in the Hola wood. The brigades of the X Austrian Corps now evacuated the villages on the Bistritz, and by 10 a.m. retired into the main position at Langenhof, so that by 10.30 the X and the III Corps were assembled about Langenhof, Lipa and Chlum, where 160 guns were

[1] Parts of the Austrian position were artificially strengthened by five batteries—two north of Nedelist, three from north-east to west of Chlum—by abattis on the edges of several woods, and by a number of fire trenches; the western portions of the villages of Lipa and Chlum had also been put into a state of defence. The forces engaged in the battle were 206,100 Austrians (including 22,000 Saxons), and 220,984 Prussians.

keeping up a steady fire against the Prussian batteries: this lasted for a considerable time, until about 12 o'clock the Prince ordered the 5th and 6th Divisions to cross the Bistritz in order to ensure the occupation of that position. But by that movement six divisions were massed on a line of only 7,000 paces' length, which gives about ten men per pace, a depth which caused very heavy losses from the Austrian artillery fire; no advance could be made against this fire, and at 1 p.m. the position seemed so dangerous, that a retreat across the Bistritz was seriously thought of.

Events on the Right Austrian Wing till 2 p.m. At 8.30 the 7th Prussian Division had arrived at Benatek with a cavalry brigade protecting the left wing, and its four batteries had opened fire against the brigade of the IV Austrian Corps, which was posted south-east of Maslowed, and held the Swiep wood, south of Benatek and Horenowes, occupied by advanced battalions. When General Festetic saw the direction of attack assumed by the 7th Division, he sent two more battalions into the wood; before these arrived, four Prussian battalions had attacked, and as two battalions of the III Austrian Corps had just then been taken towards Chlum, two battalions of the attack occupied Cistowes, the other two got a footing in the western part of the wood. The remaining battalions of the Austrian brigade Brandenstein were now sent forward to retake the wood, which they failed to do, as the Prussians had been reinforced by two battalions: the Austrian brigade retired to Maslowed.

Instead of giving up the wood, the possession of which was not necessary for maintaining the position

Chlum-Naslowed-Horenowes, which Festetic had occupied with his corps instead of the line Chlum-Nedelist prescribed by the Chief of the Staff, the IV Corps and the II as well were now employed in attempts to retake it. These did succeed in driving the 7th Division out of it, but only when the first divisions of the 2nd Prussian Army arrived in the vicinity of the battlefield, and in consequence of the dislocation of the forces found the approach to the rear of the Imperial army at Racic and Trotina almost undefended.

Comment   When Festetic took up the position Chlum-Horenowes, he was under obligation to send information to the Chief of the Staff, and no excuse can be found for the fact that the IV Corps, and subsequently the II, exhausted their forces against the Swiep wood, for the object of the order placing them so as to face north should have been quite evident to them, because on the heights of Dubenetz they had had the 2nd Prussian Army in front of them only forty-eight hours before.

Details of the Fighting in the Wood   It is doubtful whether the attack on the wood would have been carried on in the truly disastrous fashion, if Festetic had not been severely wounded and his chief staff officer been killed at an early hour, after which his successor in the command made two brigades, which at Maslowed were still facing north, follow the first two brigades in the direction of the Swiep wood. One brigade took Cistowes, but the attack on the forest failed: instead of incurring this waste of infantry, the artillery should have been ordered to prevent the enemy from sallying out of the forest. When the attacks were given up,

General Mollinari received warning from Benedek not to let the IV Corps advance, as the time for a counter-attack had not yet arrived. Nevertheless, he asked General Prince Thun, commanding the II Corps, to support him, who was posted then between Maslowed and Horenowes. Mollinari acted directly contrary to orders received, and Thun, who ought to have given his whole attention to watching and patrolling the country to the north, was foolish enough to fall in with his requests. In consequence two of his brigades attacked the forest at 11.30, and as the Prussians were now gradually giving way, he sent another half-brigade after them, when the news arrived that strong hostile columns were approaching from the north. Now Thun received orders to take position between Maslowed and Sendracic, whilst five batteries were placed on the height east of Horenowes to engage the artillery of the Prussian Guards.

Result The 7th Prussian Division had lost the wood about noon, and had fallen back to Benatek, after suffering a loss of 2,120 men in its twelve battalions; there were then in the wood ten Austrian battalions and forty-nine around Maslowed and Horenowes, of which only thirteen were intact, whilst twenty-eight had become practically useless: their total loss amounted to 13,400 men, including about 5,000 taken prisoners.

For some time Benedek also had known, that rather large bodies of the enemy were approaching from the north, and it was quite time to bring forward the VI Corps and the II Light Cavalry Division in order to prevent a catastrophe.

THE BATTLE OF KÖNIGGRÄTZ

Advance and Attack of the 2nd Prussian Army

At 5 a.m. the Crown Prince had ordered that the 1st Corps followed by the cavalry division Hartmann should march to Gross-Bürglitz, the Guards Corps to Jericek and Lhota, the 6th Corps to Welchow, whilst observing Josephstadt, and the 5th Corps—following the 6th two hours later—to Choteborek (three and a half miles north of Horenowes.)

At 11.15 the Crown Prince arrived on the height of Choteborek, observed the fighting on the Bistritz, and noticed that the 7th Division was in urgent need of support. The 1st Division of the Guards was then near Choteborek, the 11th Division (6th Corps) was, after 11 a.m., marching up against Racic, and the 12th Division was arriving on the heights of Habrina. The Crown Prince gave the order that the three divisions should take the position of Horenowes, where several Austrian batteries were placed: the four batteries of the 11th Division at once opened fire on them.

Austrian Counter-attack Planned

In the meantime Benedek had planned a counter-attack in the centre towards and beyond the Bistritz, but it did not please him that his right wing was so hotly engaged in the Swiep wood, although its occupation had to precede his absurd frontal attack. To carry it out he had brought forward his reserves (two army corps and two cavalry divisions) to the foot of the heights of Lipa and Langenhof. General Baumgarten, just returned from the right wing, advised to send one of these two corps to that part to fill " the hole in the line of battle," and Benedek ordered the VI Corps to march up between Chlum and Nedelist, but soon after he sent counter-orders to stop that movement. At 11.30 he received a telegram from the officer commanding in Josephstadt, stating that Prussian columns were passing west of that place with the evident intention of operating against the right flank of the army. Hereupon he sent orders to the IV and II Corps to evacuate the Swiep wood and to take up the partly entrenched line Chlum-Nedelist-Sendrasitz, in accordance with the original dispositions. The execution of this order could not but take up much time, as the troops after the wood fighting were much scattered and mixed up, and Sendrasitz was quite three and a half miles from the Swiep wood, nor were the generals commanding these corps willing to execute the order, for Mollinari had taken it into his head that by beating the 7th Prussian Division he was smashing the left wing of the enemy, and would be able to roll up their whole line : only after personally remonstrating with Benedek did he order his corps to assemble east of Chlum. Thun also said, he could not understand, why they should again fall back into the defensive : just then were heard the first reports of the guns at Horenowes. Benedek now ordered Ramming to march with his corps to the right wing and reinforce it ; this general replied, that he would do so slowly, hoping that the order would be countermanded and the frontal attack be executed. Then Benedek, contrary to Baumgarten's warning that the time for a counter-attack was not at hand, actually ordered Ramming to stay with his corps, where he was. Benedek was by this time so completely out of balance that he really did not know what he was doing, and showed plainly that he did not possess the qualities which make up and distinguish a great commander. Soon after, at 2.30, he received news from the Crown Prince of Saxony that the left wing had been obliged to retire.

Attack in the North   Before 12 o'clock eight Prussian batteries, posted at Zizelowes, Racic and Habrina, had opened fire against the five Austrian batteries on the dominating height south-east of Horenowes; soon after 12 they were reinforced by seven more batteries, so that then ninety guns were fighting against forty Austrian guns. The 1st Division of the Guards broke by its advance the flank march of the IV and II Corps moving into their proper position, took Horenowes at 1 o'clock, then advanced through the wood against the artillery position, and forced the Austrian batteries to retire.

The 6th Corps took Racic and the western edge of the Horickaberg without difficulty, as the defending brigade of the II Austrian Corps was posted between Sendracic and Lochenic behind the Trotinka stream. This brigade, soon outflanked on the left, retired to Lochenic; then three battalions were posted in this village, and the other battalions retired behind the Elbe; the 2nd Light Cavalry Division took up a position to the west of Lochenic, whilst the 12th Prussian Division occupied Sendracic at 2.30. Another brigade of the II Corps, on its return march from the Swiepwald, had not the time to get into proper order, and reached the line of trenches north of Nedelist with only two battalions, which, however, soon retired from that position. The 3rd Brigade of the same corps was attacked on the return march by a cavalry brigade, but repulsed the charge and got to Nedelist; the 4th

Brigade, somewhat protected by the fire of three batteries which had unlimbered near Maslowed and were attracting the fire of the Prussian artillery on the height of Horenowes, reached the heights south-east of Maslowed, and finally Nedelist at 2 o'clock. The II Corps by this time was scarcely any longer in a fit condition to fight.

Of the IV Corps, one brigade was then at Cistowes, fronting towards the Swiepwald, a second brigade in the line of trenches north of Chlum, with two battalions of the II Corps close to its right, the other two brigades north of Rosberic: near them to the south-west eight batteries of the Artillery Reserve had taken position. Two brigades of the III Corps were north of Rosberic and in Chlum; farther to the west there were still the lines of its two other brigades and of the X Corps, with two reserve corps and two cavalry divisions behind them. The front of the Austrian right wing was then 6,000 paces, that of the centre 4,000 paces.

Opposite to the right wing the front of the 6th Prussian Corps and of the 1st Guards Division extended from Trotinka by Sendracic and Maslowed, where twelve batteries were now in position against the Swiepwald, which was now again occupied by the 7th Division.

Events on the Left Austrian Wing from 8 a.m. till 3.30 p.m. By orders received at midnight, the position of the Saxon Army Corps had been fixed on the ridge of hills east of Popowic and Tresowic, but when early in the morning it was reconnoitred, it was found not to be favourable to the placing of a complete army corps, on account of limited lateral communications, whilst the ridge farther east, between Nieder-Prim and Problus,

THE BATTLE OF KÖNIGGRÄTZ

seemed well suited for the purpose. The Saxon Crown Prince asked for permission to modify his instructions accordingly: this was obtained. Only one brigade was now ordered to hold the original position, and was directed to hold Popowic and Tresovic, as well as the bridges. Alt-Nechanitz and Nechanitz were to be held also by advanced battalions, but, in the event of an attack by superior forces, all the advanced detachments were to fall back on the main position. About 8 a.m. Alt-Nechanitz, and, after a lengthy skirmishers' fire fight, Nechanitz also, had been abandoned by Saxon jäger battalions, who retired towards Lubno. Before retiring they had destroyed the bridges over the Bistritz or made them unpassable, but General Herwarth, curiously, was satisfied with repairing the one at Nechanitz instead of rapidly constructing several passages: in consequence the 15th Division did not cross the river till 9.30, and it was 11 o'clock before it was formed up for the advance, and its four batteries joined the two of the advanced guard on the heights south of Lubno.

Remark about Engineers The services of the engineers were altogether neglected in the Prussian army: they were actually used to secure the lines of communication. And yet it stands to reason, that the place of engineer companies is with the advanced guards, and that, though occasionally they may be attached to artillery under special circumstances, they should always be to the front, and be at hand to remove obstacles, repair or make bridges, work hand mortars, etc. In 1870 better use was made of the engineers, and in the last war the Japanese have shown that they knew the full value of that branch of the service: the result of their experience has been that they intend to raise the strength of engineers to three battalions for each division of infantry of twelve battalions. This certainly expensive development of their scientific corps might make us consider, whether one company R.E. is sufficient for the needs of a division of twelve [1] infantry battalions.

Attack by the Elbe Army General Herwarth determined to attack Problus, and with this object directed, at 11.30, the 15th Division with one cavalry brigade, via Hradek, against Ober-Prim, and the 14th Division, then still west of Nechanitz, against Problus, by way of Lubno and Popowic. To meet this enveloping movement, the Saxon Crown Prince determined to make a counter-attack in the direction of Hradek: it was undertaken at 12 o'clock by way of Ober-Prim by the brigade of Life Guards (foot), but they were attacked in the left flank and forced to retreat. Then brigade Schulz, of the VIII Austrian Corps, attacked the outflanking enemy at Ober-Prim, brigade Roth prolonging the line. Now the Crown Prince resolved to use also the 2nd Saxon Brigade, and to renew the counter-attack with all four brigades. It failed again, because brigade Schulz, in the centre, came at 1 p.m. upon the just arrived 30th Prussian Brigade, was hurled back by the latter in great disorder, and thus exposed the left wing of the Saxons, in consequence of which the 2nd Saxon Brigade had to retire; the brigade Roth was also entangled in the confusion and disorder, and retired into the Brizerwald. Ober-Prim was taken by the Prussians, upon which the Saxons took up a position

[1] By new Army Orders.

on the plateau of Problus, where ten batteries were unlimbered. The brigade Schulz took position to the left on the heights of Bor, and the brigade Roth as right wing at Roznitz. The brigade Wöber at Charbusic now occupied the Brizerwald with two battalions.

But in spite of all these precautionary movements, the 14th and 15th Prussian Divisions took Problus and the Brizerwald.

When the general commanding the I Austrian Corps noticed that the Saxons were gradually abandoning the heights of Problus, he sent at 2.45 one brigade to support them. It arrived near Bor after 3 o'clock, and attacked Problus, but was repulsed and retired towards Ziegelschlag at 4 p.m., as the Austrian centre had gone back meanwhile.

About this time Edelsheim, who had reached the heights of Techlowitz with his cavalry division to cover the left flank of the whole army, received orders from Benedek to turn to the centre and fill a gap in that part of the position: he went there with two brigades.

The order was senseless, for under the actual circumstances every effort had to be made to secure the line of retreat to Pardubitz: the bridge north of Königgrätz should have been barred by other forces.

On the left wing of the Austrians not much more was achieved by the Prussians, who remained almost stationary at Problus, and even the 16th Division was brought up to Stezirek, where it was not wanted, instead of being sent with the whole cavalry of the right wing to Kuklena, on the Pardubitz road. General Herwarth had stayed at Nechanitz, and did not know, what was going on in front of his divisions.

Result

During these engagements the Prussians lost 1,657 men out of a total of 25,000; the Saxons and Austrians, 4,500 out of 36,000. Advantages were fairly even on both sides, as offensive and defensive alternated, but the Prussians seem to have shown greater fighting efficiency, as the Allies in superior numbers were mostly in strong positions, and were well directed by their commander, which was hardly the case with the Prussians.

Comment on the Position

The Saxon Crown Prince selected the position at Problus, which certainly had its advantages, though it was not well adapted to the strategical circumstances. As the VIII Austrian Corps had been placed under his orders, it would have been more appropriate to allot to them the defence of the heights of Problus, and to place the Saxons from the beginning on the heights of Hradek, even if only to serve the purpose of avoiding the always precarious fact of mixing troops of different states and nationalities. It is true that the frontal extent of the heights of Problus is 8,000 paces, and that the VIII Corps was not 20,000 men strong, but the Austrian reserves were so near that a timely arrival of supports could be reckoned upon. On the other hand, tactical considerations also demanded this disposition of troops, as the dominating heights of Hradek invited the enemy to use them as starting and supporting point for outflanking the Austrian left wing; it was likewise demanded in order to cover the road to Pardubitz, which was most necessary for the retreat, especially if Königgrätz was shut to the army, as had been specially stated in the general orders.

Now, the position on the heights of Problus had been chosen on account of its capacity for defence : what was done ? Soon after the commencement of the fight the Saxon Crown Prince sent forward at first one, then gradually four brigades, to attack Hradek, and thereby used up his troops, and exhausted them so much that the intended defence itself became impossible. The normal conduct of the defensive should be, to let the enemy's forces get weakened and exhausted by attacks, during that time to find out some weak spot, and then to make a dash for it, unexpectedly and rapidly, as Napoleon did at Austerlitz.

The conduct of the fighting in the Prussian divisions was excellent, but their inaction after taking the heights of Problus seems strange ; evidently the general commanding the force was not on the spot, so that the energy slacked at the moment, when the greatest efforts were demanded. The 14th Division could without doubt have held Problus and the woods in front of it, so that the 15th could now have been directed towards Kuklena with the Cavalry Division, followed by the 16th. The Elbe Army stopped moving, just when they should have secured the most valuable results of their success. Who was to blame ?

Decision of the Battle About 2 p.m. the 1st Division of the Prussian Guards had formed up behind Maslowed, took by surprise a redoubt south of the village, and dispersed the Austrian brigade in that position ; then two battalions pushed into Chlum from east and south, and scattered two Austrian battalions in the village which were facing north and west : the other five battalions of the brigade Appiano were but 1,000 yards south of the village. But the blame for the miserable measures of defence does not fall on General Appiano alone. Chlum formed the salient angle in the Austrian line of battle, and the protracted fight for the Swiepwald, as well as the artillery duel at Horenowes, should have made it certain that the junction of the two Prussian armies would be effected by the capture of Chlum. But neither Benedek, though on the height near the village gazing at Sadowa and dreaming of counter-attack, nor any Staff officer, seems to have thought it worth the trouble to examine the measures for defence taken at Chlum or to observe the surrounding ground. Benedek, who at the moment of the surprise attack on the village was close to it, ordered two battalions instead of a whole brigade to advance on it; the attack failed and could not be supported, as the five battalions of Appiano's brigade near Rosberitz were not only prevented from advancing by an attack of a brigade of Prussian Guards, but were even forced to give up that village also. Nothing was now more necessary and important than to extend the left wing so as to facilitate escape to the south: the defeat was now unavoidable, there could be only the question of lessening it as much as possible, but no measure was taken in that direction.

Advance of Troops of the 2nd Prussian Army — About 1.30 the Prussian Crown Prince rode from Choteborek to Horenowes, which had then been taken, ordering the 5th Corps, meanwhile arrived, to follow him. From Horenowes he rode towards Maslowed and Chlum, and on hearing of the capture of the latter place (3 p.m.), he ordered the 2nd Division of Guards,

THE BATTLE OF KÖNIGGRÄTZ 167

just arrived at Maslowed, to advance on Chlum and Rosberitz, and the artillery reserve of the Guards to unlimber on the heights east of Chlum. In the meantime, the 6th Prussian Corps had advanced from Sendracic, taken Nedelist, and forced the remnants of the II Austrian Corps to retreat behind the Elbe.

As soon as the attempts to retake Chlum had failed, the two brigades of the III Austrian Corps, still at Lipa, began to retreat to Langenhof and Roznitz, and the X Corps followed this movement. Now Benedek gave orders to Ramming to attack the heights of Chlum with the VI Corps, which was absurd, for if troops of the 1st Prussian Army occupied the heights of Lipa, now abandoned, and followed the retreating III and X Corps to Langenhof, the VI Corps in its attack would be fired on in flank and rear. When deploying his regiments Ramming received a new order, directing him to attack Chlum and Rosberitz: this he did with two brigades. Rosberitz was taken, and both brigades attacked Chlum, but were driven back, as the advanced guard of the 1st Prussian Corps had arrived there in the meantime. Once more Ramming ordered three brigades to attack Chlum, but parts of one of them were thrown into disorder by the retreating battalions of the III and X Corps: of course this attack also failed with enormous losses, whereupon the retreat of the decimated VI Corps was much endangered by the advance of the 11th Prussian Division against Sweti, whilst the 12th Division had already occupied Lochenitz and seized the bridge over the Elbe at that place.

Comment Altogether Benedek had but little tactical skill, and now he had lost every trace of circumspection. After the loss of Chlum and the abandonment of the heights of Lipa and Langenhof by the III and the X Corps, the following dispositions should have been made: the VI Corps to extend between Sweti and Lochenitz to cover the right flank, the III Corps with the Artillery Reserve to hold Wsestar, the X Corps to join the Saxons under the orders of their Crown Prince, to take the place of the I Corps, which should have marched on Kuklena. Chlum and Rosberitz were now no longer of any importance for the army, threatened as it was now in both its flanks.

Last Attempts to Retake Chlum In the meantime, the I Corps had deployed and tried, upon Benedek's orders, to regain possession of Chlum and Rosberitz: as these two places are in the salient angle between the heights of Langenhof, Lipa and Sweti, which were already occupied by the Prussians, the attack naturally proved a failure. In the twenty minutes which this futile attempt lasted, the Austrians lost, under the heavy converging fire to which they were exposed, 270 officers, 10,000 men and 23 guns. What would have been the use of the best breech-loaders under such circumstances?

Comment The fact that, with such suicidal proceedings, the Austrian army escaped utter destruction, is certainly not Benedek's merit, but the result and consequence of the lack of decision and energy of action on the part of the Prussian chief command. To command troops well means to perform with a certain given strength things which it would have been impossible to carry out with a smaller force. But here it would have been possible to do much more; nay, it can be safely maintained, that it was almost impossible to attain less than the actual result.

The course which the battle would take could be foreseen, and was indeed foreseen by Moltke; for when the King began to feel uneasy about noon, on account of the advance of the 1st Army being stopped, Moltke remarked: "You are going to win to-day not only a battle, but the whole campaign." Therefore dispositions ought to have been made beforehand to have fixed certain lines and limits for the advance of the three converging armies, so as to forestall the disorder and confusion which could not be avoided under the circumstances.

Moltke indeed stated once that it had been intended to throw the Austrians on to the Elbe, to cut them off from Josephstadt and Königgrätz, and to annihilate them if possible. But nothing had been done to bring about such a result; on the contrary, Moltke remained perfectly passive all day long. The causes of many omissions may be different, but the most important one was certainly Moltke's inexperience in the matter of conducting a battle; in fact, he had replied to a criticism on General Hess' conduct at Solferino with the remark that the chief of the staff had to direct the armies to the suitable place for battle, that his functions then ceased, and his place was taken by the leaders of the troops. If the general is monarch at the same time, as was the case with Frederick and Napoleon, then the conduct of the battle is naturally wielded by him, and all orders emanate from him as a matter of course. But the King had no experience as a general, and Moltke was too much a man of the world to push himself forward too much; besides, he did not on the morning of the 3rd enjoy the same authority as in the evening of the same day: only great merits, or at least successes, confer authority.

End of the Battle
At 4.30, after the last fatal attempts against Chlum and Rosberitz, all the Austrian troops were in full retreat, when parts of the 2nd Prussian Cavalry Division attacked the I Austrian Reserve Cavalry Division at Stresetic: as the Prussian cavalry were greatly inferior in numbers at the first encounter, they had to retire to Langenhof, but when more regiments came up to the attack and the Austrian cuirassiers came under infantry fire from Langenhof, they were driven back to Bor, pursued, fallen upon by new squadrons, and finally retired to Rosnitz. Two other regiments of the same Prussian cavalry division came upon the III Austrian Reserve Cavalry Division at about the same time and also near Langenhof: here also the Austrian horsemen were driven back after a sharp encounter; they also had to sustain infantry fire, and when pursued the various masses of cavalry continually came under the fire of Prussian batteries, some also met with fresh Prussian squadrons, so that they suffered heavy losses, were much broken up, and scattered in all directions.

After these fights all parts of the Austrian army were in full retreat across the Elbe, with the exception of the II and I Light Cavalry Divisions on the right and left wing, and the II Reserve Cavalry Division in 'the centre; these divisions covered the retreat, together with twenty-eight batteries, till about 6.30, but the artillery duel with about thirty-four Prussian batteries did not quite cease till the approach of darkness.

The retreat of the Austrian troops was at first carried out in quite orderly fashion, but the bonds of discipline and the tactical units got loosened by the restricted space on which such a mass of men, horses and vehicles were hemmed in: the banks of the Elbe had been inundated by the opening of flood-gates, and Königgrätz remained closed to the retreating troops till the fall of night; in consequence many troops were forced to break off in the direction of Opatowic and Pardubitz. The Prussian army corps did not advance beyond the line Sweti-Briza-Charbusic, and were in bivouac for the night as follows: The three divisions of the Elbe Army, with their reserve artillery, at Problus, Prim and Stezirek; the infantry divisions of the 1st Army at Bor, Problus, Wsestar, Lipa, Langenhof, Stresititz, and at the wood of Sadowa; their reserve artillery went back to Klenitz, and the cavalry divisions were at Rosnitz and Nechanitz. Of the 2nd Army, the 1st and 5th Corps were about Rosnitz, the 6th at Briza and Sweti, the Guards between Wsestar and Langenhof, the cavalry at Briza and Rosberitz. The outposts during the night extended from Techlowitz by Stösser and Freihöfen as far as Plotist.

The losses of the Prussians amounted to 359 officers and 8,794 men; those of the Austrians and Saxons to 44,200, of whom 19,800 were taken prisoners.

The Austrians lost 160 guns and 5 colours, the Saxons 1 gun. The losses of the Austrian army up to July 4 were 70,987 men; those of the Saxons, 2,100 men; those of the Prussians, 15,533 men; therefore the Austrians had lost more than a quarter, the Saxons one-tenth, and the Prussians one-seventeenth part of their original forces, and comparison allows us to form an opinion on the skill of leadership and the fighting capacity of the troops.

After the battle the Royal Headquarters were again established at Horiz, and Moltke, with the General Staff, even returned to Gitschin, instead of remaining on the field of battle, e.g. at Dohaliczka. This is the greatest mistake that can be committed, for only on the battlefield it is possible to gain a full view and perception of the situation, and to discuss, without loss of time, with the generals the actual condition of affairs, and take resolutions and order movements accordingly. And thus indeed Moltke did act in the night after the battle of Gravelotte!

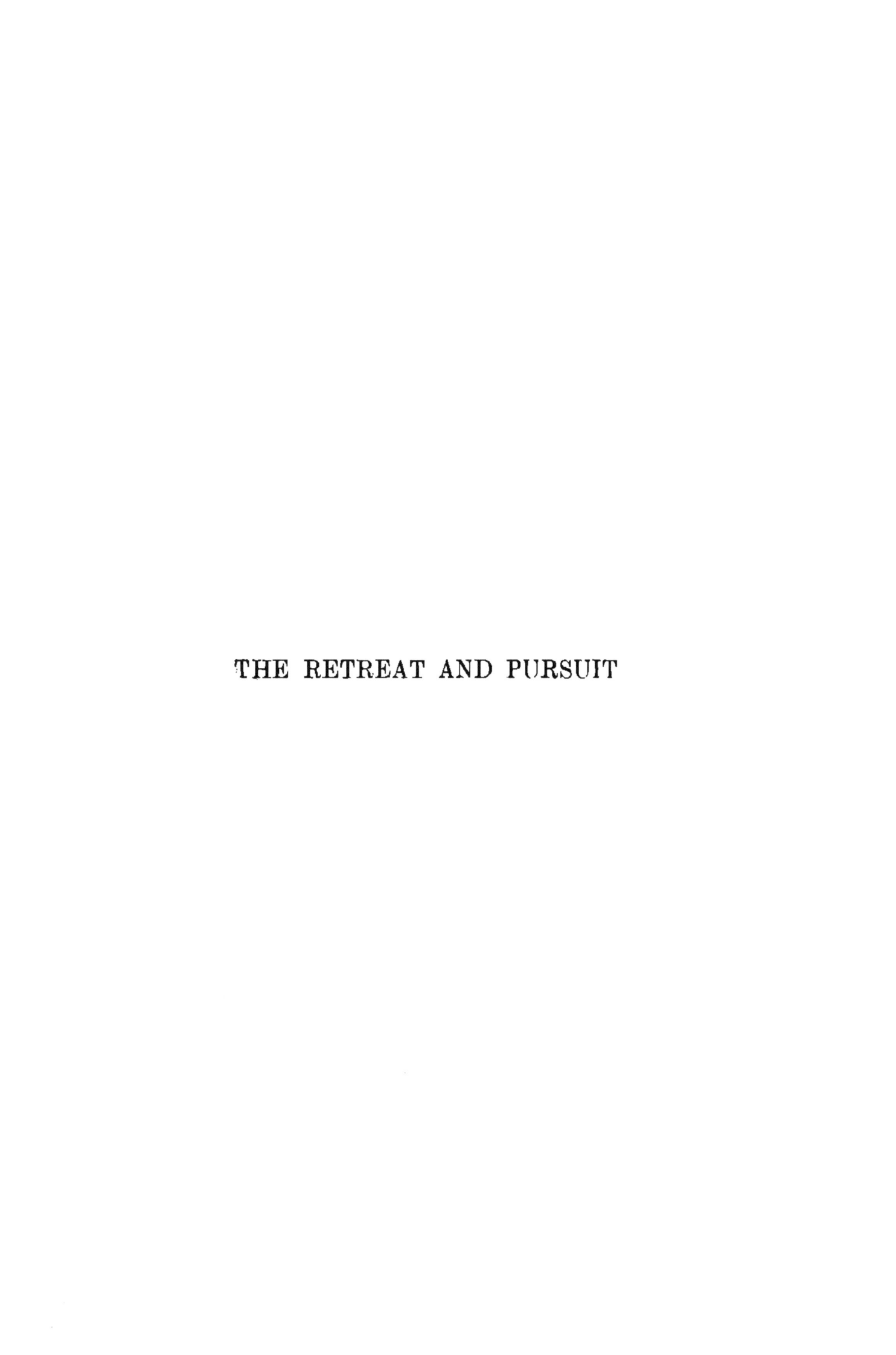

THE RETREAT AND PURSUIT

CHAPTER IX

The Retreat and Pursuit

Inactivity of the Prussians — CRITICS have blamed the Prussian chief command for not having begun the pursuit at once on the 4th by making the 2nd Army march on Prossnitz via Hohenbruck, and letting the Elbe Army camp on the left bank of the river at Pardubitz, whilst the 1st Army, which had suffered most severely in proportion, could have followed the forward movement on the following day. They say, that by doing so the order in the organisation of the various units would have been most quickly restored, and that by rapidity of pursuit the Austrian army would probably have been destroyed, though it had escaped that fate in the battle.

But only the troops of the Elbe Army had been moved from the early morning of the 4th, with the intention of separating them from the other corps and thus avoiding disorder: they reached Urbanitz and Libcan during the day. In the afternoon the order was given for the other two armies to take up a position between Pardubitz and Podebrad, after the morning had been spent in making all arrangements which are necessitated by a battle of such dimensions—as for the care of the wounded, the disposal of the unexpectedly large number of prisoners, the bringing up of the supply trains and columns, completing the ammunition supply in the regimental transports.

Again critics have said: " The order to march up between Pardubitz and Podebrad was distinctly absurd; the forward march on Brünn should have been commenced with energy on the 4th with the endeavour of cutting the Austrians off from Vienna, if they went off aside to Olmütz. It was the duty, and should have been the business of the numerous cavalry, never to lose the enemy out of sight and to find out the directions they had followed. At the Royal Headquarters they had no idea of the extent of the victory, but just on that account energetic measures ought to have been taken all the more keenly for a close pursuit, in order to increase the results and prevent scarcity of provisions. A few words or verbal messages on the evening of the 3rd would have sufficed to issue the necessary directions."

Retreat of the Austrians The retreat of the Austrians had been executed in three columns: the right wing column, the II Army Corps and a cavalry division got to Hohenbruck in the night of the 3rd, and continued its march on the 4th to Kosteletz, with the rearguard at Tynist; the IV Corps had remained near Neu-Königgrätz; the main column, I, III and VI Corps, with the greatest part of the Saxons and the Artillery Reserve, took the road to Hohenmauth, a portion remaining at Holic; the left wing column, VIII and X Corps, with part of the Saxons and the greatest part of the cavalry, had marched to Pardubitz, and its last detachments had crossed the Elbe there between 6 and 7 a.m.: all these troops left this town by the night of the 4th, one

[1] When turned about to face the pursuing enemy.

part marching for Hohenmauth, there to join the main column, the other part, including the Saxons, taking the road to Zwittau.

Choice of Line of Retreat The choice between the farther direction of retreat lay between Vienna and Olmütz: on the 140 miles to Vienna the army, in its condition after the battle, would for certain have dissolved itself, unless a halt could be made to re-establish order, to reorganise units, to obtain ammunition and other necessaries; but if that proved possible, one was again sure to see the Prussians catching up the fugitives, and there was no position north of the Danube, where a permanent resistance could be offered, so that all the land north of that river would fall into the hands of the enemy. It is true, that at Vienna a direct connection with the victorious Southern Army would be established, whose assistance alone could equalise the enemy's superiority; but it could hardly be expected, that the Italians would allow of a large portion of that army to be free for disposal in the north.

The fortified camp of Olmütz offered, at only half the distance, a safe place of refuge, where the army could again assemble and refit. More than 100,000 men in a flanking position could not but create great difficulties to the enemy's advance towards Vienna, and would protect a considerable portion of the Austrian monarchy, or force him to divide his forces. Of course the flanking position could only be effective, if the army could again resume the offensive from it, which was doubtful, as the moral condition of the troops hardly warranted a renewal of offensive operations. It was also doubtful, whether Olmütz possessed all the resources required for the complete refitting and provisioning of the troops. However, Benedek decided in favour of Olmütz, and only ordered the X Corps and the greater part of the cavalry to proceed to Vienna for the protection of that city.

Events on July 5

On July 5 Benedek arrived at Zwittau; the rearguard of his right wing column reached Wamberg, the centre column Leitomischl, the left wing column Krouna.

On the part of the Prussians the cavalry division Hartmann passed the Elbe near Pardubitz by fords, a bridge at Nemcitz was repaired, and horse artillery crossed the river by that means. Hartmann at once commenced repairing the bridges at Pardubitz, which was next occupied by the advanced guard of the 5th Army Corps. The other troops of the 2nd Army halted near Hradist and Opatowitz, with the exception of the 6th Corps, the 11th Division remaining on the battlefield, the 12th in observation near Josephstadt. The divisions of the 1st Army reached Prelauc and other places on the Elbe, and those of the Elbe Army got to Chlumetz and Zizelitz, with the advanced guard at Kladrub.

The field artillery of the 12th Division was ordered to bombard Königgrätz from a distance of 5,000 paces, but as no appropriate result could be obtained, the firing was stopped in the evening.

As the time seemed to have arrived now to take possession of Prague and its resources, the Elbe Army received orders in the evening to direct the division Rosenberg from Podiebrad to that city, and to occupy the passages over the river at Elbe-Teinitz and Neu-

Kolin : railways and rolling stock were to be protected against destruction. It may be stated at once, that the division marched via Sadska, and on July 8 reached Prague, which was found abandoned by Austrian troops. The occupation of this city was of great importance, because the railway line, Turnau-Prague-Pardubitz, could now be put in use. On the same day General Mülbe, commanding at Dresden, received orders to march with the division Bentheim via Teplitz to Prague, where he arrived on the 18th.

July 6   The Austrian Headquarters remained at Zwittau, the rear of the right wing column reached Wildenschwerdt, that of the centre column Leitomischl, the left wing column Policka.

Advanced Prussian cavalry reported Hohenmauth abandoned by the enemy, the 5th Corps reached Holitz, the 1st Corps Chrudim, the Guards went through Pardubitz and Dasitz to Zwing. The 1st Army did not move during the day except the Cavalry Corps, which marched to Zdechowitz, and a newly formed strong advanced guard of six battalions, three cavalry regiments and three batteries horse artillery, which reached Choltitz in the afternoon. The advanced guard of the Elbe Army advanced to Elbe-Teinitz, the 14th Division to Neu-Kolin, to give eventual support to the division Rosenberg marching on Prague; the other troops went into bivouacs between Chlumetz and the Elbe.

The reports received from the advanced troops had now made it certain that the main body of the enemy's forces was retiring on Olmütz, and King William determined to follow them there only with the left wing army, and to direct the other two armies straight against

Vienna, in order to bring the campaign to an early conclusion.

It was not the intention to lay regular siege to this strong place, nor could it be fully invested without a dangerous splitting up of the Prussian forces; therefore the only task of the 2nd Army could be to cover the advance of the 1st and the Elbe Army on Vienna.

It was assumed, though not correctly, that the defeated hostile army had still sufficient fighting efficiency to be able to resume the offensive after a short rest in the entrenched camp. As it was still numerically much superior to the army of the Crown Prince, it was thought that the latter might be forced to retreat. However, all the previous fighting should have convinced the General Staff that the fighting efficiency of their soldiers was much greater than that of the Austrians, and the result of the great battle following upon all the previous blows could but have had very different effects on the morale of the two armies. Anyhow, even if a temporary retreat of the 2nd Army should have been necessitated, it would have drawn the Army of Olmütz in the direction of Silesia and away from the chief operation, which it was necessary to carry out rapidly, so as to appear on the Danube before the Austrian Government could draw large reinforcements from Italy, which could be done safely after the victory of Custozza. The 2nd Army was therefore ordered to take up such a position that it could observe the enemy and fall back in case of attack by superior numbers, or follow him, if he marched off towards Vienna. It would have been much better, and more appropriate to the actual circumstances, to have taken rapid and decisive action to prevent the junction of the North Army with the forces near the capital by risking, without hesitation, another battle before the disorder, confusion and discouragement of the Austrians could be effaced and supplanted by better conditions and feelings. In spite of the great victory, the conduct of the operations was still marked by strange, unaccountable timidity and half-heartedness.

The 2nd Army received the order to advance on Mährisch-Trübau and to establish a line of communication with Glatz via Mittenwalde, so that the line via Königinhof passing near the two Elbe fortresses could be given up, and the bulk of the 6th Army Corps could be drawn from that part to join the other corps of the army.

During the farther progress of the retreat and pursuit small skirmishes occurred occasionally, in most of which numerous Austrians were taken prisoners.

July 8. Armistice Proposed

The 1st Army received orders to march on Brünn on the road Policka-Kunstadt, the Elbe Army to proceed to Iglau. On this day the Austrian General Gablenz, *persona gratissima* at the Prussian Court, arrived at the Royal Headquarters at Pardubitz with "instructions" from the Prime Minister, Count Mensdorff, which proposed the immediate conclusion of an armistice of at least eight weeks, at the most of three months. If one takes in consideration the actual situation at that time in Bohemia (as well as in South Germany), it is hard to believe that the Austrian Government had the illusion that Prussia would enter upon such proposals. They had already ceded the province of Venice to France, which offered the chance of transferring considerable forces from the southern to the northern theatre of war, and it could hardly be expected that Prussia would blindly grant the time in which to do this. The proposals were refused by the King.

July 11   In the course of this day the Austrian North Army was assembled at Olmütz, with the exception of the portions which had been directed to Vienna. They had obtained a start of twenty-eight miles on the 1st Prussian Corps, and of fifty miles on the Guards Corps. But although by this uninterrupted retreat of about 100 miles they had avoided all serious fighting, yet it had surely more and more deteriorated the moral and material fighting efficiency. The overcrowding also of the camp at Olmütz could not but cause serious difficulties of all sorts. Besides, the 1st Prussian Army had reached the line Kunstadt-Bobrau, and its advanced guard was within one day's march of Brünn; within a few days the last connection of the North Army with Vienna could be interrupted from Brünn at Lundenburg, and the capital itself be then threatened. The 2nd Prussian Army had reached the line Mährisch-Trübau-Landskron, the Elbe Army was at Iglau, Wollein and Pirnitz.

The dangers of the situation were now perceived by the Austrians, and it was resolved to draw the greatest part of the North Army to Vienna, leaving only one corps in Olmütz, instead of leaving the greatest part there, in order to operate in the rear of the enemy. This change of plan was quite correct, because only a complete change in the highest command and in the conduct of the operations could possibly awaken new hope in the discouraged masses, and nothing can be done without a certain show of self-confidence. Therefore, as the newly appointed Commander-in-Chief, Archduke Albrecht, demanded the concentration of the army on the Danube, Benedek had received the order to send off by rail to Vienna one corps after the other, with the exception of one, as before mentioned, as long as the railway was open; in case this should be interrupted, he was to march on Vienna behind the river March with the troops not yet despatched. In consequence the III Corps was sent off on the 11th, and was to be followed by the Saxon Corps. Benedek fixed upon the line Hullein-Hradisch-Ostrau-Göding for the infantry and artillery to march to Pressburg, and for the cavalry, which was to start last and cover the flank and rear of the marching troops, the road Prossnitz-Eisgrub-Walkersdorf, west of the March. The VI Corps, which was to remain at Olmütz, was to protect, during the time of the departure of the other corps, the railway line from Olmütz to Prerau; the I Corps was to cover the neighbourhood of this place, and for a similar purpose the brigade Mondl had already been detached at Lundenburg.

From all the reports received at the Headquarters of the 2nd Army, it had become known that the enemy was in such a condition, that an offensive movement on his part was not to be expected; therefore, although the despatch of troops to Vienna had not yet become known, it was resolved for this army to occupy the line Prossnitz-Urtschitz, instead of the line Littau-Konitz, which would stop all communication between Olmütz and Vienna on the right bank of the March. However, the line of communication with Glatz could then no longer be considered secure, which was all the more precarious, as the railway connection with Turnau was blocked by Josephstadt, and damages on the line Prague-Pardubitz had not yet been repaired. Thus the troops of the 1st and the Elbe Army could only subsist by a continuous advance into districts which had not yet sustained requisitions.

There was a small cavalry skirmish on the advance to Brünn at Tischnowitz, in which Austrian lancers were driven back by dragoons of the Prussian Guard.

July 12 Archduke Albrecht handed over the command of the South Army at Vincenza to General Maroicic, and started for Vienna with Archduke John, the Chief of his Staff. Brünn was occupied by the advanced guard of the 1st Prussian Army, and the King's Headquarters came to Czernahora. The advanced brigade of the 1st Corps, 2nd Army, reached Oppatowitz, Hartmann's cavalry being farther ahead. The advanced guard of the Elbe Army reached Lispitz, after the vanguard had had a slight encounter with the enemy; the mainguard reached Mährisch-Budwitz; the three divisions reached Startsch, Trebitsch and Gross Meseritsch.

July 13 The Headquarters of the 2nd Army were moved forward to Oppatowitz. The advanced guard of the Elbe Army entered Znaim, and General Schœler had a temporary bridge made acros the Thaya, close to the one destroyed by fire. The King entered Brünn, where the 5th, 6th and 7th Divisions were billeted, and the advanced guard of the 1st Army was pushed forward to Modritz. In the evening a cavalry patrol, which had advanced up to the works of Olmütz, reported that they had not found any enemy, but that some forces were said to be encamped east of the place.

Archduke Albrecht arrived in Vienna. There were on that day still 92,000 men with 364 guns about Olmütz, 41,000 men with 106 guns on the way to Vienna, 9,400 cavalry with 72 guns on the Thaya; the X Corps, 16,700 men with 56 guns, near Vienna, including the Brigade Mondl at Lundenburg. There were also on the road from the southern theatre of war 57,000 men with 120 guns, so that all these forces, if assembled on the Danube, would have formed an army of 216,000 men with 718 guns. One may think about the chances of the continuance of warlike operations as one likes, but the safety of the Austrian states seems to have depended less on the doubtful efficiency of this army of the Danube than on the actual dissension at the Prussian Headquarters produced by Bismarck's intrigues; for from the date of Count Benedetti's arrival there, all dispositions became marked by uncertainty and their execution defective, a proof of how dangerous it is to introduce into the simple military headquarters the turbulent current of court cabals.

Defence of Vienna
At the beginning of the hostilities the Austrian engineers began the construction of a vast line of fortifications to form a bridgehead at Florisdorf, north of Vienna, which is stated to have been completed on July 13, and to have been armed with 387 guns. The outer line had an extent of fourteen miles—about 30,000 paces—the two reduits forming the inner line an extent of together 15,000 paces: 50,000 men were required at least to man these lines.

Advance of the Prussian Armies to the Danube

On July 14 orders were issued from the Royal Headquarters that the 1st Army was to advance on Vienna by the three roads Eibenschütz-Laa - Ernstbrunn, Dürnholz-Ladendorf, Muschau-Nikolsburg-Gaunersdorf, and that a detachment was to be directed to Lundenburg to destroy the railway line leading to Prerau, taking care to keep intact, or even to repair on its advance the line leading to Gänserndorf. The Elbe Army was to advance on the two roads Jetzelsdorf-Hollabrunn and Joslowitz-Enzersdorf-Thaleim and send a detachment to Maissau to demonstrate against the Upper Danube, near Krems. The main bodies of both armies were to cross the Thaya on the 17th at Muschau and Znaim. All the pontoon columns of the 1st and the 2nd Army were to be sent by train to Brünn as soon as possible.

Of the 2nd Army the 6th Corps reached M. Trübau, the Guards Oppatowitz only; but the 5th Corps was close to Laschkau, and the 1st Corps approaching Prossnitz. The Cavalry Division halted at Kosteletz, but its advanced detachments reported " no enemies " at Ollschann or south of Prossnitz, whereupon Hartmann sent a detachment to reconnoitre towards Tobitschau. The consequence was a slight cavalry skirmish at Kralitz: the report of it was accompanied by the information that some infantry and artillery of the enemy were advancing from Tobitschau. The first reports were given to the Crown Prince by General Hartmann in the afternoon at Neustift, from where he sent orders to the 1st Army Corps to send the same evening one infantry brigade with one battery to Tobitschau, in order to support the advance of the Cavalry Division on Prerau, which was to be executed early on the 15th. In General Hartmann's absence the main body of the Cavalry Division was marched to Prossnitz, and the 1st Cuirassier Regiment sent forward towards Tobitschau. When darkness was setting in, the squadrons came upon Austrian infantry formed in a square, which was attacked vigorously, but not with great success : the regiment was retired to Prossnitz, when more Austrian troops, coming from Biskupitz, opened infantry and artillery fire upon the cuirassiers. The infantry encountered belonged to the flank-guard of the II Austrian Army Corps, which had started its march upon Göding under the following circumstances.

Benedek leaves Olmütz

At noon on the 13th, Benedek had received from the Archduke Albrecht this telegram : " Have to-day taken over the chief command. Order that without contradiction all troops shall be started on the march to Pressburg on the left bank of the March, to-morrow and on the next day ; ten battalions, one cavalry regiment and one battery are to be left as garrison at Olmütz." But Benedek had already ordered and commenced the march of four army corps on the right bank of the March to Göding, where they had to cross the river and then proceed to Pressburg via Stampfen.

All the news received by the Prussian Crown Prince during the day made it probable that the greater part of the North Army had already left Olmütz for Vienna, and he therefore ordered the 6th Corps and the Guards to march on Brünn, as it seemed unsuitable to him to assemble his whole army at Prossnitz. This resolution seems ill advised, for the 1st and the 5th Corps ought to have first made sure whether the enemy had really left Olmütz, and in which direction he had gone. If it was found that he had gone off to the south, he had to be followed as rapidly as possible on the roads to Hradisch and Holics, as the main object should have been to gain touch with him at last. The distance from Königgrätz to Prossnitz is eighty-four miles, which had been covered in eleven days: thus the pursuit had not been particularly fast, although it had the object of cutting off the North Army from the South.

Combat of Tobitschau, July 15

The Austrian II Corps had started from Tobitschau at 2 a.m. and got to Kremsier without being molested, the IV Corps likewise, from Kojetein to Zdannek. The VIII Corps was to move from Olmütz to Kojetein, and started at 4 a.m., brigade Rothkirch, with three squadrons, being the advanced guard, whilst brigade Wöber was to move as flank-guard via Kralitz to Niemtschitz. When the advanced guard had entered Tobitschau, the flank detachment received fire near a wood outside the place. A part of the cavalry division Hartmann and one brigade of the 1st Army Corps had arrived there. The Austrian flank-guard of two companies, though reinforced by the remainder of the battalion, was driven out of the wood in which it had taken position. The brigade Rothkirch now deployed on the heights north of the town, and its battery opened fire on three Prussian batteries; the left wing had begun to retire, when Benedek ordered the artillery reserve of the VIII Corps (four batteries) to form up west of the road, to silence the Prussian guns. They had scarcely commenced firing, when they were fallen upon by the 5th Prussian Cuirassier Regiment, who took two batteries whilst the other two had time to escape. The Austrian infantry soon after began to retreat.

Meanwhile the Austrian flank-guard, brigade Wöber, had come up and deployed, but when the approach of strong columns from Prossnitz was observed, it retired on the main body of the VIII Corps, which meanwhile had deployed on the heights of Dub. An artillery duel, without much result, was then carried on, till the 1st Prussian Army Corps appeared deployed for the attack, when Archduke Leopold ordered the retreat of his corps behind the March, in obedience to instructions, which caused him to march to Prerau. An attack of eight Prussian squadrons on part of the infantry and cavalry of the I Austrian Corps in marching column at Prerau was repulsed, though successful at first, and they had to retire: they lost 10 killed, 97 wounded, and 113 horses, but their unexpected appearance and attack had produced the most complete confusion in the Austrian columns, so that they brought back 5 officers and 250 men as prisoners. The total loss in the day's fighting to the Prussians was 12 officers, 235 men; whilst the Austrians lost 1,956, including 1,070 missing. The attack of the cuirassiers, which resulted in the capture of 18 guns, 15 limbers, 7 ammunition wagons, 2 officers and 168 men, only caused the loss of 10 men.

Comment on the Situation The VI Austrian Corps had meantime marched unmolested from Olmütz to Leipnik, the 5th Prussian Corps had occupied Prossnitz, the Guards and the 6th Corps had arrived at Boskowitz and Lettowitz. By the fight at Tobitschau the head of the 2nd Prussian Army had put a wedge between the two echelons of the Austrian North Army, had forced that part of it marching on the right bank of the March to retire behind that river, and its cavalry had even crossed it. But the favourable situation thus created was not taken advantage of : the general in chief command seems to have been blind to the fact that he had in front of him the largest and most important portion of the enemy's forces, that there was urgent necessity not to let them escape, and that he could never bring about a more decisive event. It surely was his duty to keep in touch with the enemy, and to make full use of every favourable opportunity to make an attack on the disheartened enemy's masses.

The order was given that the 5th Corps and the cavalry division Hartmann should pursue the Austrians, and that the 1st Corps should observe Olmütz, but nothing really was done, chiefly owing to the absence of the commanding general from the scene of action : without personal exertion nothing can be accomplished. General Bonin brought up the 1st Corps at Tobitschau, but neglected to follow up the advantage gained, and inflict a serious, perhaps fatal blow on the enemy. Instead, he retired to the bivouac, and even evacuated Tobitschau, leaving there only a rearguard. He then wasted the 16th and 17th by a reconnaissance to Prerau, which he might have taken already on the 15th, and he destroyed the railway leading to Silesia.

Advance of Other Troops on the 15th During the fight at Tobitschau the 5th Prussian Corps had occupied Prossnitz, the Guards and the 6th Corps had arrived at Boskowitz and Lettowitz. The 1st Army had continued the march towards Vienna : the advanced guard found the Thaya bridge at Muschau destroyed by fire, so that only one cavalry regiment and two battalions could cross the river during the afternoon. The 6th, 7th and 8th Divisions were marching on Pohrlitz, Gross Niempschitz and Klobank, but in consequence of an order from the Royal Headquarters directing the advance on Lundenburg, the 7th Division was ordered to march to Auspitz, the 5th from Brünn to Mönitz, the 8th to occupy Göding on the following day, and to secure the railway and interrupt the transport on it of the enemy's troops. On receipt of this order at Klobank, General Horn, commanding the 8th Division, at once detailed a detachment of 150 men of the 6th Lancers on the best horses of the regiment, together with a section of mounted engineers, to proceed to a point on the railway south of Göding. They arrived there at 6 p.m., having seen two trains pass from the north, removed some rails and cut the telegraph; a third train then approaching, halted and steamed back; but when several bodies of the enemy's infantry and cavalry came up, the detachment retired and went back to Klobank, where they arrived at midnight, having covered fifty-eight miles since they left their bivouac at 3 a.m.

The appearance of Prussian troops at Göding caused a telegraphic order being sent from Vienna to the effect that the brigade Mondl, till then stationed at Lundenburg, should destroy the bridge at that place and go back to Marchegg by rail the same night. The Elbe Army continued the march on Znaim, which was occupied during the day by the 14th Division; its advanced guard got to Jetzelsdorf, where it had a slight skirmish with cavalry and artillery, who retired after the exchange of a few shots.

On the side of the Austrians the IV and the II Corps had arrived unmolested at Zdaunck and Kremsier. When Benedek, who was with the I and VIII Corps at Prerau, as shown above, heard in the evening that Göding had been reached by Prussian troops, he gave up the idea of continuing his march in the valley of the March, and issued the following instructions: the IV Corps was to proceed to Mijava via Hradisch and Welka, the II Corps to Neustadt-on-the-Waag via Hradisch and Strany, the I Corps from Prerau via Slawitschin to the Wlar Pass, the VIII Corps to the Hrosenkau Pass via Holleschau and Boikowitz; the VI Corps, still left at Olmütz, to Klobank via Leipnik, Meseritsch and Wsetin; the latter was to be followed by about 10,000 Saxons and men of the VIII Corps still remaining at Olmütz.

July 16   The Headquarters of the 2nd Prussian Army moved to Prödlitz; the Guards and the 6th Corps, continuing the march in westerly direction, reached Czernahora and Raitz; the 5th Corps had to march to Prerau, and was to be supported by a division of the 1st Corps, and its flank to be covered to the south by the Cavalry Division : by these wise dispositions the heads of the two halves of the 2nd Army were forty-two miles apart, and their line was forty-six miles north of that occupied by the other two armies on this same day! Prerau was, of course, found abandoned by the enemy, whereupon the 10th Division and part of the 1st Corps marched back to their bivouacs; but, evidently with the intention of doing something, they destroyed 1,000 yards of the railway line and blew up the iron bridge across a tributary of the March, whereby the connection with Upper Silesia was interrupted, contrary to the spirit of the instructions from the General Staff!

The 8th Division reached Göding and put a bridge across the March, the 7th Division occupied Lundenburg, whilst the specially formed *advanced guard* of the 1st Army, under Duke Wilhelm of Mecklenburg, was stopped at Eisgrub, five miles to the *rear* of the 7th Division, through the delay caused by throwing a bridge across the Thaya. The 5th Division followed the 7th, the Cavalry Corps advanced to Feldsberg, the 6th Division to Nicolsburg, the 2nd Army Corps to Danowitz, the Headquarters of the 1st Army moved to Pawlowitz, eleven miles north of Lundenburg. The divisions of the Elbe Army reached various places round Laa, having marched off to the left from their original direction in accordance with the latest instructions.

The Austrian IV Corps had reached Hradisch by a night march, and proceeded as far as Ostrau; the II Corps got to Hradisch via Napagedl; the I and VIII Corps, under Benedek, to Holleschau; the VI Corps left Leipnik; the II Saxon Division marched from Olmütz to Leipnik, and continued the march during the night to Weisskirchen.

July 17 After Benedek had seen himself obliged to attain his junction with the army near Vienna by the long *détour* across the Little Carpathians, he strove to make up for the unavoidable loss of time by forced marches, which reflect greatly to the credit of the endurance of his army. Thus, in spite of the difficult progress along mountain roads, the rearguards of

o

his corps reached Welka (the IV), Strany (the II), Boikowitz (the I and the VIII), Meseritsch (the VI).

The 1st Prussian Corps left Tobitschau and went back to its cantonments near Urtschitz, because these had been fixed by orders received four days previously (*sic!*); the 5th Corps and the Cavalry Division had a day's rest, and were to start on the next day down the March; the Guards and the 6th Corps reached Brünn. Of the 1st Army the 8th Division went to Holics, the 5th to Göding, the 7th remained in occupation of Lundenburg; the 2nd Army Corps and the 6th Division marched forward towards the Danube; the Cavalry Corps advanced down the March to Hohenau, sixty-three miles ahead of the cavalry division Hartmann, with the 5th Corps! The advanced guard, under the Duke of Mecklenburg, went south on the Vienna road, but finding Wilfersdorf on that road occupied already by the advanced guard of the Elbe Army, moved off five miles to its left to Hauskirchen. The three divisions of the Elbe Army reached Erdberg, Ameis and Staatz; the vanguard of its advanced guard had a slight skirmish at Schrick with Austrian cuirassiers.

Special Orders

Late in the evening the following orders were despatched from the Royal Headquarters: "His Majesty intends to make a general advance on the Danube; the 1st Army will march on both banks of the March, and has the task of preventing the retreat of hostile troops from Olmütz to Pressburg. The 2nd Army will assemble along the line Nikolsburg-Lundenburg, and will immediately follow the movements of the 1st and the Elbe Army. The 1st Army has to take into consideration, that one of its divisions may be ordered to advance from Malaczka, with forced marches, on Pressburg, to obtain possession of it and of the passage of the Danube, and, if possible, also of the places Hainburg and Kitsee."

Comment On July 12 a council of war had been held at the Royal Headquarters at Czernahora, in which the question of attacking the entrenched lines of Florisdorf, north of Vienna, was discussed; Moltke wanted to get fifty heavy guns from Dresden for the purpose of bombarding them, but their transport was calculated to take fourteen days, and thereupon Bismarck stated, that they could not lose so many days without dangerously increasing the possibility of imminent French arbitration proposals, and proposed to effect the crossing of the Danube; finally, the above royal order decided in favour of this proposal rather against military opinion. As a matter of fact, the lines of Florisdorf were armed with old guns, and were so extensive that they could not have been effectively defended and might have been carried by assault, as those of Düppel had been carried two years previously. But Bismarck wanted to prevent the triumphal entrance of the Prussian army in Vienna, in order to spare the feelings of the Austrians, and to facilitate a reconciliation in the future.

July 18 In conformity with these orders the following movements were carried out by the Prussian troops : on the west of the March the advanced guard to Spannberg with the Cavalry Corps on its left, behind them the 7th Division at Drösing, the 6th at Zistersdorf, the 2nd Army Corps near Feldsberg ; on the eastern side of the March the 8th Division was pushed forward to St. Johann and the 5th to Holicz. The Elbe Army was concentrated on the line Aspern-Wilfersdorf, with its advanced guard at Gaunersdorf. Of the 2nd Prussian Army the Guards and the 6th Corps continued their march south from Brünn, the 5th Corps reached Kojetein, whilst the cavalry division Hartmann pushed forward to Kremsier and Hullein. In front of Olmütz the 1st Corps took up the positions required for the investment of the place.

The Austrian IV Corps got that day as far as Mijawa, the II to Waag-Neustadtl, the I and VIII were approaching the valley of the Waag at Boikowitz, whilst the VI reached Klobank. In the evening the II Corps received special orders to hurry on to Pressburg in order to support the brigade Mondl, which had gone to Blumenau, and to secure the possession of Pressburg, which seemed endangered by the advance of considerable hostile forces from Göding.

July 19 The Elbe Army was to keep during the day their position about Aspern and Wilfersdorf, pending the approach of the two corps of the 2nd Army towards Muschau: the 1st Army also was not to advance far beyond the line Malaczka-Gaunersdorf, and in consequence its advanced guard and cavalry only took up a line near Schönkirchen on the Weidenbach; the 8th Division, on the left bank of the March, advanced to Gross Schützen, the 5th to Kuti; the cavalry division Hartmann advanced to Napagedl, and was followed by the two divisions of the 5th Corps: advanced cavalry detachments took a large quantity of rolling stock at the station of Altstadt.

The II Austrian Corps continued its march on the

road to Pressburg as far as Koztolan; part of the IV halted at Mijawa, part was sent to Jablonitz on the road Göding-Tyrnau; the I Corps went down the Waag to Trencsin, the VIII got to Choholna, whilst the VI Corps reached Nemsova, leaving one Saxon division behind at Klobank.

New Prussian Orders
In the Prussian Headquarters no certain information had as yet been obtained as to the number of Austrian troops which had been sent by rail from Olmütz to Vienna, before the line was interrupted, nor was it known, whether a reserve army had already been formed behind the Danube of the 4th (garrison) and the newly raised 5th battalions of the infantry regiments. Again, it was not known, how great a part of the Southern Army had lately been brought to Vienna from Italy, whence the Italian army was reported to be inactive, and to do nothing to prevent such withdrawal of forces from that theatre of war. It was therefore not impossible, that by means of using all these resources a large army was already assembled near Vienna, which, to save the capital, might sally out on the Marchfeld from the lines of Florisdorf.

These considerations caused the Prussian Headquarters at Nikolsburg to issue the following orders (abridged) :—

" It is the intention of His Majesty to concentrate the army behind the Russbach, the Elbe Army at Wolkersdorf, the 1st Army behind Deutsch Wagram, the 2nd Army as reserve at Schönkirchen.

" In this position the army is to be capable of opposing an attack which the enemy might be able to undertake with 150,000 men from Florisdorf; further, the army is either to reconnoitre and attack the enemy's entrenched lines at that place or, leaving a corps of observation opposite the lines, to march off to Pressburg as quickly as possible.

" For this purpose all the available detachments move to-morrow to the Weidenbach, and send their advanced guards forward to Wolkersdorf and Deutsch Wagram. At the same time the general commanding the 1st Army has to make the attempt to take possession of Pressburg by a surprise attack, and to secure the passage across the Danube."

Comment   These circumstantial dispositions, and altogether the assembly of the whole army previous to the intended actions, seem to have been not justified by the circumstances. Prince Frederick Charles and General Herwarth could have been shortly ordered to surprise Pressburg and the Florisdorf bridgehead respectively, early in the morning of the 21st, with all available forces: these two armies alone possessed quite enough fighting efficiency to cope with the Austrian corps without waiting for the 2nd Army, whose much delayed arrival near the probable scene of final operations was perhaps partly the cause of these orders for assembly and concentration at a time, when circumstances demanded energetic decision and rapid action to strike a few blows to influence the conditions of an armistice, for which negotiations had commenced some days previously to the issue of the order. Materials for assaulting the Florisdorf lines and for bridging the Danube had been got ready, and were partly already at Lundenburg, where the railway line from Dresden via Prague to Vienna was still interrupted.

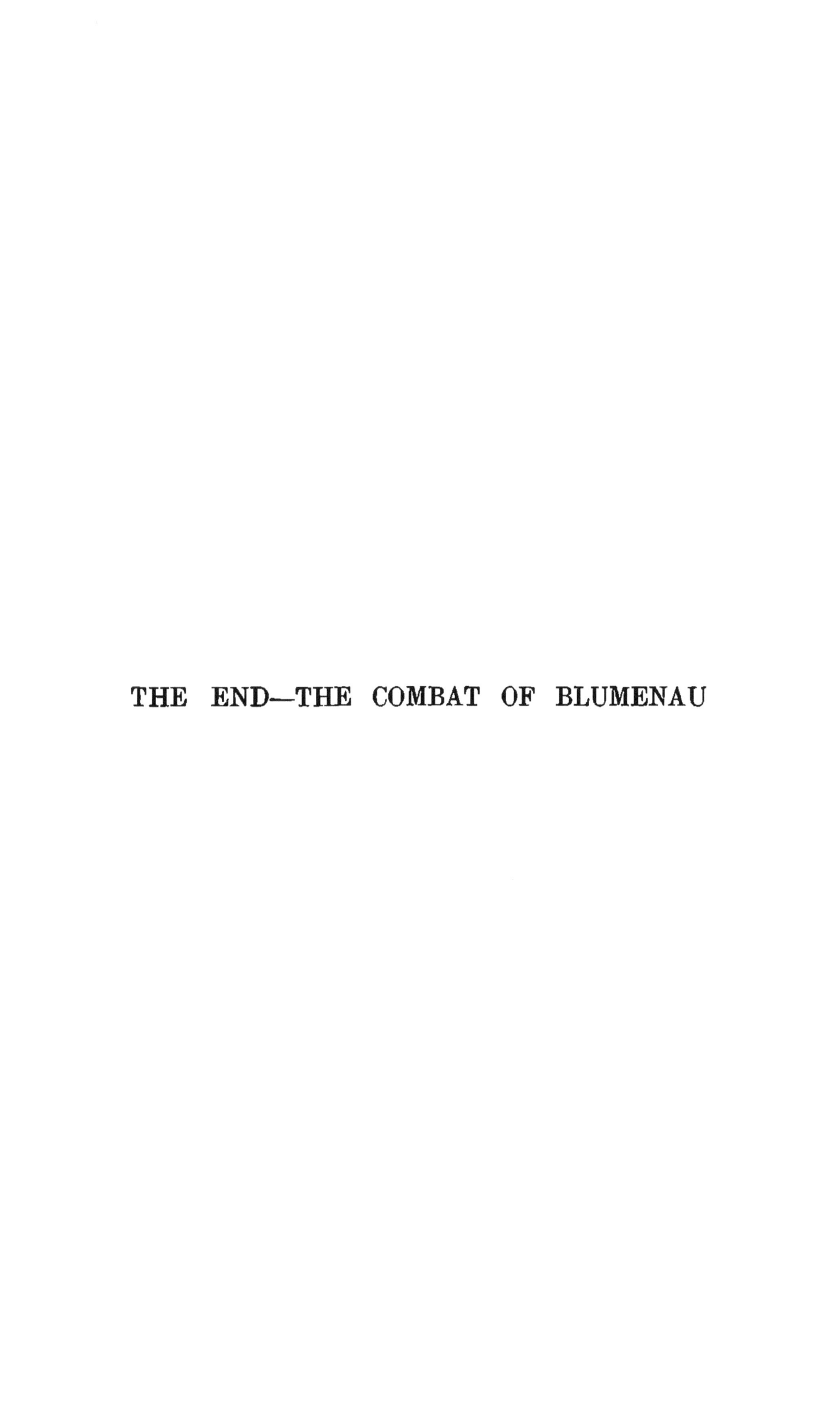

THE END—THE COMBAT OF BLUMENAU

CHAPTER X

THE END

THE COMBAT OF BLUMENAU—JULY 22

Previous Movements On the 20th the advanced brigade of the II Austrian Corps reached Tyrnau, where 1,000 vehicles had been got ready to take them on to Pressburg without delay: there they arrived at 8 p.m., and were posted as reserve to the brigade Mondl in the Mühlenthal (valley of the mill). Mondl was further reinforced on the 21st by four batteries and some cavalry, besides two jäger battalions, and, in the course of the following night till 2 a.m., by nine battalions of infantry, so that he commanded altogether twenty-four battalions of infantry and three of jägers.

On the 21st the 7th and 8th Prussian Divisions were joined at Stampfen, under the command of General Fransecky, and at his request the cavalry division Hann also was placed under his orders at Marchegg; the 8th Division then advanced the same evening as far as south of Bisternitz.

The Combat Fransecky, who had under his orders eighteen battalions, twenty-four squadrons and seventy-eight guns, had found when reconnoitring with General Bose, that an attack against the front of the enemy's position would demand great sacrifice of life on account of their strong artillery position, and had therefore determined on a containing attack in front, to have the enemy's right wing outflanked, and then to join both attacks at the suitable moment. The outflanking movement was to be made by Beneral Bose from Bisternitz and Marienthal through the Mühlenthal into the rear of the position of Blumenau; he started on the flank march at 6 a.m. At 7.30 Fransecky received the order to stop all movements at 12 a.m. noon, at which hour the armistice had been arranged to begin, and at the same time to inform the enemy of the agreed upon cessation of hostilities.

He now ordered two containing attacks against the two wings of the brigade Mondl to be carried out slowly, and to be connected in the centre by the fire of ten batteries: in the left attack a farm was taken at 11 a.m. by four and a half battalions, who then advanced against a ridge north of Blumenau, occupied by three Austrian batteries, without gaining any further results; the right attack failed to make any impression on the infantry holding the ground. In the meantime Bose's brigade had carried out the flanking movement in two columns of three battalions each, and had occupied, after 10 a.m., the southern slopes of the Gemsenberg, but the hurried up troops of the II Austrian Corps maintained the position between the Kalvarienberg and the Eisenbründl till noon, when hostilities ceased on both sides: the Austrians had lost 489 men, the Prussians, 207 men.

Comment Fransecky had expected to fight against the one brigade Mondl of nine battalions with cavalry and artillery, not knowing that they had been reinforced by a brigade of the 2nd Corps, and that eight more battalions were held in reserve, who had only arrived early that morning. Under the actual circumstances he would have done better, if he had advanced with one brigade on Blumenau via Franzhof, and with another brigade against the ridge west of Kaltenbrunn ; in fact, he should have shortened the length of his whole line so as to throw finally his whole infantry into the space between the Kunstmühle and the Danube, which was only 4,000 paces wide, instead of spreading his 16,000 men over a line of more than 12,000 paces ; he might in that case have taken the heights between the Schlossberg and Kalvarienberg, and might have got to the Danube bridge before 12 o'clock : however, this would not have been a great advantage, and the losses would certainly have been heavier.

Armistice
Negotiations had been carried on for several days at the Royal Headquarters at Nikolsburg, with the immediate object of arranging a cessation of hostilities for five days. The chief object was to gain time for diplomacy. The course of events had constantly changed a situation which could have been treated as a base for negotiations. Now, when the Prussian armies marched into the Marchfeld—the plain of Wagram—a new catastrophe was dangerously imminent. The French Ambassador at the Court of Berlin had arrived at Headquarters on the 13th, and had offered the intervention of his Emperor, and had passed several times between the Royal Headquarters and Vienna, before he could find the most necessary and

yet acceptable basis, upon which serious proposals of peace could be made. The hostilities were to cease at noon on Sunday, the 22nd, and were not to be recommenced before noon of the 27th. The armistice was signed by the delegates from the two Headquarters at the very time when the treaty was to take effect. The cessation of hostilities was on the 26th supplanted by the armistice of Nikolsburg, after the preliminaries of peace had been signed under the pressure of French intervention.

Peace The peace between Prussia and Austria was concluded at Prague on August 26, and contained the following conditions:—

1. The Emperor of Austria recognises the dissolution of the German Bund, gives his consent to a new constitution of German states without Austria, recognises in advance the changes in territory which Prussia is going to carry out in North Germany, but imposes the condition, that the kingdom of Saxony remains intact and unimpaired as a member of the new North German Confederation.

2. He transfers his share of the claims on Schleswig-Holstein to Prussia, on the sole condition that the northern districts of Schleswig shall be reunited with Denmark, if their population declare their wish of such re-incorporation by free voting (cancelled in 1878).

3. Austria pays to Prussia a war indemnity of three million pounds.

4. Prussia imposes the condition of the surrender to Italy of the province of Venetia.

As by the first condition Prussia was given a free hand to annex the territories of her late enemies amongst the smaller states of Germany, the following were irrevocably incorporated with the Prussian monarchy: the kingdom of Hanover, the electorate of Hesse-Kassel, the duchy of Nassau, and the free city of Frankfurt. By these annexations Prussia was increased by one-fourth of her size, and her population augmented from 19 to $23\frac{1}{2}$ millions.

APPENDICES

APPENDIX I

A. SUMMARY OF EVENTS ON THE WESTERN THEATRE OF WAR

Langensalza AFTER the capitulation of the Hanoverian army on June 29, the King and Crown Prince were allowed free departure and the army was dissolved; the officers retained arms and horses, the rank and file had to give them up, and all alike had to promise not to serve again during the war against Prussia.

Prussian Advance The three Prussian divisions, amounting, together with contingents from the allied smaller states, to about 46,000 men, were henceforth called the army of the Main, and under the command of General Falkenstein. Their advance into South Germany proved everywhere victorious, although the South German states had more than 100,000 men under arms, including one Austrian brigade. The passage across the Franconian Saale was forced by successful engagements at five places on July 10. After another small fight on the 13th, the Hessians of Darmstadt and of Kassel, joined by the Austrian brigade, were defeated on the 14th at Aschaffenburg: this was a rather important fight, in which the Prussians lost 17 officers, 163 men, whilst the Allies had 23 officers, 687 men killed and wounded, besides 21 officers, 1,738 men taken prisoners.

Frankfurt-on-the-Main was occupied on the 16th, Darmstadt on the 17th; after the defeat of the Würtemberg contingent and a few more successful engagements with the Bavarians, Würzburg and Nürnberg were occupied by the Prussians, after which an armistice was concluded, which took effect from

August 2. Prussia concluded separate treaties of peace with the different states which had each to pay a very small war indemnity.

B. CAMPAIGN IN NORTH ITALY

The Italian army, nominally under King Victor Emanuel, was defeated by the Austrians under Archduke Albrecht at Custozza on June 24: the Austrians lost about 6,500 killed and wounded, 1,500 prisoners; the Italians had 4,200 killed and wounded, but also 4,000 were taken prisoners. The defeat of the Italians was caused by bad command: two of their divisions close to the scene of fighting were not employed, two others had stopped on their march at short distance from the field of battle, whilst three more divisions gave way too soon and at once broke into hasty flight; hence the great number of prisoners lost by them. They had to retreat across the Mincio, but were not pursued by the Austrians, whose attention was soon occupied by the events in Bohemia.

At sea also the Austrians were successful: their fleet, though inferior in the number and the quality of ships, defeated the Italian fleet at Lissa on July 20.

APPENDIX II

ORDRE DE BATAILLE OF THE PRUSSIAN ARMIES ON JUNE 16 UNDER THE COMMAND OF HIS MAJESTY KING WILLIAM.

HEADQUARTERS OF THE KING

Chief of the General Staff: General v. Moltke.
Quartermaster-General: Major-General v. Podbielski.
Inspector-General of Artillery: Lieut.-General v. Hindersin.
Inspector-General of Engineers: Lieut.-General v. Wasserschleben.

1ST ARMY

UNDER THE COMMAND OF H.R.H. GENERAL PRINCE FREDERICK CHARLES OF PRUSSIA

Chief of the Staff: Lieut.-General v. Voigts-Rhetz.

2nd Army Corps:
  Lieut-General v. Schmidt.
  3rd Infantry Division: Lieut.-General v. Werder.
  4th Infantry Division: Lieut.-General Herwarth v. Bittenfeld.

	Total Battalions.	Squadrons.	Guns.
	26	16	78
5th Infantry Division:			
Lieut.-General v. Tümpling	13	4	24
6th Infantry Division:			
Lieut.-General v. Manstein	13	5	24
7th Infantry Division:			
Lieut.-General v. Fransecky	13	4	24
8th Infantry Division:			
Lieut.-General v. Horn	10	4	24

Cavalry Corps:
    H.R.H. General Prince Albrecht of Prussia.
  1st Cavalry Division:
    Major-General Hann v. Weyhern . . . 21 squadrons.
  2nd Cavalry Division:
    Major-General v. Alvensleben . . . . 20 ,,
  5 batteries Horse Artillery . . . . . . 30 guns.

Army Reserve Artillery:
  Major-General Schwarz . .
  16 batteries . . . . 96 guns.

  Total of strength of the 1st Army:—
        69 battalions of infantry.
        3 battalions of jägers.
        74 squadrons of cavalry.
      300 guns.
        3 battalions of engineers.

2ND ARMY

UNDER THE COMMAND OF GENERAL H.R.H. THE CROWN PRINCE OF PRUSSIA

Chief of the Staff: Major-General v. Blumenthal.

	Battalions.	Squadrons.	Guns.
1st Army Corps:			
General v. Bonin.			
1st Infantry division:			
Lieut.-General v. Grossmann. . .	13	5	24
2nd Infantry Division:			
Lieut.-General v. Clausewitz . . .	13	4	24
Reserve Cavalry Brigade:			
Colonel v. Bredow	—	12	6
Reserve Artillery—7 batteries:			
Colonel v. Oertzen	—	—	42
Guards' Corps:			
General Prince August of Würtemberg, R.H.			
1st Guard Infantry Division:			
Lieut.-General Hiller v. Gärtringen .	13	4	24

	Battalions.	Squadrons.	Guns.
2nd Guard Infantry Division:			
Lieut.-General v. Plonski	14	4	24
1st Heavy Cavalry Brigade:			
Major-General Prince Albrecht (son)	—	8	6
Reserve Artillery—5 batteries:			
Colonel Prince Kraft of Hohenlohe-Ingelfingen	—	—	30
5th Army Corps:			
General v. Steinmetz.			
9th Infantry Division:			
Major-General v. Löwenfeldt	10	5	24
10th Infantry Division:			
Lieut.-General v. Kirchbach	13	4	24
Reserve Artillery—7 batteries			
Lieut.-Colonel v. Kameke	—	—	42
6th Army Corps:			
General v. Mutius.			
11th Infantry Division:			
Lieut.-General v. Zastrow	13	4	18
12th Infantry Division:			
Lieut.-General v. Prondzynski	7	4	12
Reserve Artillery—5 batteries			
Colonel v. Scherbening	—	—	30
Cavalry Division of the 2nd Army:			
Major-General v. Hartmann	—	24	12

Total: 87 battalions infantry.
       5 battalions jägers.
      76 squadrons.
      342 guns.
      4 battalions of engineers.

ARMY OF THE ELBE

General in Command: General Herwarth v. Bittenfeld.
Chief of the Staff: Colonel v. Schlotheim.

	Battalions.	Squadrons.	Guns
14th Infantry Division:			
Lieut.-General Count Münster Meinhövel	$13\frac{1}{2}$	4	24

	Battalions.	Squadrons.	Guns.
15th Infantry Division:			
Lieut.-General v. Caustein	13	5	24
16th Infantry Division:			
Lieut.-General v. Etzel	13	—	12
Reserve Cavalry Brigade:			
Major-General v. Kotze	—	8	6
14th Cavalry Brigade:			
Major-General Count v. d. Goltz	—	9	—
Reserve Artillery, 7th Army Corps:			
Colonel v. Bülow	—	—	36
Reserve Artillery, 8th Army Corps:			
Colonel Hausmann	—	—	42

Total: 36 battalions of infantry.
2 battalions of jägers.
26 squadrons.
144 guns.
1½ battalions engineers.

1st Reserve Army Corps

Lieut.-General v. d. Mülbe.

	Battalions.	Squadrons.	Guns.
Combined Landwehr Infantry Division:			
Major-General v. Bentheim	12	—	—
Guard Landwehr Infantry Division:			
Major-General v. Rosenberg-Grusze-zynski	12	—	—
Combined Landwehr Cavalry Division:			
Major-General Count Dohna	—	24	54

Total: 24 battalions of infantry.
24 squadrons.
54 guns.

ORDRE DE BATAILLE OF THE IMPERIAL ROYAL AUSTRIAN NORTH ARMY UNDER THE COMMAND OF FELDZEUGMEISTER RITTER V. BENEDEK

Chief of the General Staff: Field Marshal-Lieutenant v. Henikstein.
Chief of Operations: Major-General v. Krismanic.
Director of Artillery: Field-Marshal-Lieutenant Archduke William I.R.H.
Director of Engineers: Colonel v. Pidoll.

	Battalions. Infantry.	Jäger.	Squadrons. Cavalry.	Guns.	Rocket Battery.
I Army Corps: General Count Clam-Gallas.	30	5	5	88	1
II Army Corps: Field-Marshal-Lieut. Count Thun	24	4	5	72	1
III Army Corps: Field-Marshal-Lieut. Archduke Ernst I.R.H.	23	5	5	80	1
IV Army Corps: Field-Marshal-Lieut. Count Festeticz	24	4	5	72	1
VI Army Corps: Field-Marshal-Lieut. v. Ramming	24	4	5	72	1
VIII Army Corps: Field-Marshal Archduke Leopold I.R.H.	24	3	5	72	1
X Army Corps: Field-Marshal v. Gablenz	25	3	—	72	—
I Light Cavalry Division: Major-General v. Edelsheim	—	—	30	24	—
II Light Cavalry Division: Major-General Prince Thurn and Taxis	—	—	20	16	—
I Reserve Cavalry Division: Field-Marshal-Lieut. Prince Schleswig-Holstein	—	—	26	16	—

II Reserve Cavalry Division :
    Major-General v. Zaitsek . —   —   26   16   —
III Cavalry Division :
    Major-General Count Coudenhove . . . . . —   —   26   16   —
Army Artillery Reserve :
    Colonel v. Tiller . . . —   —   —   128   —

Total strength of the North Army :—

    174 battalions of infantry.
    28 battalions of jäger.
    158 squadrons of cavalry.
    744 guns.
    6 rocket batteries.

THE ROYAL SAXON ARMY CORPS

General commanding : H.R.H. the Crown Prince of Saxony.

	Inf. Batt.	Jäger Batt.	Squadrons.	Guns.
1st Division : Lieut.-General v. Schimpff . .	8	2	2	12
2nd Division : Lieut.-General v. Stieglitz . .	8	2	2	12
Cavalry Division : Major-General v. Fritsch . .	—	—	12	6
Reserve Artillery : Colonel Köhler	—	—	—	28

Total strength of the Saxon Army Corps :—

    16 battalions of infantry.
    4 battalions of jäger.
    16 squadrons of cavalry.
    58 guns.

APPENDIX III

DETAILS OF THE LOSSES IN THE BATTLE OF KÖNIGGRÄTZ, JULY 3, 1866.

IN THE PRUSSIAN ARMIES

	Dead. Offi-cers.	Dead. Men.	Wounded. Offi-cers.	Wounded. Men.	Missed. Offi-cers.	Missed. Men.	Total. Offi-cers.	Total. Men.
A. Losses of the 1st Army	52	1,013	154	3,921	—	120	206	5,054
B. Losses of the Elbe Army	22	328	49	1,174	—	55	71	1,557
C. Losses of the 2nd Army	25	489	57	1,593	—	101	82	2,183
	99	1,830	260	6,688	—	276	359	8,794

IN THE AUSTRIAN ARMY

	Dead.	Wounded	Missed.	Total.
In the II Army Corps	872	2,678	2,588	6,138
In the IV Army Corps	1,270	3,161	6,214	10,645
In the Saxon Army Corps	135	940	426	1,501
In the I Army Corps	621	1,449	3,447	5,517
In the III Army Corps	755	2,195	3,489	6,439
In the VI Army Corps	352	839	3,614	4,805
In the VIII Army Corps	289	628	1,737	2,654
In the X Army Corps	352	1,596	2,399	4,347
In the Cavalry Divisions	138	297	1,143	1,578
In the Artillery Reserve	76	130	228	434
In the Engineers, Medical Service, etc.	1	7	134	142
Total losses	4,861	13,920	25,419	44,200

APPENDIX IV

Some Stray Reflections

1. The campaign of the Italians had mainly miscarried, because General Lamarmora misjudged the political military situation. He thought that Austria would oppose her whole field army to the Prussians, and that Italy would thus have time to take one of the fortresses of the quadrilateral after the other, and in this way gain possession of the province of Venetia; he forgot, that if Austria should be victorious in the north, all hopes of Italy would be dashed to the ground. His aim should have been to aid the Prussian invasion as much as possible, therefore to carry out the Italian attack in such a way that at least the Austrian army stationed in Italy—only three army corps—would be cut off from Austria or be pursued vigorously. The Italian army ought to have reached the Semmering Pass by the time the Prussians arrived at the Danube.

2. In Prussia an imposing army was put into the field and the offensive was adopted, but the fact was left out of consideration that the ultimate object could only be attained by crossing the Danube, and that 80,000 men or more would be required to secure the communications, to invest five fortresses and to garrison Prague, Brünn and other large towns. For these objects newly formed units were sufficient, but they should have followed so closely behind the field army that its strength was never seriously impaired. It is a rule that an invasion of the enemy's country must be supported so as to prevent the field army from being gradually consumed. But the King had little confidence in extemporised units formed of but partly trained men, and would not listen to their employment; but in war iron neces-

sity reigns supreme, and the people's war in France after Sedan and the disappearance of the entire imperial army, has shown that such extemporised troops can do good service, even on the field of battle. Those who object to such a course being taken in case of necessity, may argue that the strength of the army in peace should be increased; but national economy protests against this expedient, because work only—industry and commerce—produces wealth and no war can be carried on without ample financial resources.

3. Where should the executive functionaries of the Government be during a war? This seems to be a momentous question. What was the proper place for Bismarck and Roon, the Foreign Secretary and the War Minister? The Royal Headquarters or Berlin, the seat of government and centre of administration? The conduct of the business of state during a war demands the greatest energy, and does not allow of any waste of time. But all the executive authorities are in the capital, where alone the organisation of conquered provinces and the utilisation of their resources can be initiated, especially if this eventuality has not been taken into consideration before the outbreak of war. The same is the case with diplomatic incidents of all kinds: in the capital only are the permanent diplomatic officials with the information they possess, and it is just the enforced separation of the Foreign Minister from his monarch in the field which affords the sometimes desirable expedient and excuse of inoffensive delay and procrastination. And the case of the War Minister seems to be on the same footing: the formation and equipment of new units, the arming of fortresses, the constant steady refilling of magazines are so important for the efficient progress and conduct of the war that the War Minister should not leave the capital for a moment. Did Frederick or Napoleon ever take their ministers into the field?

The following statement has been made by a famous historian: " A king at the head of an army who is a thoroughly good general is almost irresistible; in the opposite case he is a tremendous incumbrance on the chief command, which is then beset by all the evils of court life." The best combination obtains, when they are as great diplomatists as generals, as Gustavus Adolphus,

Frederick and Napoleon. If they are only generals, as Charles XII, their enterprises may easily become fruitless or even pernicious; but the greatest dilemma is produced, when they are neither the one nor the other and yet want to conduct everything: then a crowd of advisers must be carried along with the headquarters, and court life with its intrigues supervenes.

How the presence of powerful personages at headquarters can influence the military events, is shown by the action of the Crown Prince at the moment, when the 2nd Prussian Army arrived before Olmütz on its march southward to intercept the retreat of the Austrians to the Danube. The officer who at 6.30 a.m. on July 14 brought to him the orders from Headquarters, also handed to him letters from the King and from Bismarck. The latter informed him that Benedetti, the French Ambassador, had arrived, and that he himself was determined to conclude peace with Austria in order to anticipate and prevent the interference of France. This information evidently determined the Crown Prince to proceed personally to Brünn in order to put forward his own opinions.[1] Therefore, under the pretext that the junction of the Austrian North and South Armies could now no longer be prevented, he set two army corps marching towards Brünn, although under the actual circumstances forced marches in the direction of Pressburg were required in order to push the Austrians into the Little Carpathians and to reach the passage of the Danube before them. Thus military necessities and the action demanded by them were entirely neglected on account of a matter of political concern, the efficacy of the chief command and with it the possibility of military success was placed in jeopardy: in order not to offend the Crown Prince, his Chief of the Staff pronounced the clear and distinct orders received to be unintelligible and disregarded them, and thus court intrigues frustrated the supreme conduct of operations.

---

[1] I wish my readers to believe me, when I state that, although I have been led to proffer these criticising remarks, my belief and trust in the Crown Prince as a leader of men was unbounded and that such was also the general feeling in his army in 1870 amongst all officers and the rank and file.

The situation as just described is clearly shown by a report from General Steinmetz to the Crown Prince on the same day: "In the moral condition in which the Austrians are performing their march from Olmütz to Vienna, I consider it absolutely necessary to pursue them rapidly and to attack them wherever they are met with, and I foresee good results. I have authorised Hartmann to push forward to Prerau."

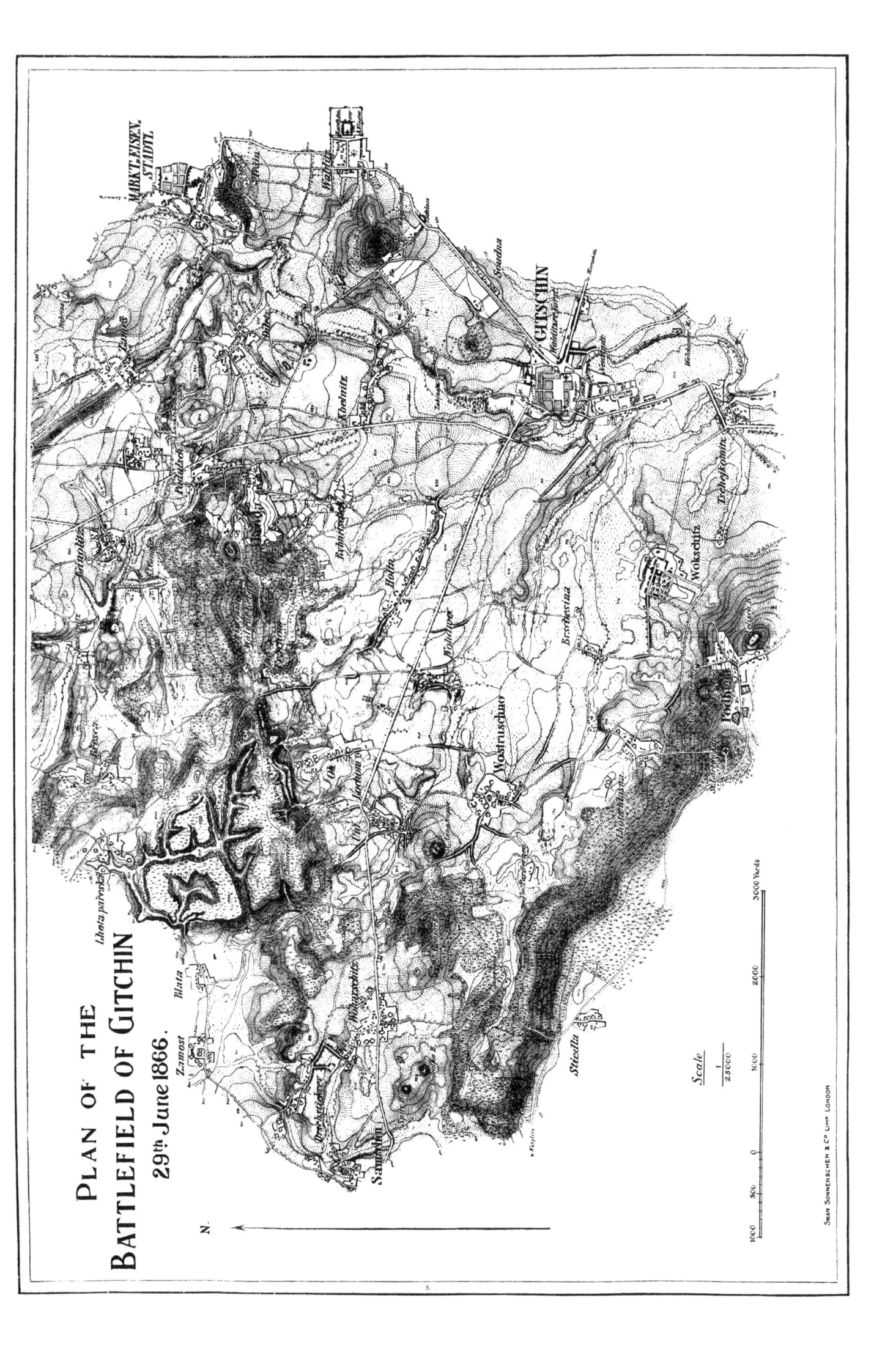

PLAN OF THE BATTLEFIELD OF GITCHIN
29th June 1866.

PLAN OF THE BATTLEFIELD OF GITCHIN

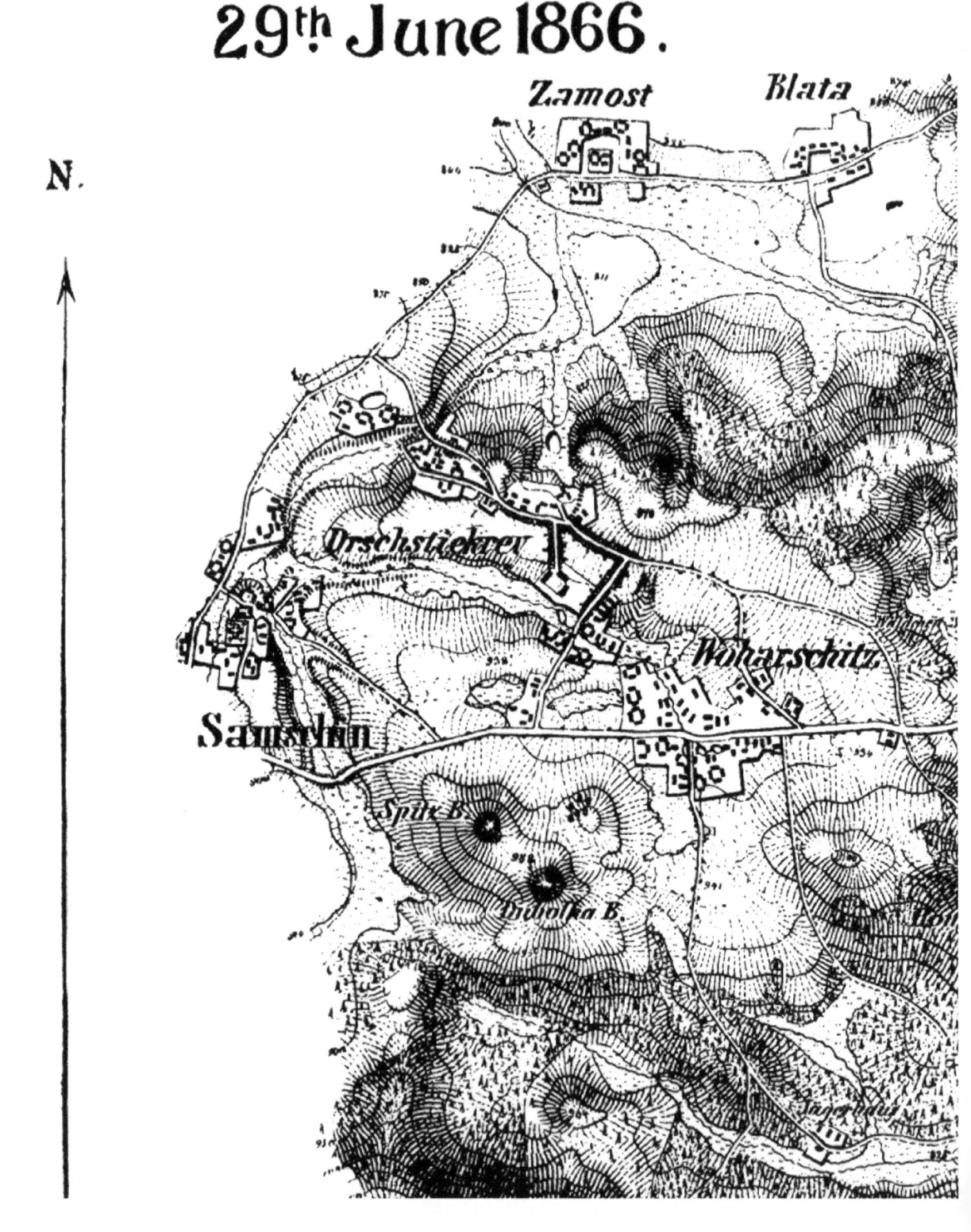

29th June 1866.

N

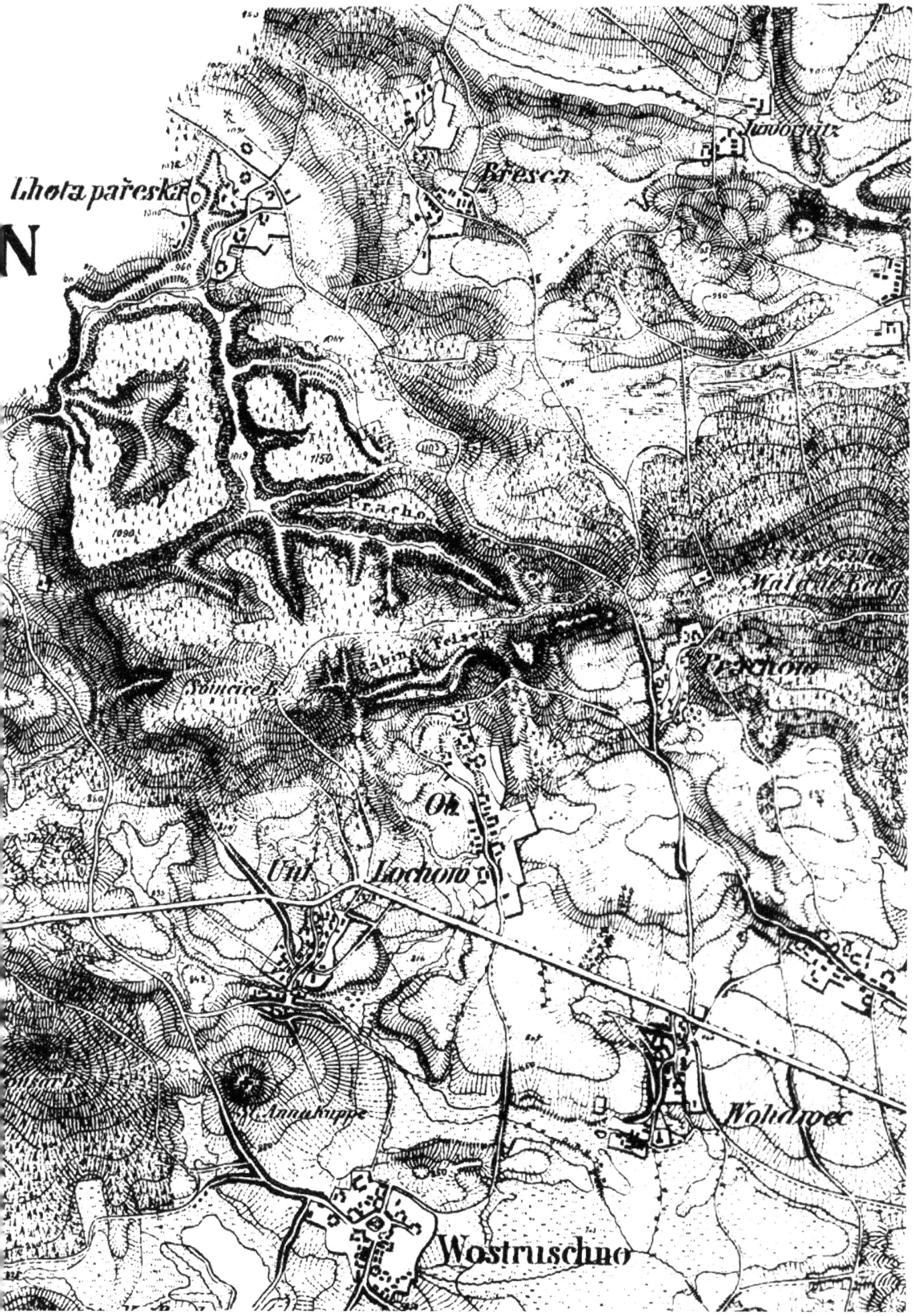

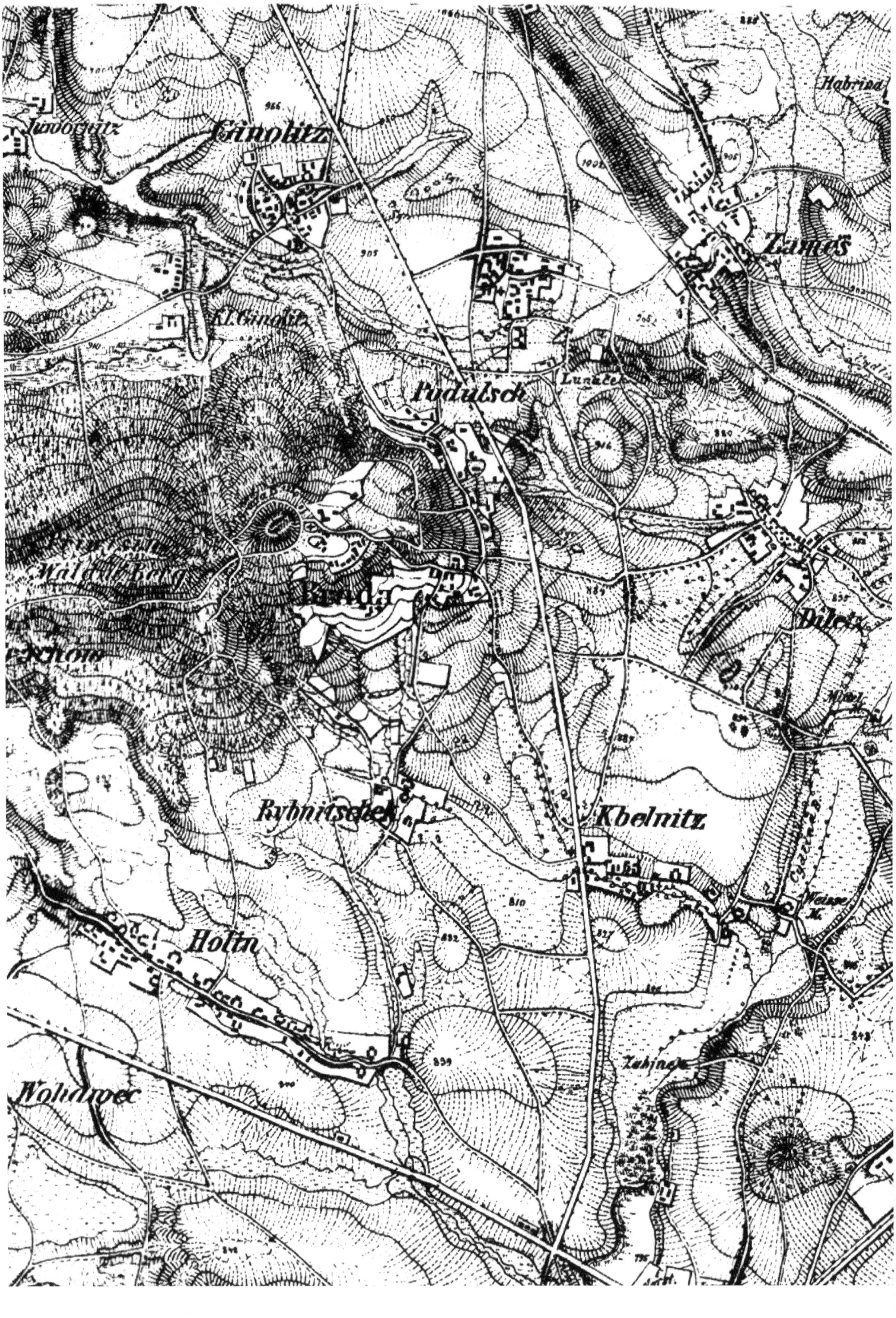

Ginolitz
Kl. Ginolitz
Zames
Podulsch
Rybnitschek
Kbelnitz
Holin
839
810

MARKT=EISEN=
STADTL

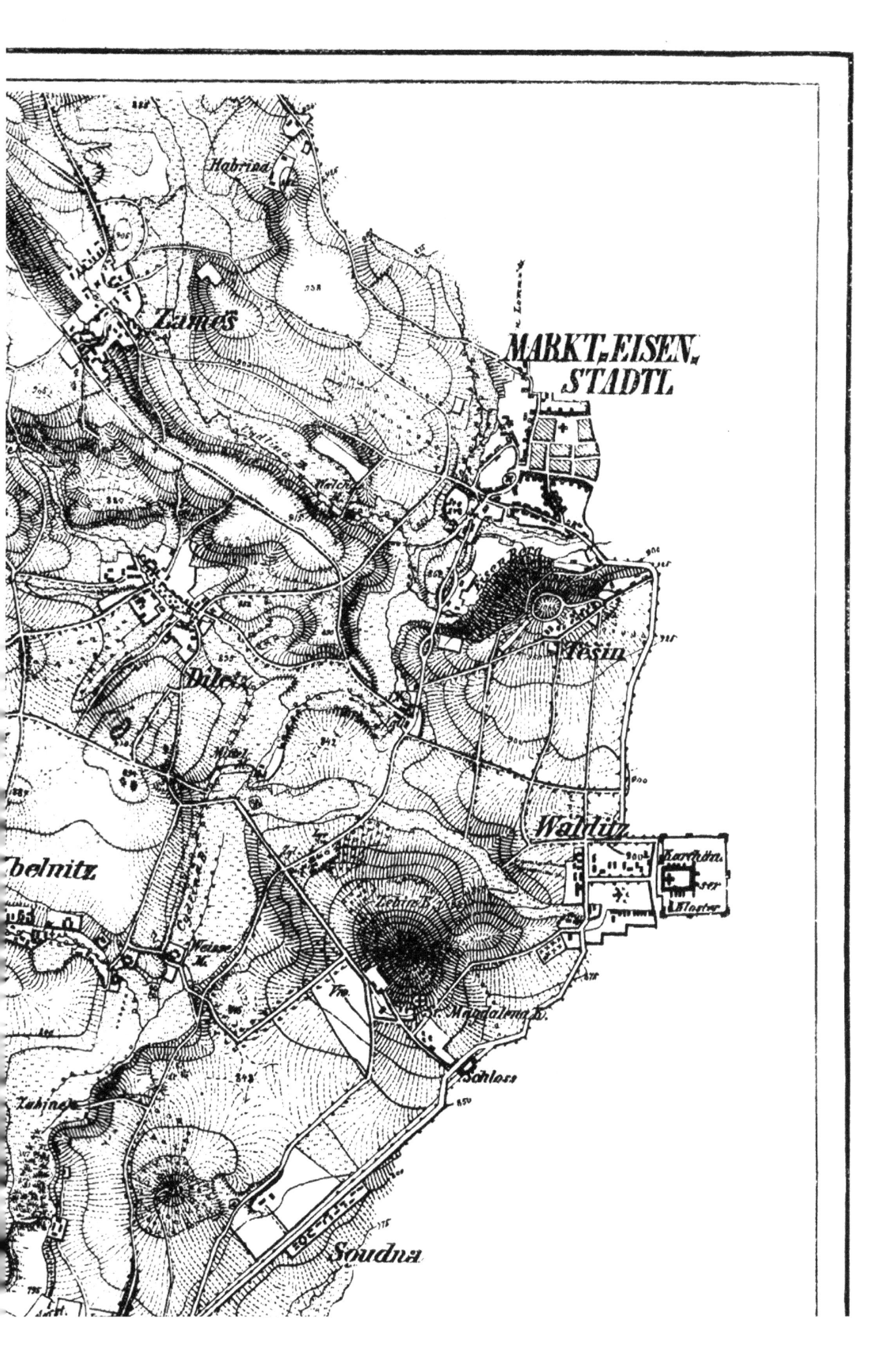

Zames

Hobrina

Dilctz

belnitz

Tesin

Waldltz

Soudna

Scale

$$\frac{1}{25000}$$

| 1000 | 500 | 0 | 1000 | 2000 |

SWAN SONNENSCHEIN & Cº LIMD LONDON

3000 Yards

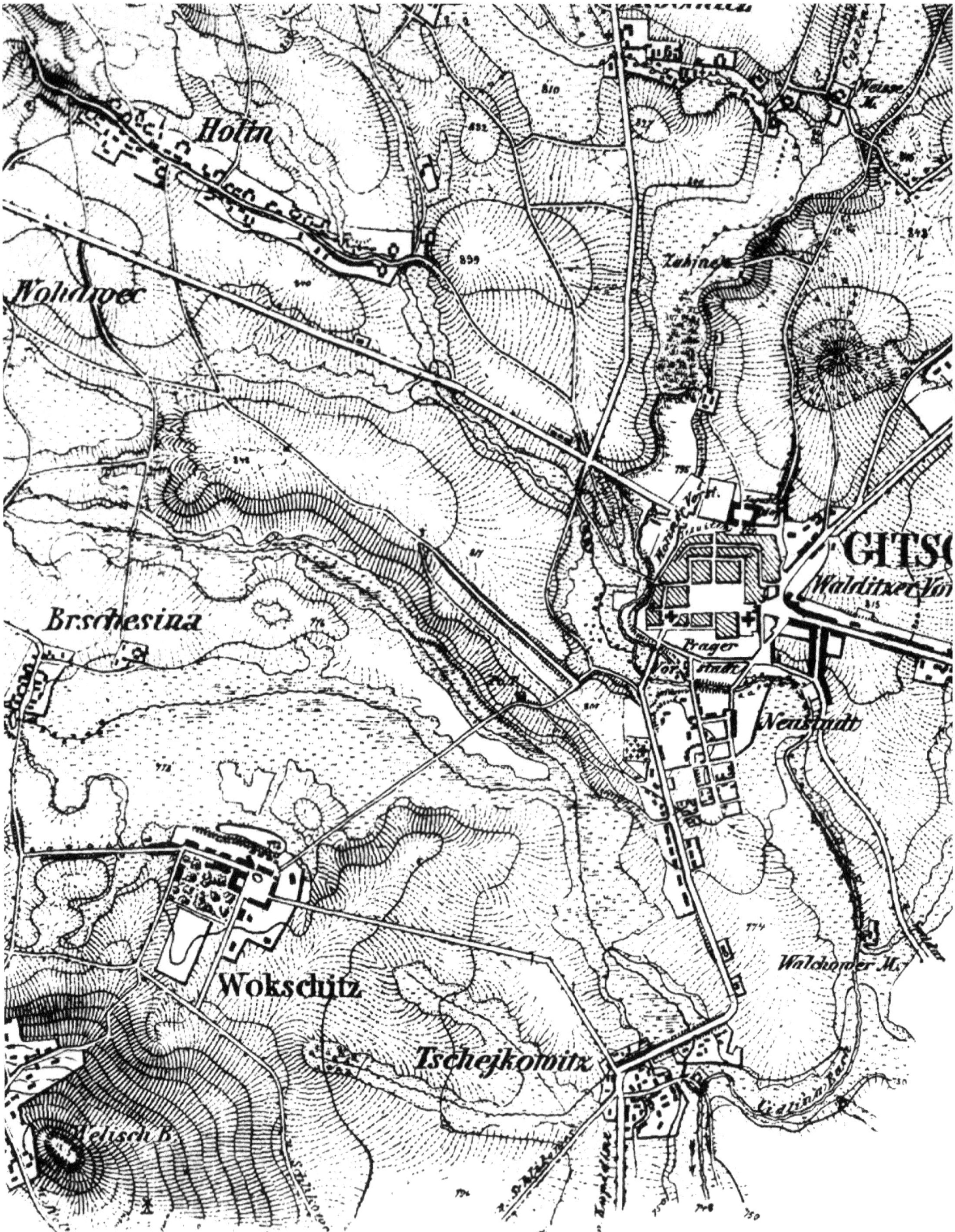
Holin
Brschesina
Wokschitz
Tschejkowitz
GITSC
Neustadt
Prager
Walchower M.

GITSCHIN

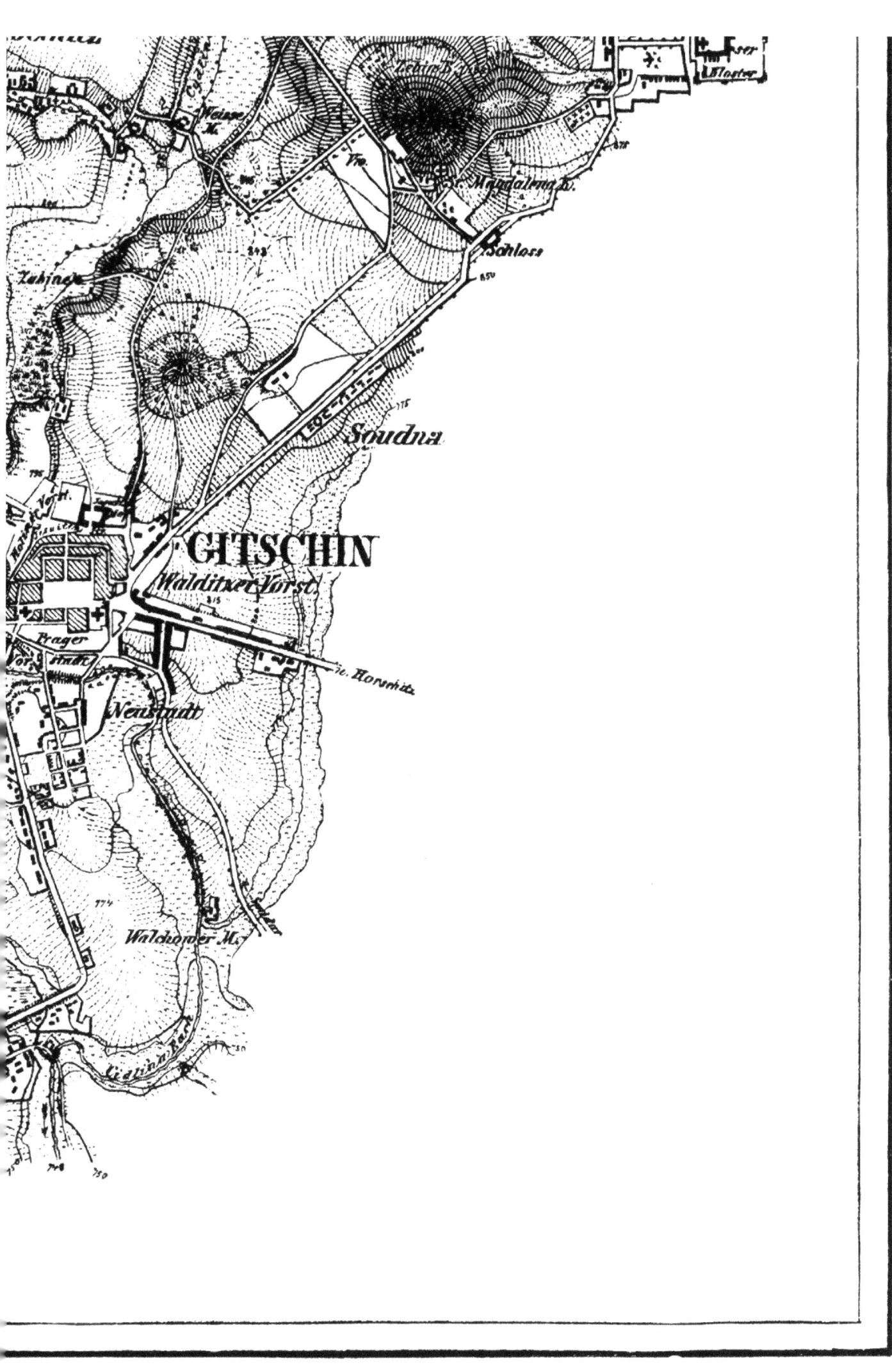

PLAN OF
NACHOD, SKALITZ & SCHWEINSCHAEDAL,
for the Battles on the 27th, 28th, 29th, June 1866.

Horicka

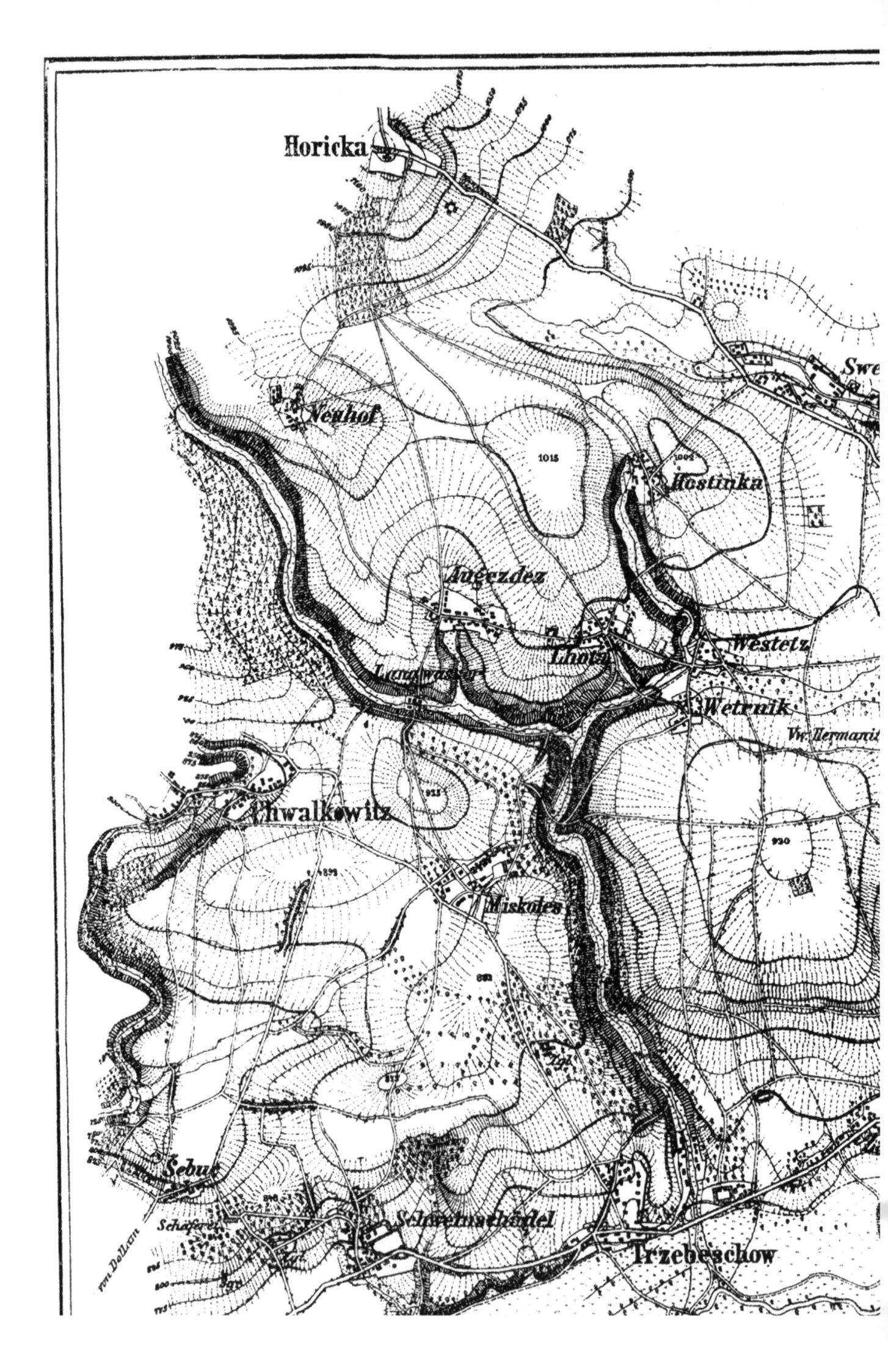

Neuhof

Swe

Hostinka

Aueczdez

Lhota

Westetz

Langwasser

Wetrnik

Vw. Hermanic

Chwalkowitz

Miskoles

930

Sebuc

Schafe

Schwetischedel

Trzebeschow

von Dollen

PLAN OF
NACHOD, SKALITZ & SCHWEINSCHAEDAL,
for the Battles on the 27th, 28th, 29th June 1866.

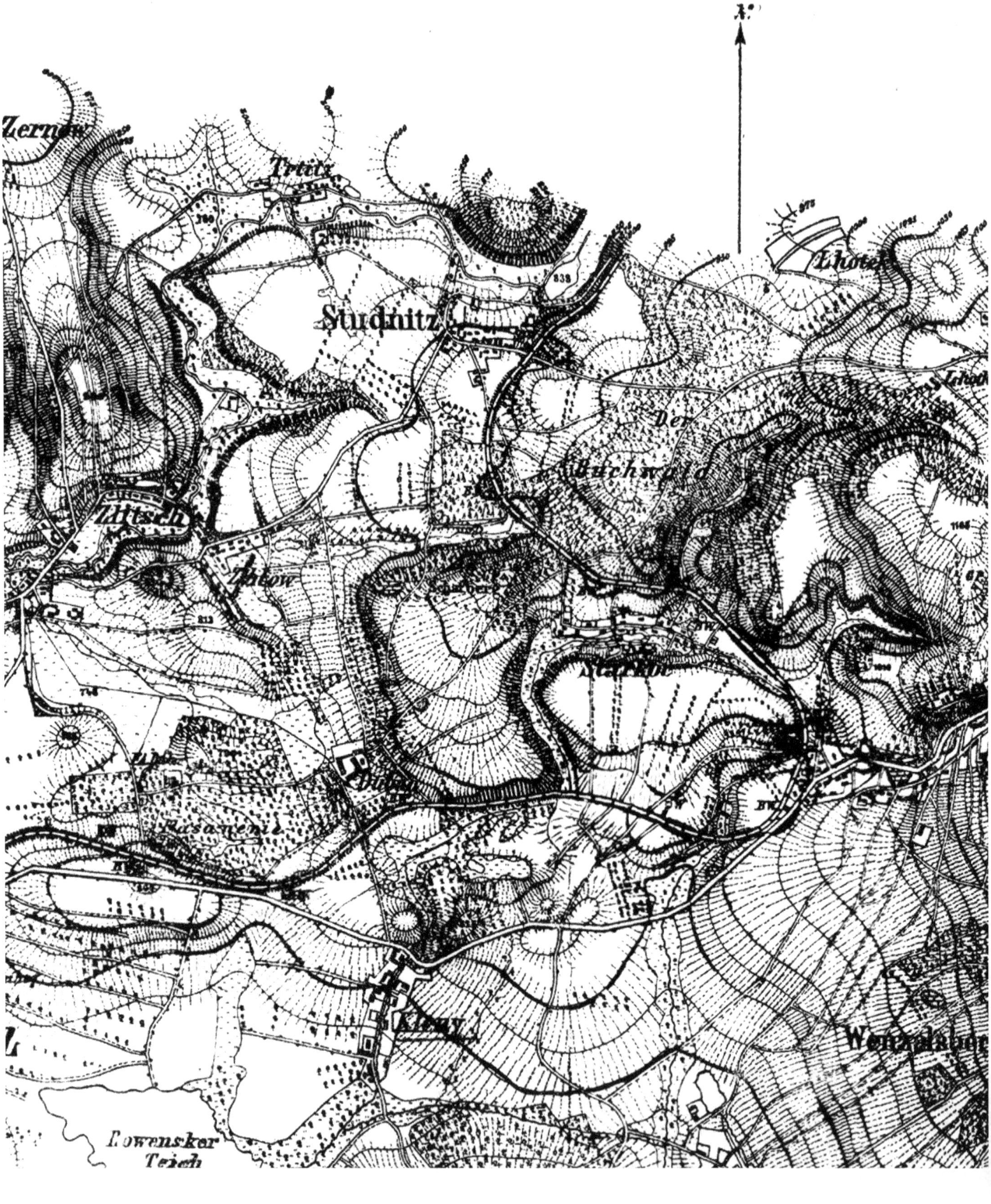
Studnitz
Zittsch
Der Buchwald
Wenzelsberg
Rowensker Teich

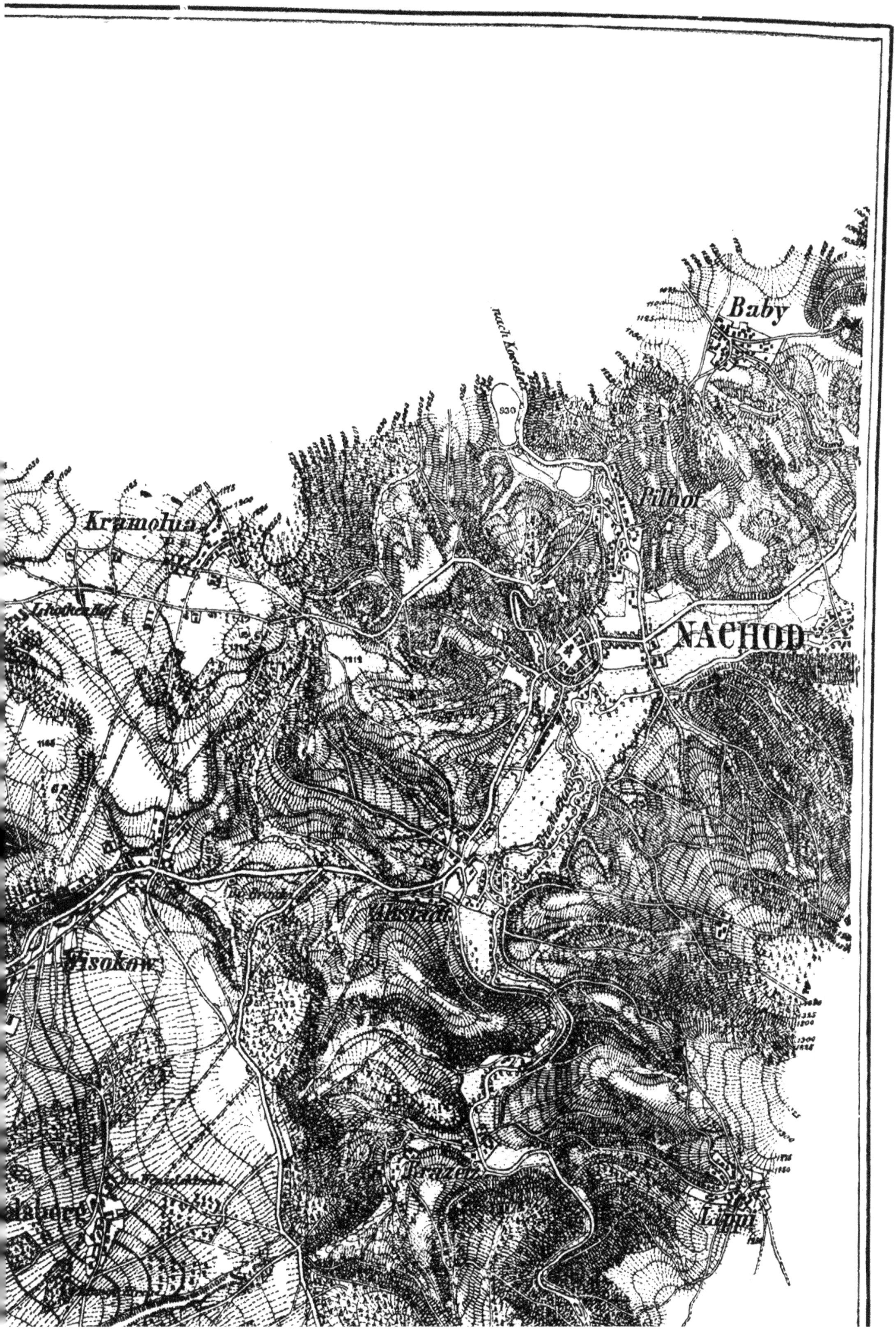

Baby
Kramolna
Pilnot
NACHOD
Wisokow
Lippi

Scale
$$\frac{1}{25000}$$

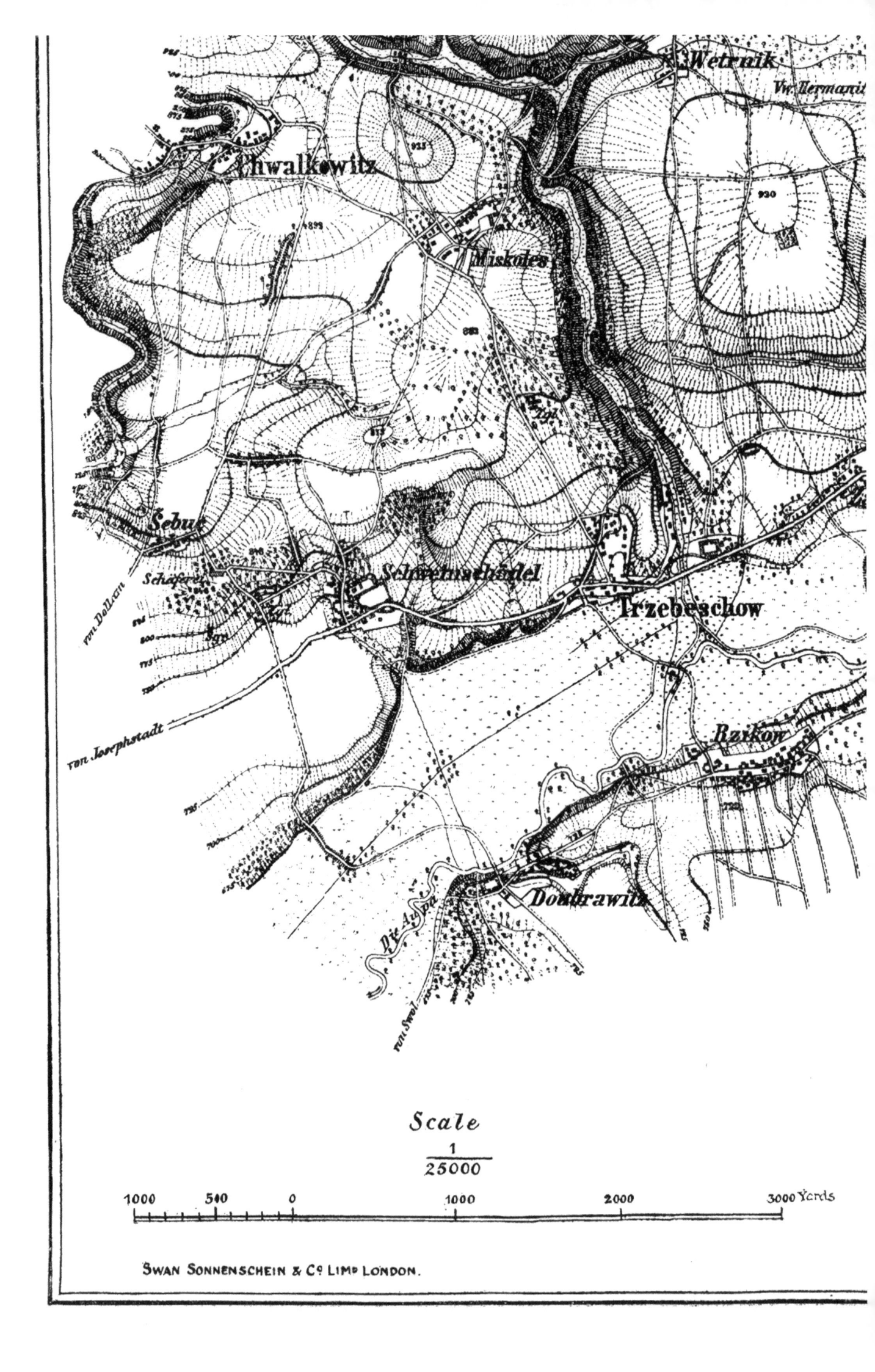

1000 500 0   1000   2000   3000 Yards

SWAN SONNENSCHEIN & Cº LIMD LONDON.

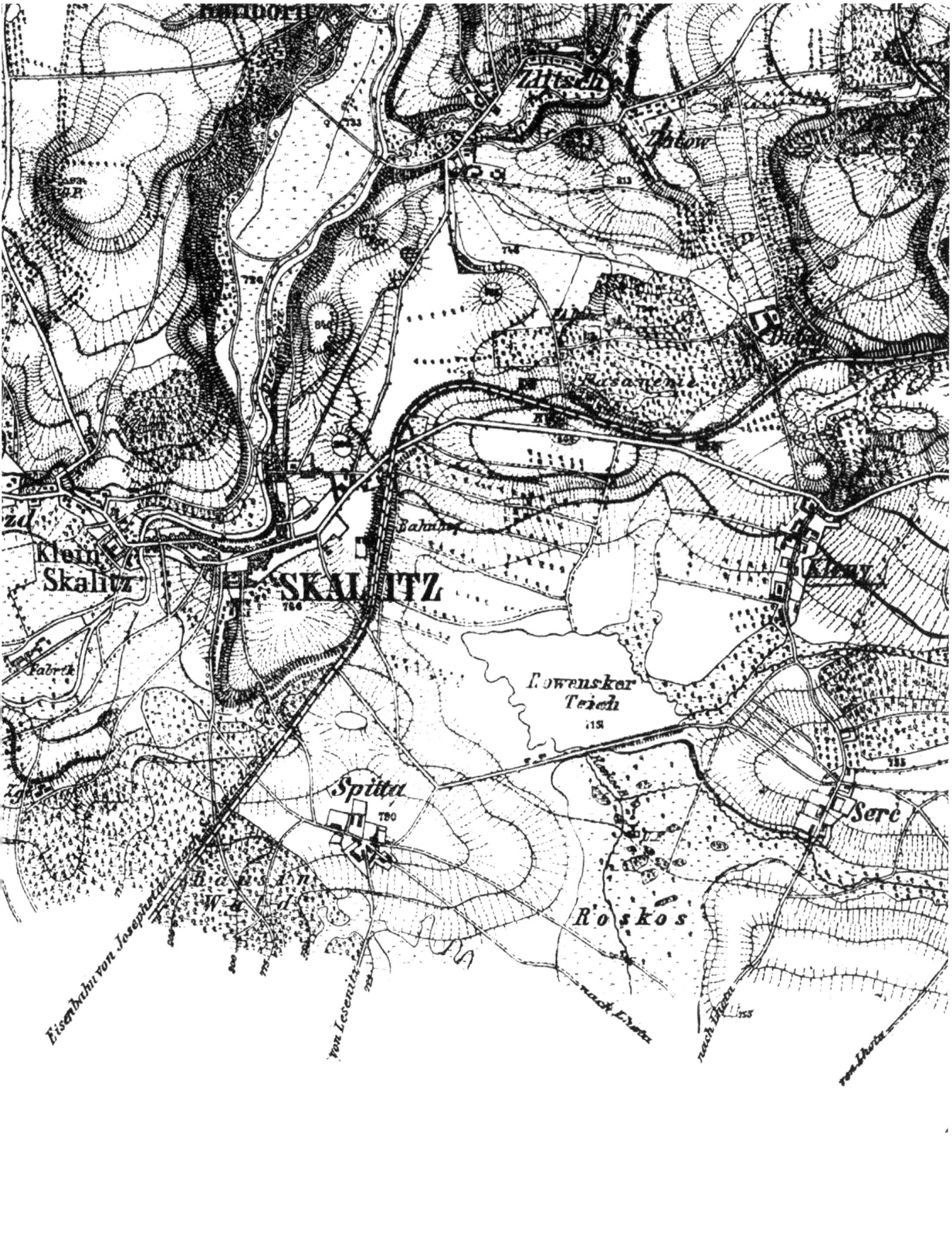
Zlitsch
Klein Skalitz
SKALITZ
Bahnhof
Fabrik
Rowensker Teich
Spitta
Roskos
Serč
von Lesenitz
nach Lhota
von Lhota

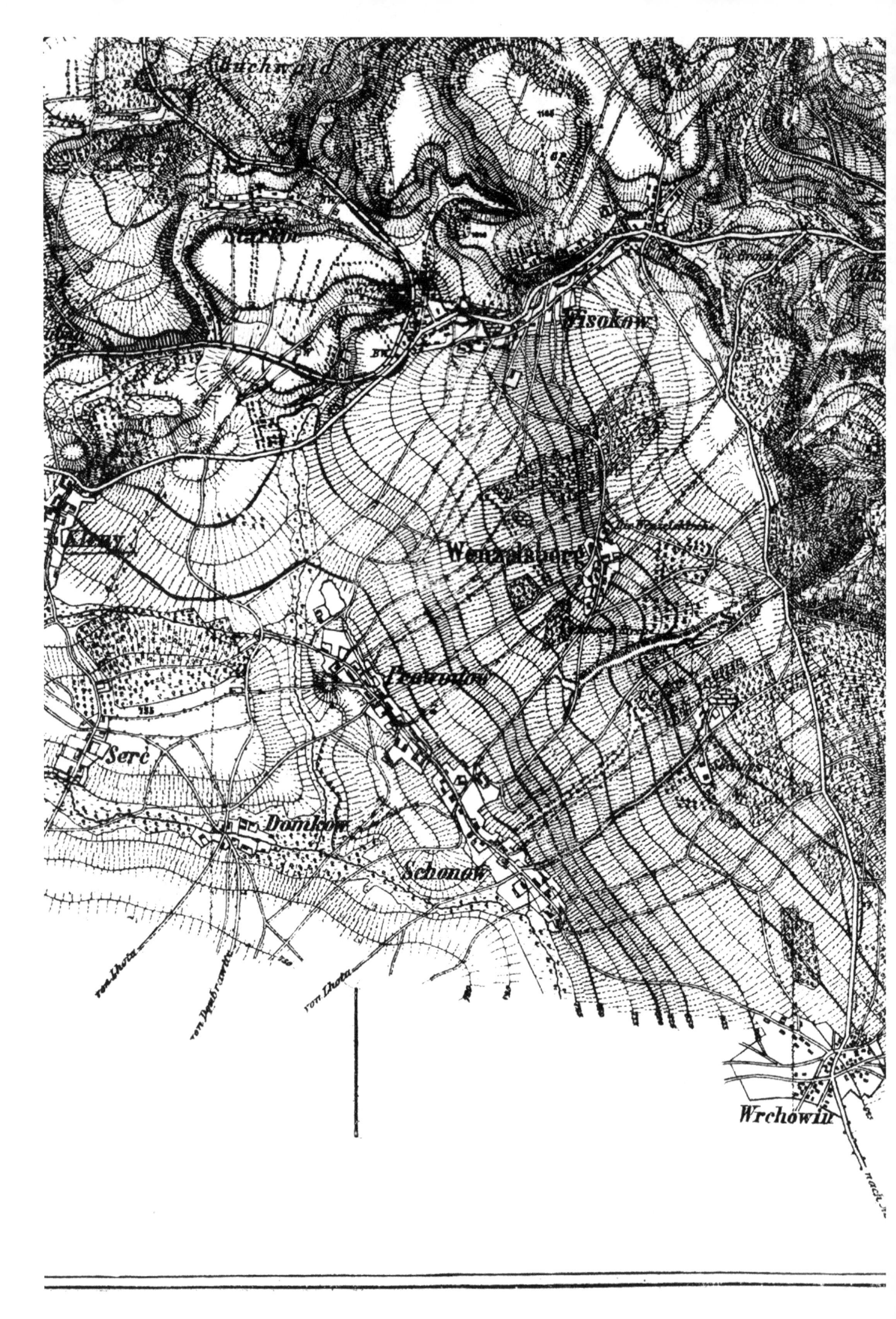
Buchwald
Wisokow
Wenzelsberg
Serč
Domkow
Schonow
von Lhota
von Lhota
Wrchowin

Wrchowin

PLAN OF PODOL-MÜNCHENGRÄTZ
26th & 28th June 1866.

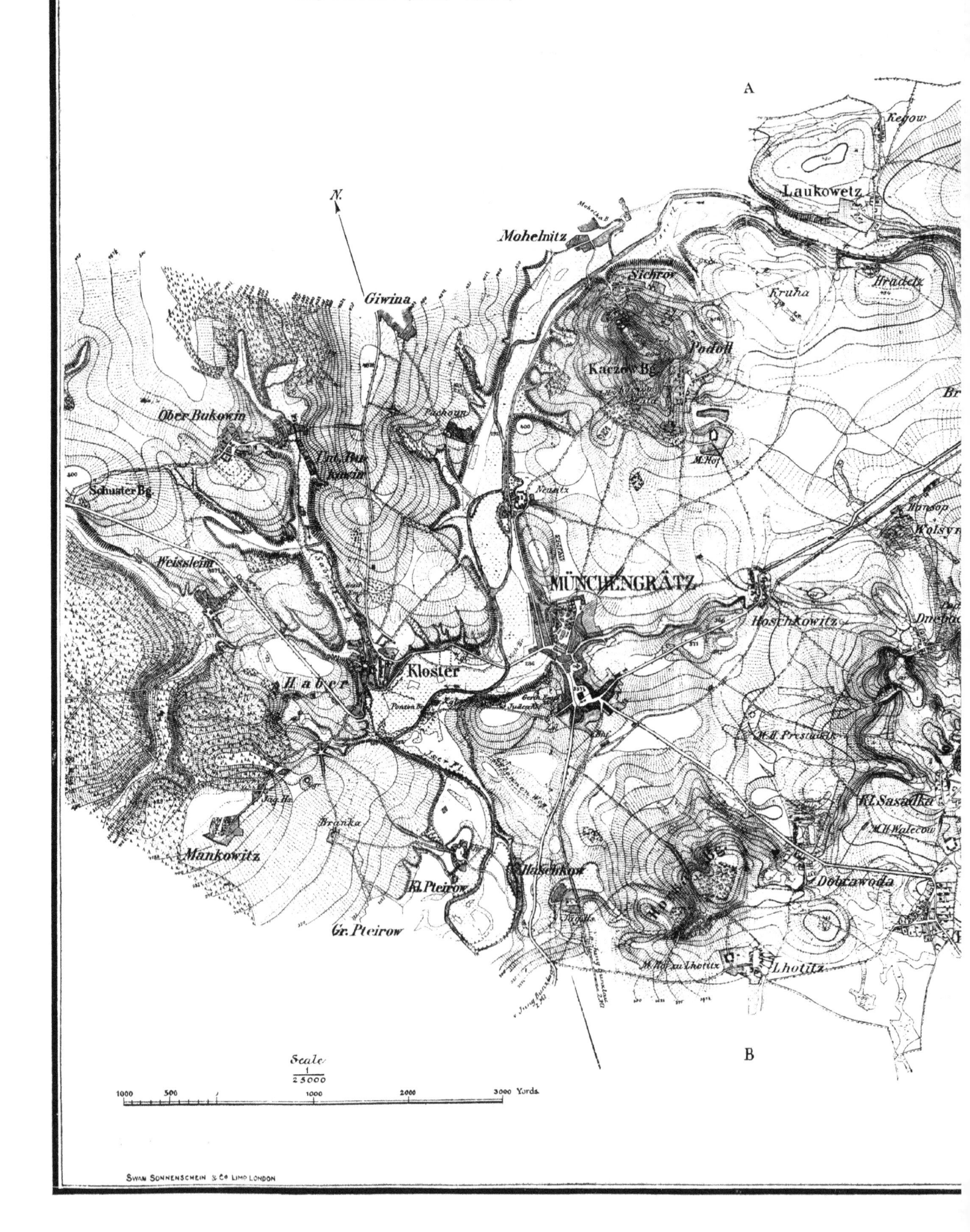

A
Swigan
Kepow
Laukow
Laukowetz
Mohelnitz
Sichrow
Hradetz
Kruha
Podoll
Kaczow Bg.
Brezina
M.Hof
MÜNCHENGRÄTZ
Hoschkowitz
Wolsyna
Dnebach
Musky Bg.
Kloster
Musky
Kl. Sasadka
Zapadow
Branžez
Dobrawoda
Kl. Pteirow
Bossin
Lhotitz
B

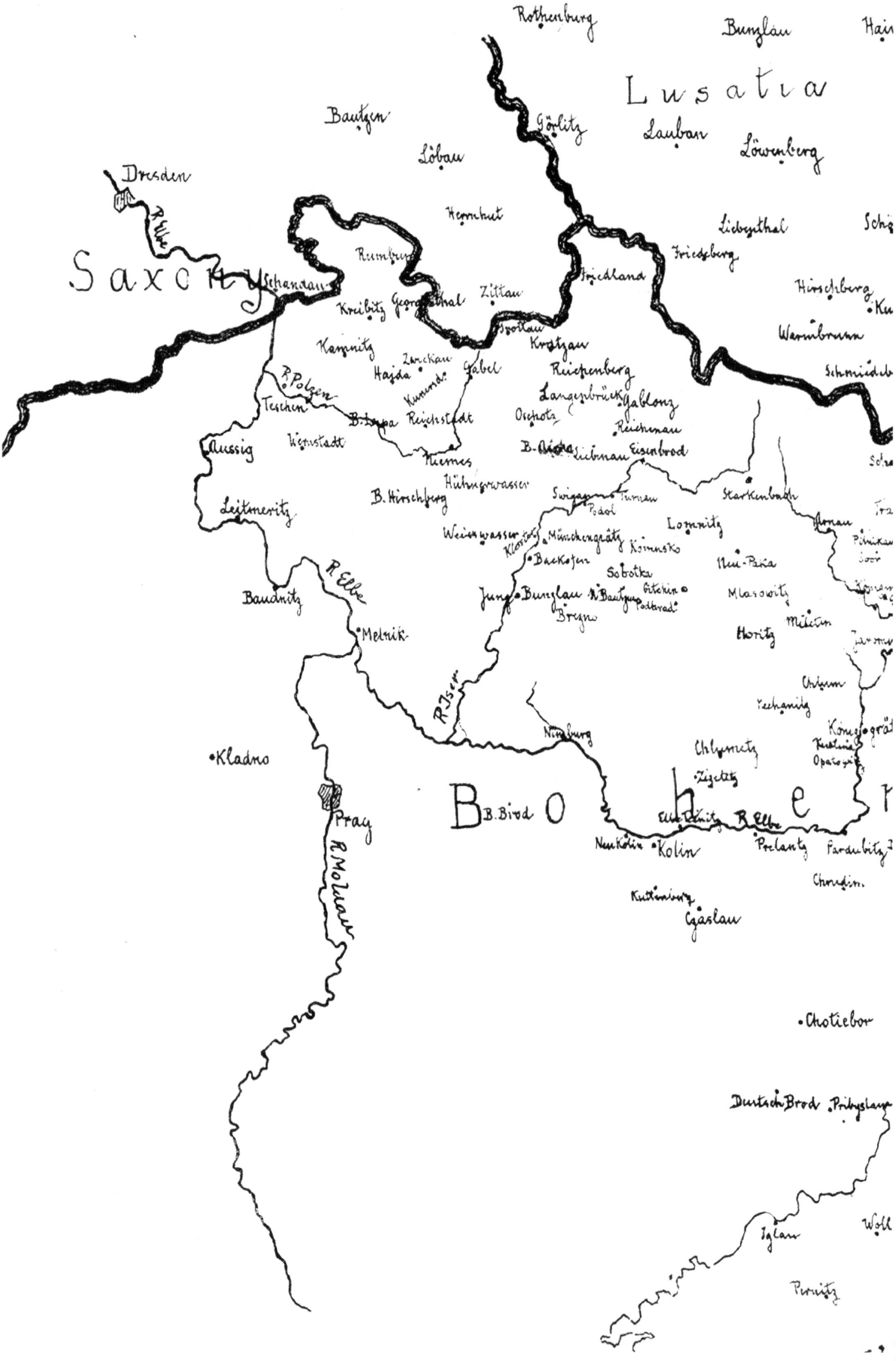

Rothenburg
Bunzlau
Lusatia
Bautzen
Görlitz
Lauban
Löwenberg
Löbau
Dresden
R. Elbe
Herrnhut
Liebenthal
Saxony
Schandau
Rumburg
Friedsberg
Friedland
Hirschberg
Zittau
Kreibitz
Georgenthal
Grottau
Warmbrunn
Kamnitz
Kratzau
Reichenberg
Zwickau
Hajda
Gabel
R. Polzen
Langenbrück
Gablonz
Teschen
B. Leipa
Reichstadt
Oschotz
Reichenau
Aussig
Wernstadt
B. Aicha
Liebnau
Eisenbrod
Niemes
Hühnerwasser
B. Hirschberg
Swigan
Turnau
Podol
Starkenbach
Leitmeritz
Lomnitz
Weisswasser
Kloster
Münchengrätz
Arnau
Backofen
Sobotka
Neu-Paka
R. Elbe
Baudnitz
Jung-Bunzlau
Gitschin
Mlasowitz
Brezno
Miletin
Melnik
Horitz
Chlum
Nechanitz
R. Iser
Nimburg
Chlumetz
Königgrätz
Opatowitz
Kladno
Zizelitz
B. Brod
Elbeteinitz
R. Elbe
Pray
Neu Kolin
Kolin
Prelautz
Pardubitz
R. Moltau
Chrudim
Kuttenberg
Czaslau
Chotiebor
Dutsch Brod
Pribyslaw
Iglau
Polnitz
B o h e

Theatre of Operations in Bohemia
June and July 1866.
N
Hainau
Liegnitz
Schönau
Striegau
Kupferberg
Freiburg
Schweidnitz
Silesia
Breslau
Ohlau
R. Oder
Brieg
Landshut
Waldenburg
Gottesberg
Reichenbach
Strehlen
Liebau
Charlottenbrunn
Nimptsch
Langenbielau
Schömberg
Friedland
Grottkau
Schatzlar
Braunau
Neurode
Frankenstein
Münsterberg
Trautenau
Silberberg
Wartha
R. Neisse
Reichenstein
Ottmachau
Neisse
Köstelitz
Nachod
Lewin
Rückerts
Glatz
Patschkau
Steinau
Skalitz
Reinerz
Weidenau
Josephstadt
Neustadt
Ziegenhals
Opocno
Habelschwerdt
Freiwaldau
Leobschütz
Mittelwalde
Reichenau
Senftenberg
Jägerndorf
Geiersberg
Brandeis
Wildenschwerdt
Hohenmauth
Freudenthal
Schildberg
Schönberg
Troppau
Trübau
Landskron
Römerstadt
Friedland
Leitomitsch
Hohenstadt
Aussee
Neustadt
Zwittau
Trübau
Liebau
Zittau
Sternberg
Olmütz
Oppatowitz
Weisskirchen
Neustadt
Lettowitz
Bystritz
Kunstadt
Boskowitz
Prossnitz
Meseritsch
Bobrau
Tobitschau
Wollein
Meseritsch
Moravia
Kunowitz
Tischnowitz
Prodlitz
Kojetein
Holleschau
Wsetin
Wischau
Kremsier
Zlin
Wisowitz

Scale
$$\frac{1}{850,000}$$

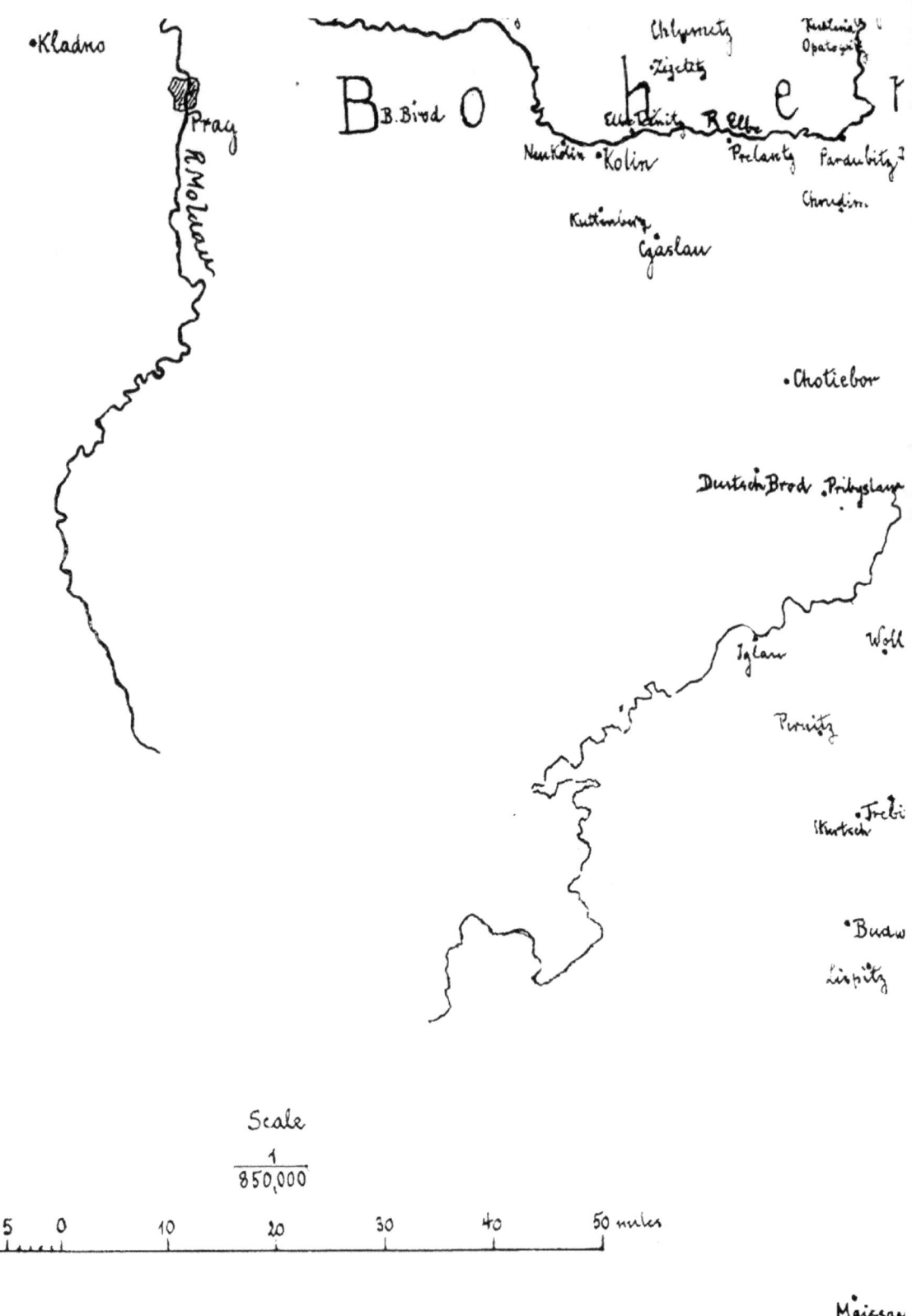

SWAN SONNENSCHEIN & CO LIMD LONDON

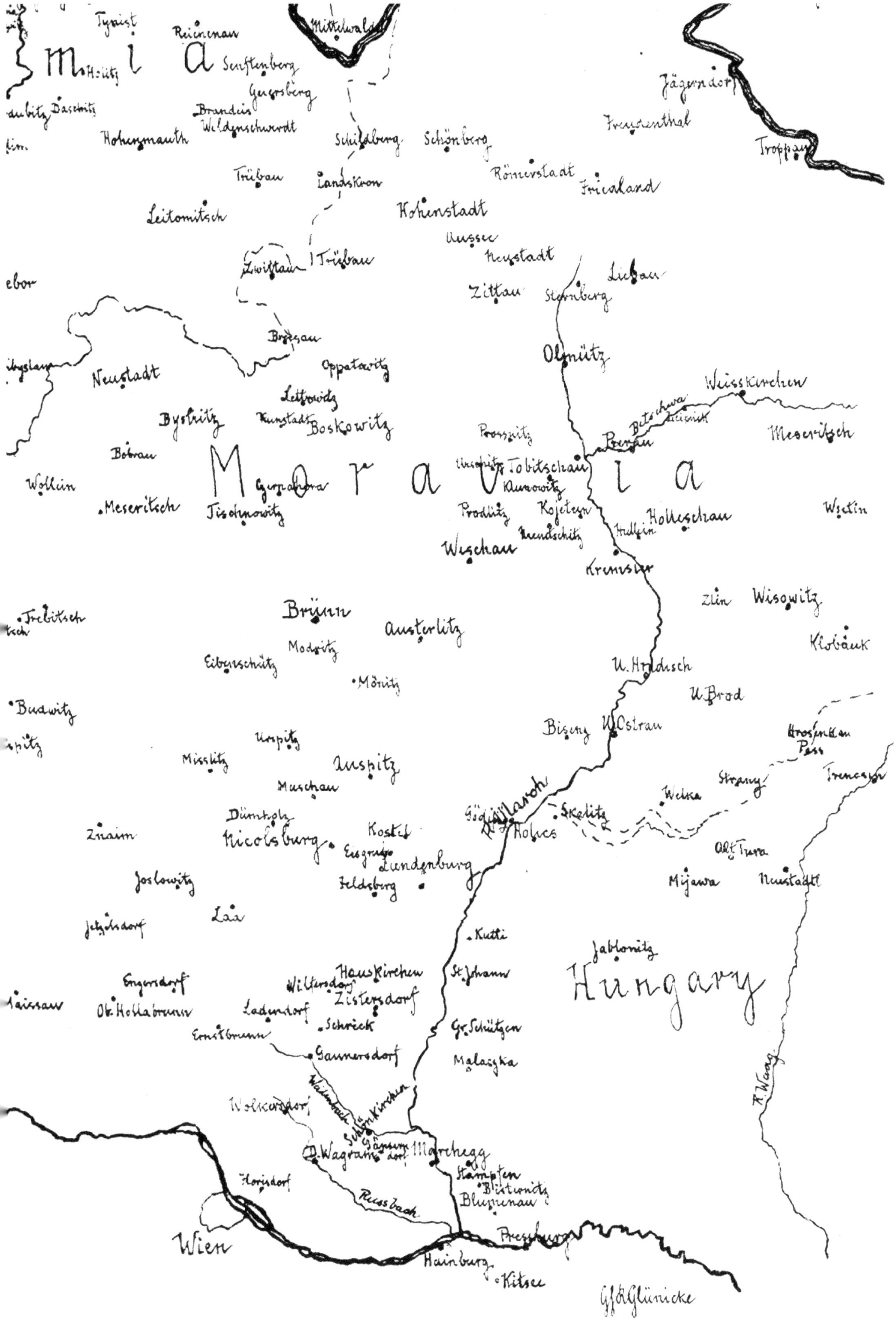
Mittelwald
Jägerndorf
Freudenthal
Troppau
Senftenberg
Brandeis
Schildberg
Schönberg
Hohenmauth
Landskron
Römerstadt
Leitomitsch
Hohenstadt
Zwittau
Neustadt
Zittau
Sternberg
Oppatowitz
Olmütz
Neustadt
Weisskirchen
Bystritz
Boskowitz
Meseritsch
Bobrau
Moravia
Tobitschau
Meseritsch
Tischnowitz
Kojetein
Holleschau
Wischau
Kremsier
Zlin
Wisowitz
Brünn
Austerlitz
Klobauk
Modritz
U. Hradisch
Mönitz
U. Brod
Budwitz
U. Ostrau
Auspitz
Muschau
Skalitz
Znaim
Nicolsburg
Kostel
Holics
Lundenburg
Alt Tura
Joslowitz
Feldsberg
Mijawa
Laa
Kutti
Jablonitz
St. Johann
Hungary
Zistersdorf
Ladendorf
Schrick
Gr. Schützen
Ernstbrunn
Gaunersdorf
Malaczka
Wolkersdorf
R. Waag
D. Wagram
Marchegg
Floridsdorf
Russbach
Wien
Pressburg
Hainburg
Kitsee
G. F. R. Glünicke

PLAN OF THE BATTLEFIELD OF BLUMENAU
22nd July 1866.

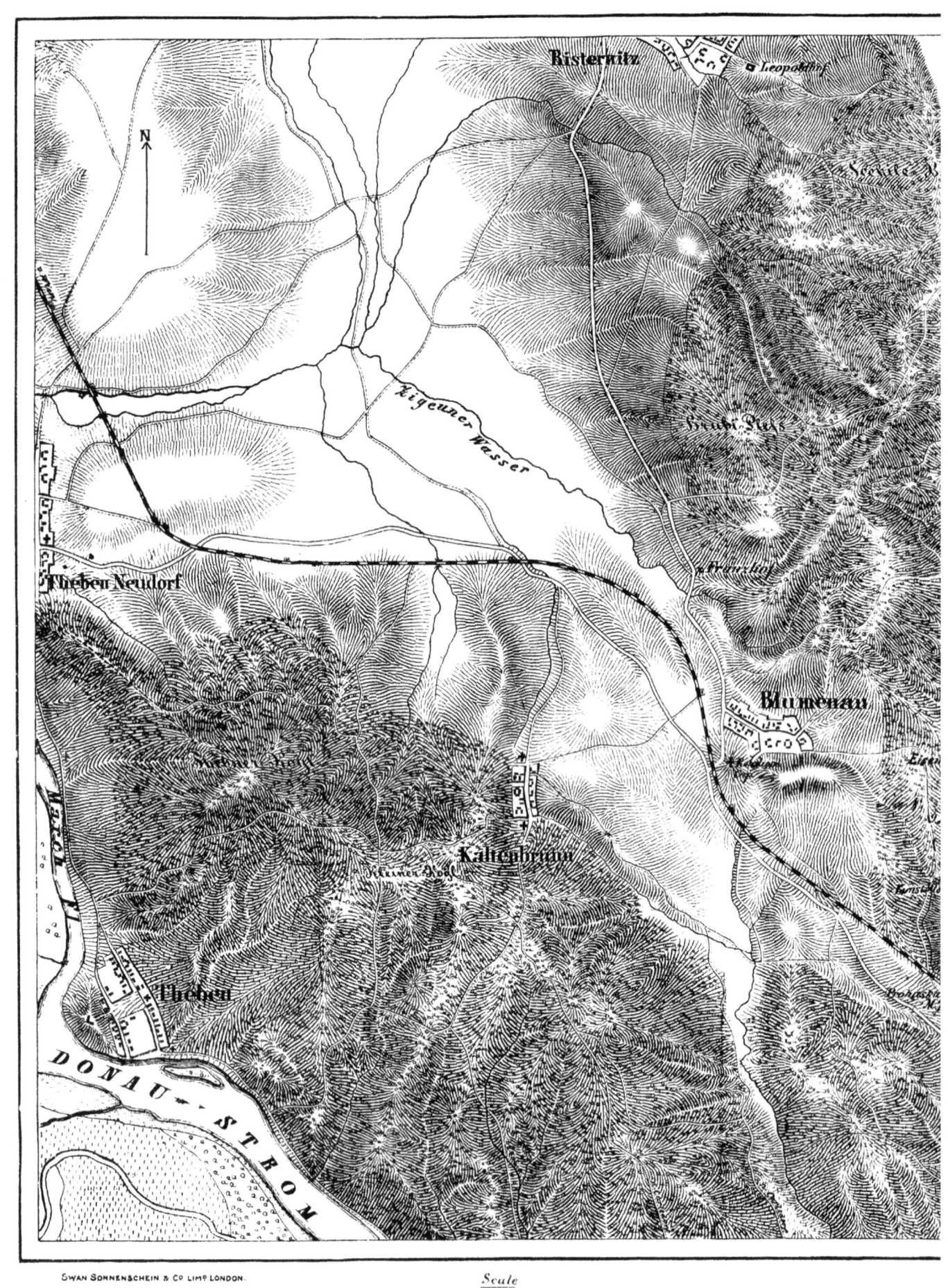

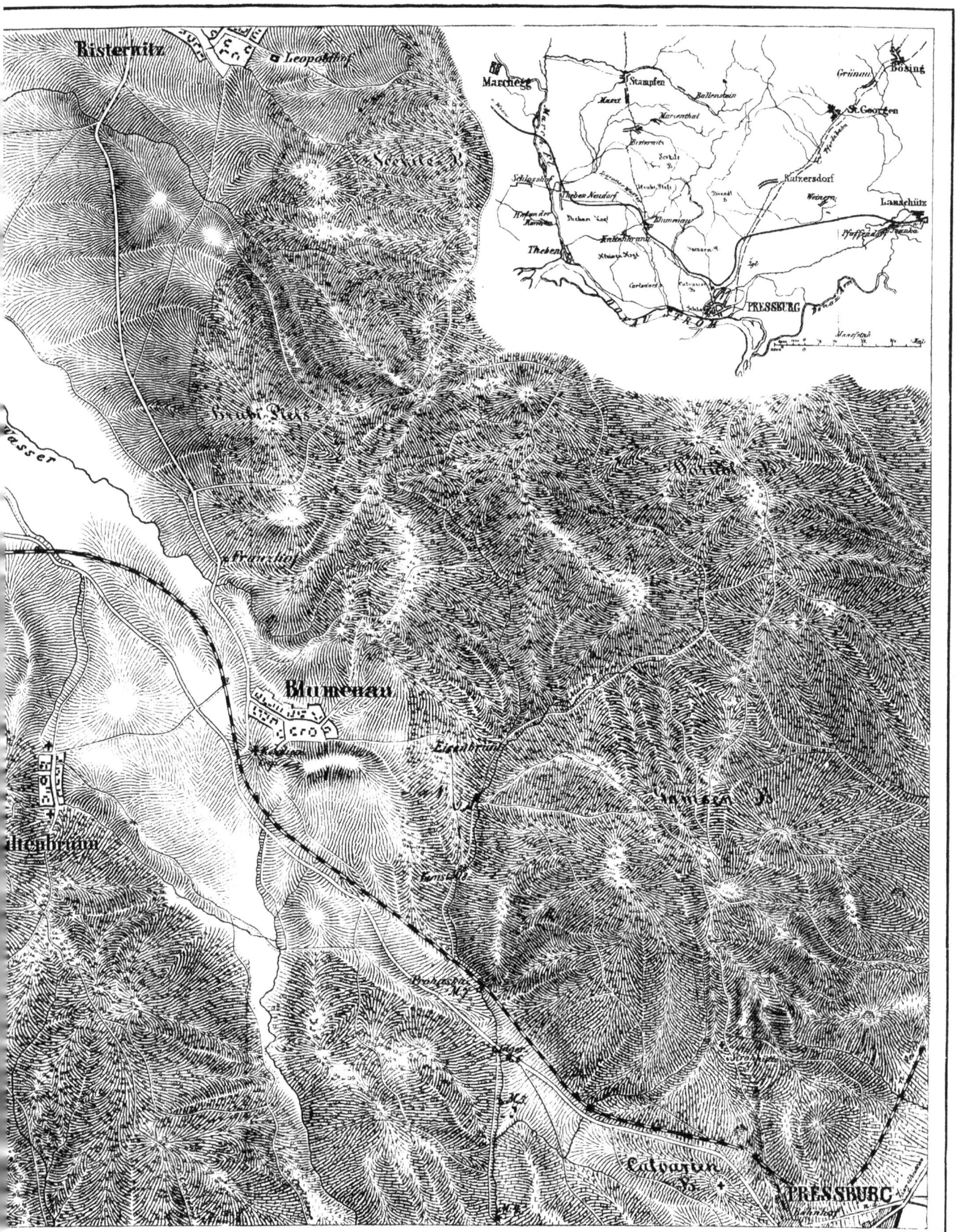
Bisternitz
Leopoldhof
Franzhof
Blumenau
Eisenbrunn
Calvarien B.
PRESSBURG
Marchegg
Stampfen
Ballenstein
Marienthal
Grünau
Bösing
St. Georgen
Ratzersdorf
Weinern
Lanschütz
Schlosshof
Theben Neudorf
Theben
Pfaffendorf

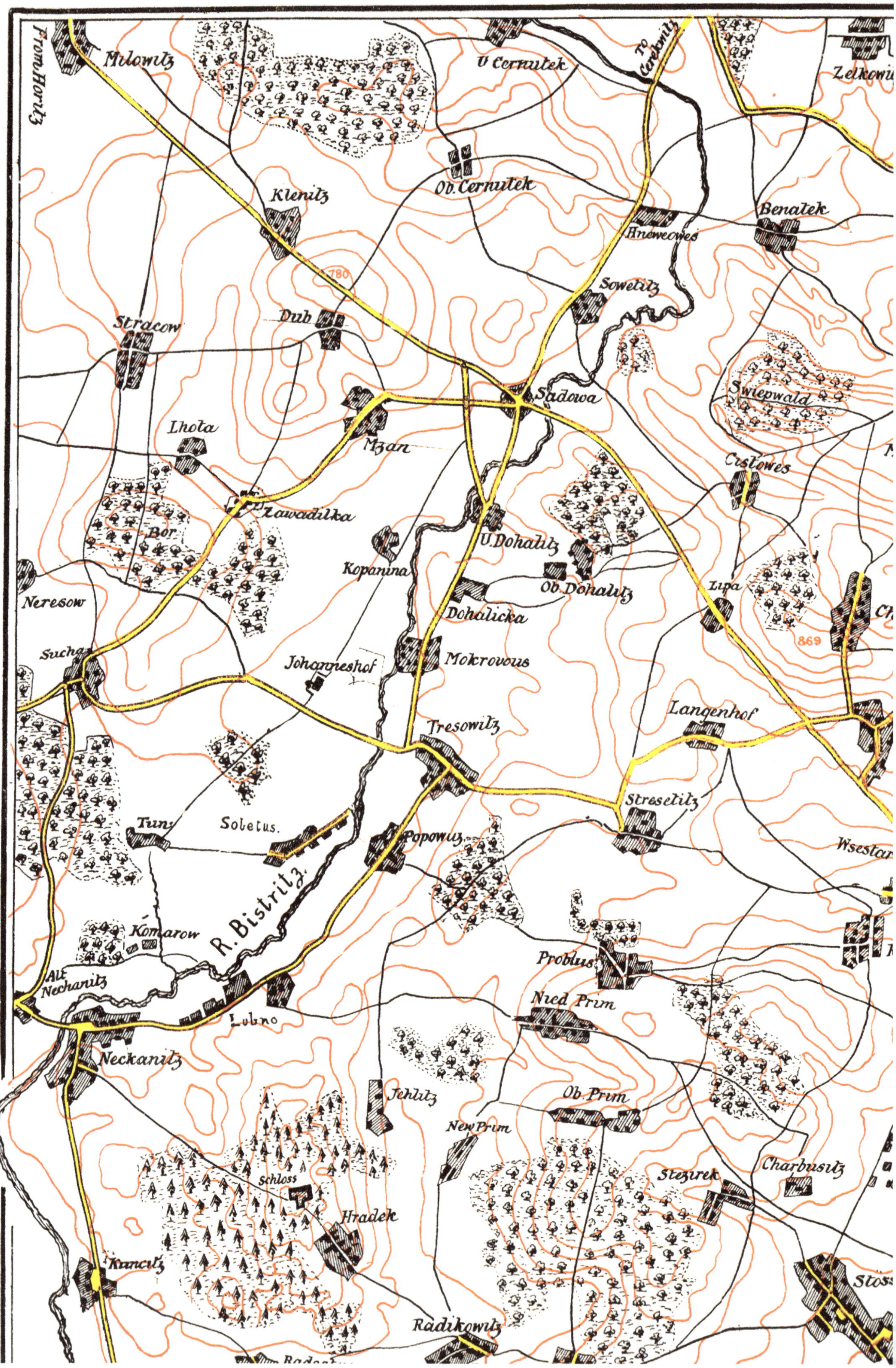

From Horitz
Milowitz
U Cernutek
To Cerekwitz
Zelkowitz
Ob. Cernutek
Klenitz
Benatek
Hneweowes
780
Sowetitz
Stracow
Dub
Swiepwald
Sadowa
Mzan
Lhota
Cistowes
Zawadilka
Bor
U. Dohalitz
Kopanina
Ob. Dohalitz
Neresow
Lipa
Dohalicka
869
Suchá
Mokrovous
Johanneshof
Langenhof
Tresowitz
Stresetitz
Tun
Sobetus
Popowitz
Wsestar
R. Bistritz
Komarow
Problus
Alt Nechanitz
Nied Prim
Lubno
Neckanitz
Jehlitz
Ob. Prim
New Prim
Charbusitz
Schloss
Stezirek
Hradek
Kancitz
Radikowitz

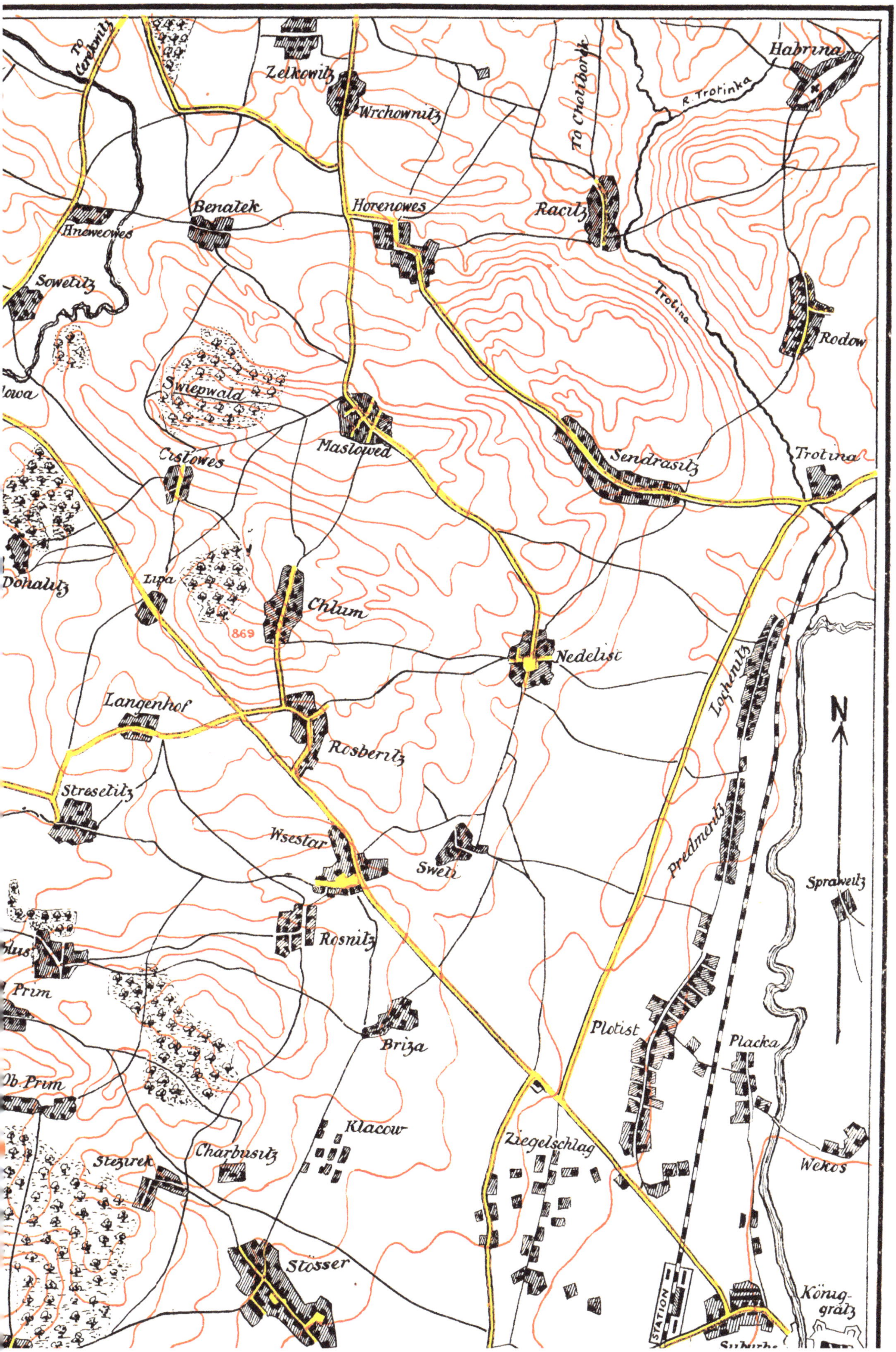
To Cerekwitz
Zelkowitz
Wrchownitz
Habrina
R. Trotinka
Benatek
Hnewcowes
Horenowes
Racitz
Sowetitz
Trotina
Rodow
Swiepwald
Maslowed
Sendrasitz
Trotina
Cistowes
Dohalitz
Lipa
Chlum
869
Nedelist
Lochenitz
N
Langenhof
Rosberitz
Stresetitz
Predmeritz
Wsestar
Swetí
Sprawcitz
Rosnitz
Prim
Plotist
Placka
Briza
Ob. Prim
Klacow
Ziegelschlag
Wekos
Stezirek
Charbusitz
Stosser
STATION
Königgrätz

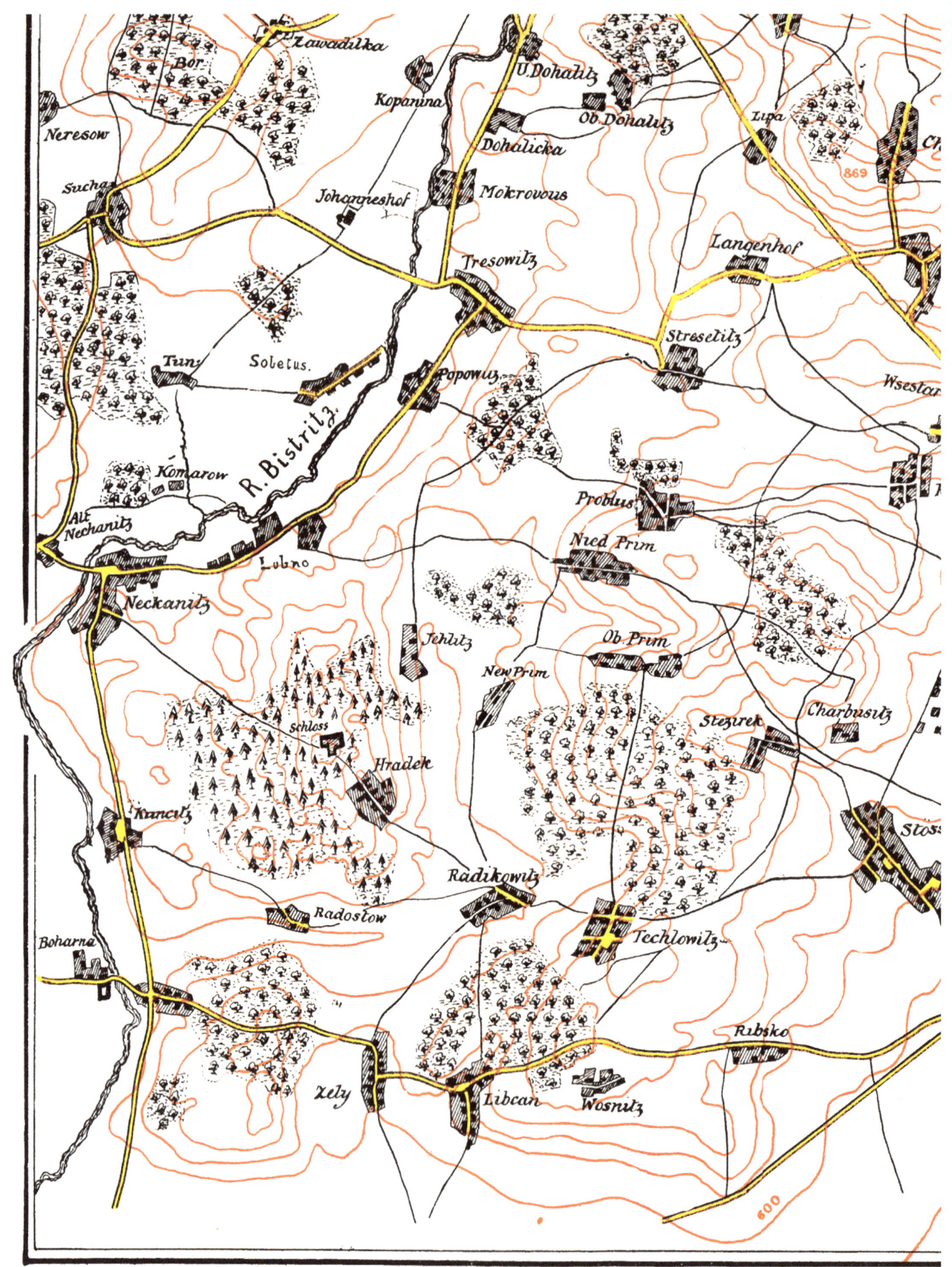

Plan of the Battlefield of Königgrätz (Sadowa)

Scale 1/50,000   Contours 25 ft. V.I.

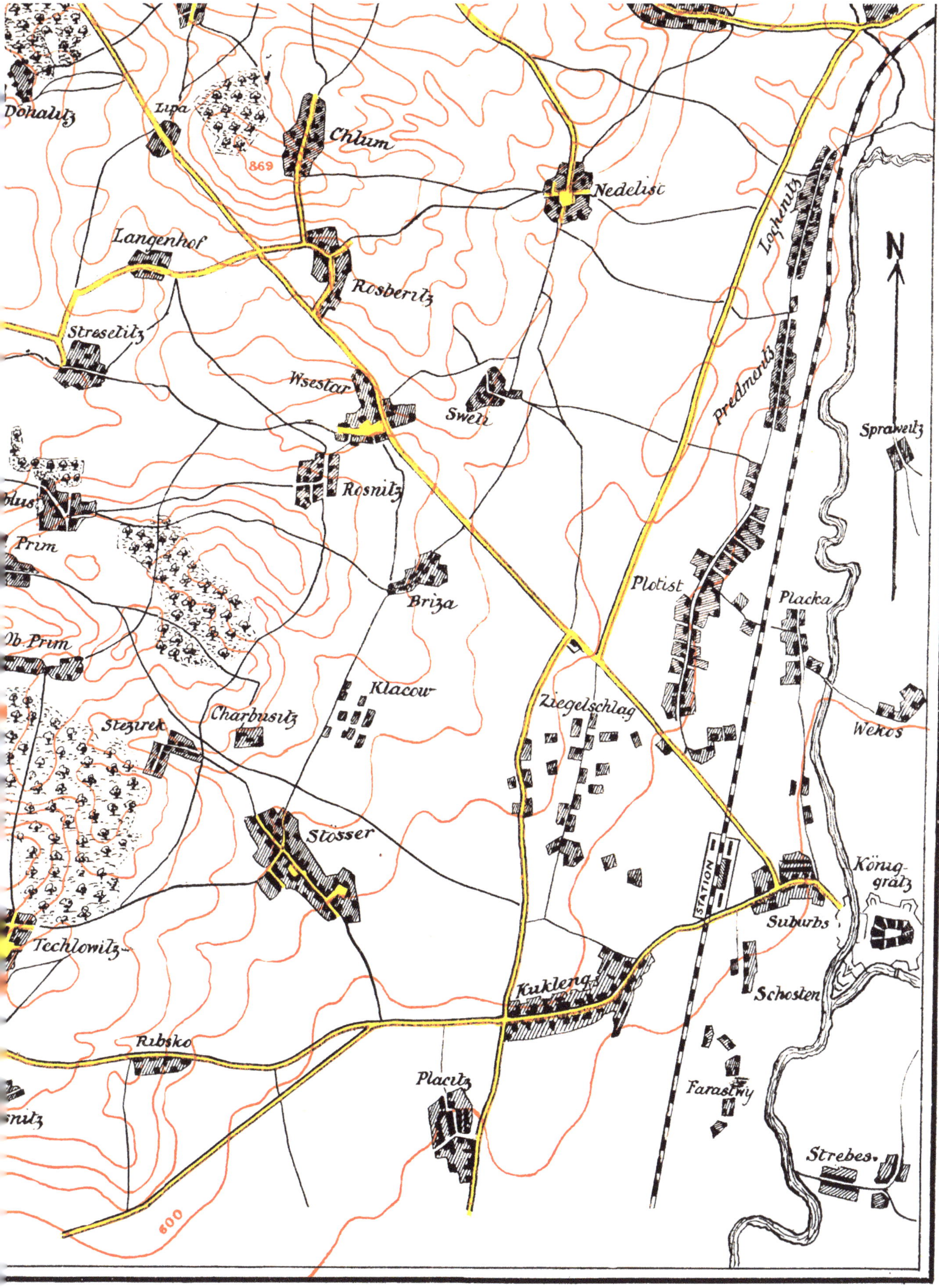
Dohalitz
Lipa
Chlum
869
Nedelist
Langenhof
Rosberitz
Lochenitz
N
Stresetitz
Wsestar
Sweti
Predmeritz
Sprawetz
Rosnitz
Prim
Briza
Plotist
Placka
Ob. Prim
Klacow
Ziegelschlag
Wekos
Charbusitz
Stezirek
Stosser
Königgrätz
STATION
Suburbs
Techlowitz
Schosten
Kuklena
Ribsko
Placitz
Farastwy
Strebes
600

PLAN OF KÖNIGINHOF
29th June 1866

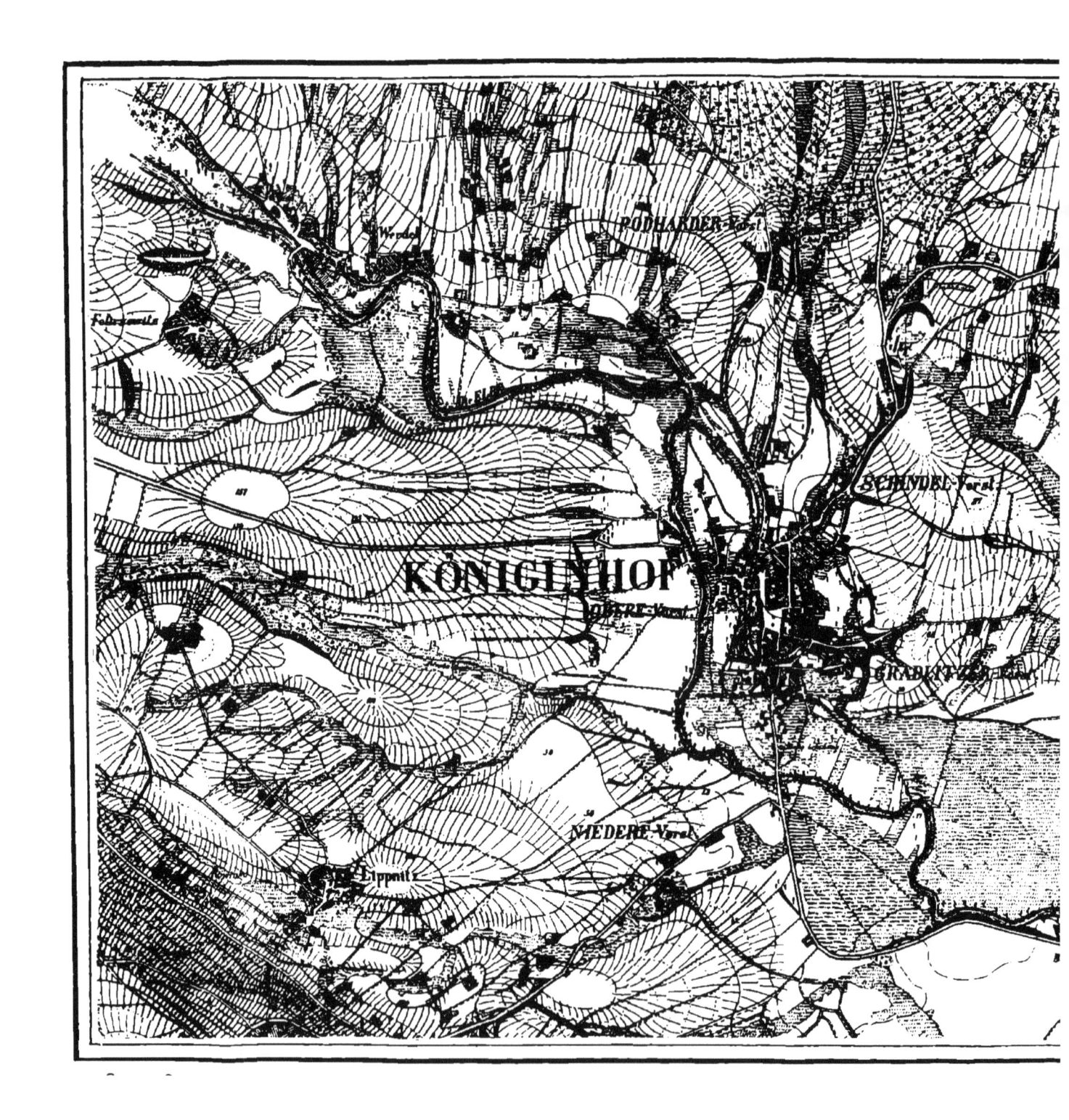

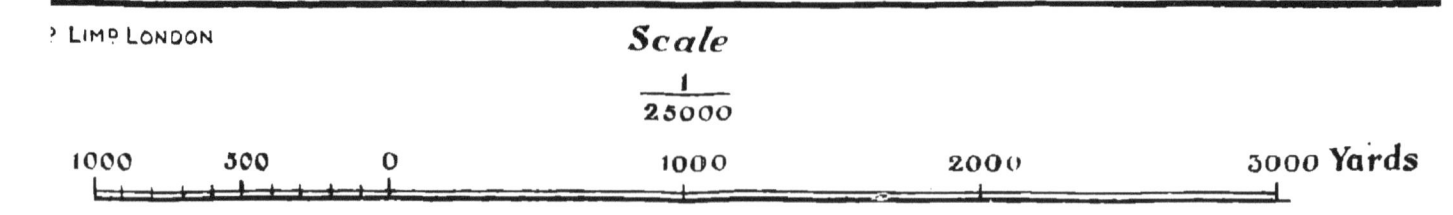

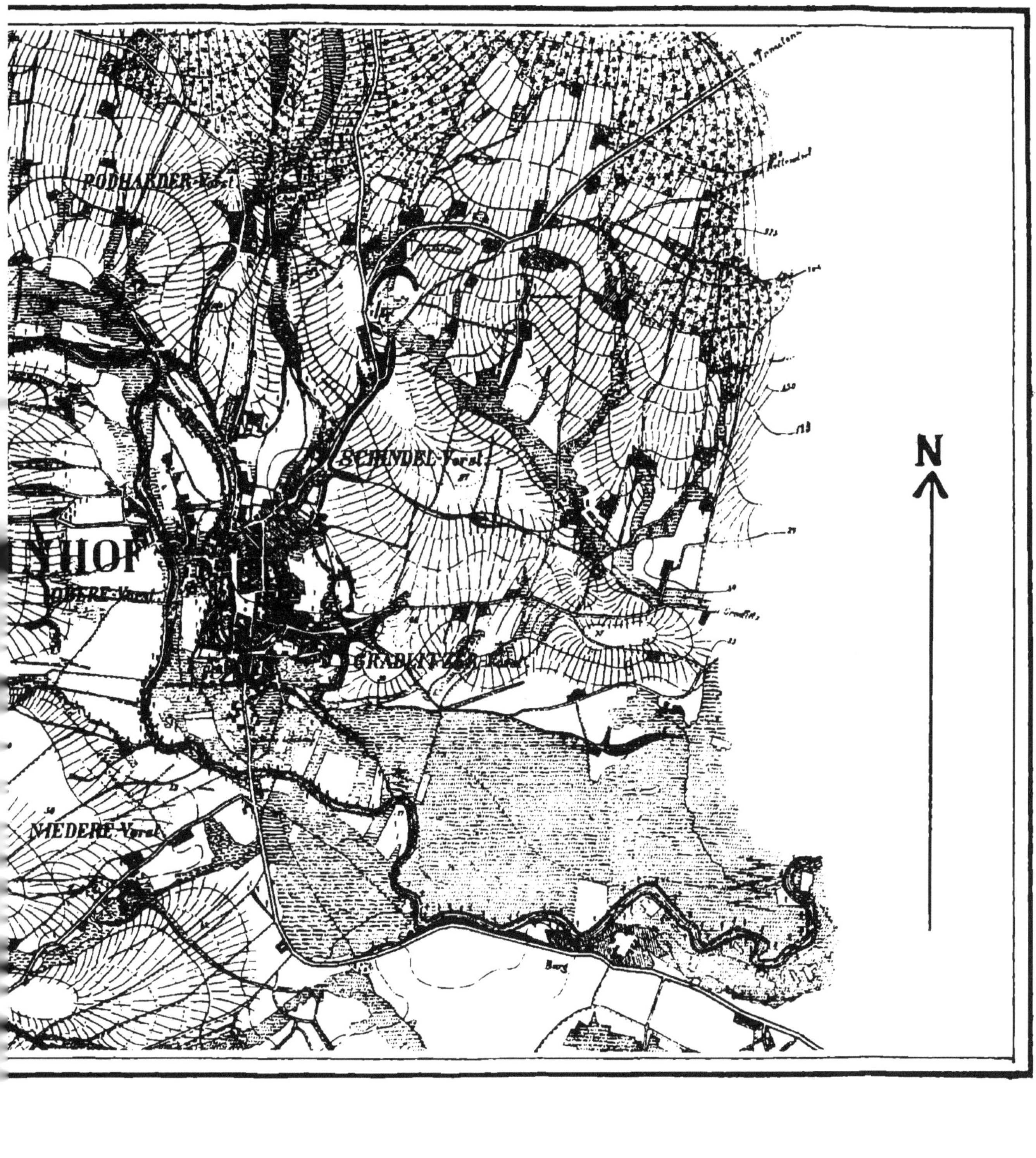
PODHARDER-Vorst.
SCHINDEL-Vorst.
NIEDERE-Vorst.
N

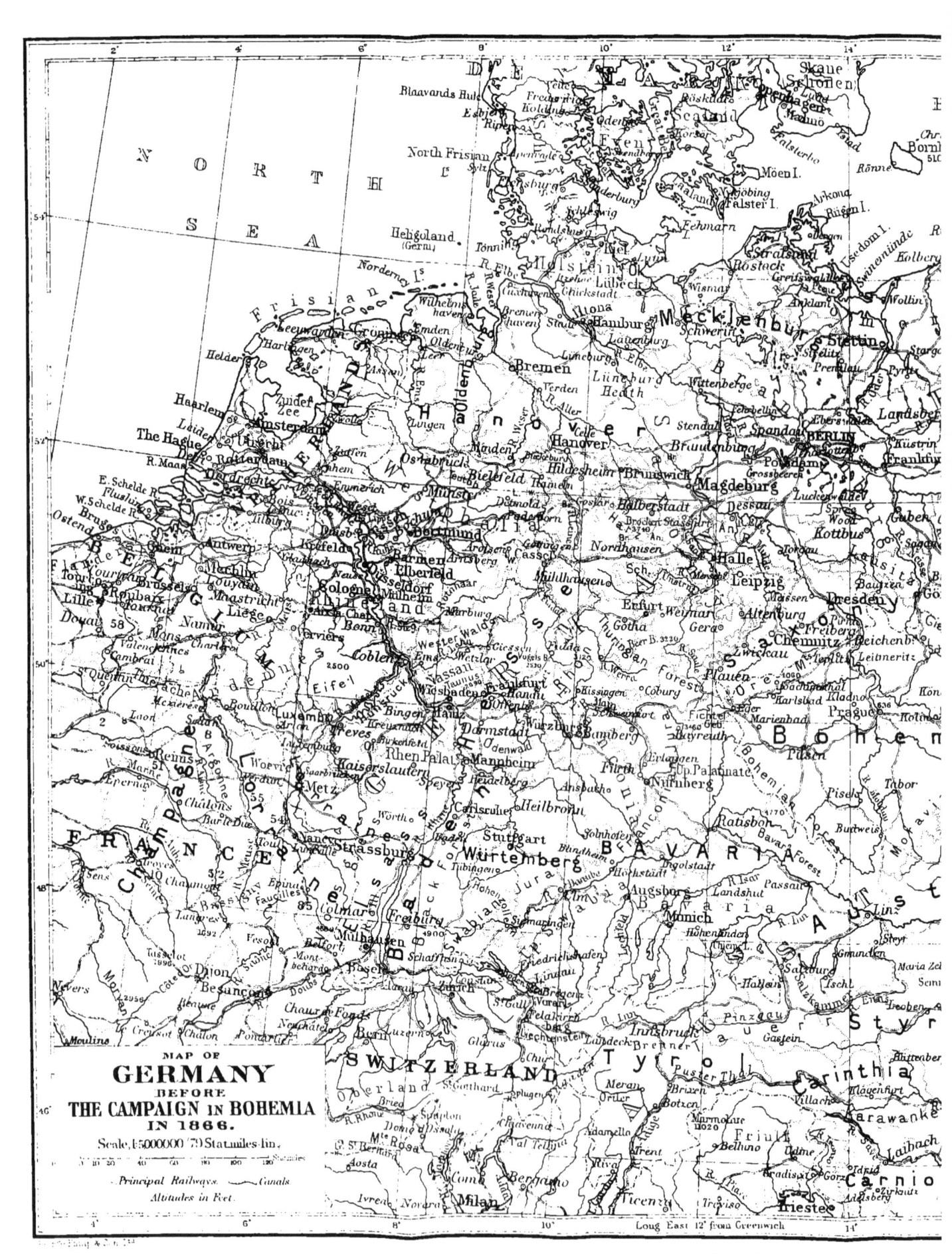

MAP OF
GERMANY
BEFORE
**THE CAMPAIGN IN BOHEMIA
IN 1866.**

Scale, 1:5000000 (79 Stat miles 1 in.)

Principal Railways.   Canals
Altitudes in Feet.

Sonnenschein & Cº Ltd London

The London Geographical Institute

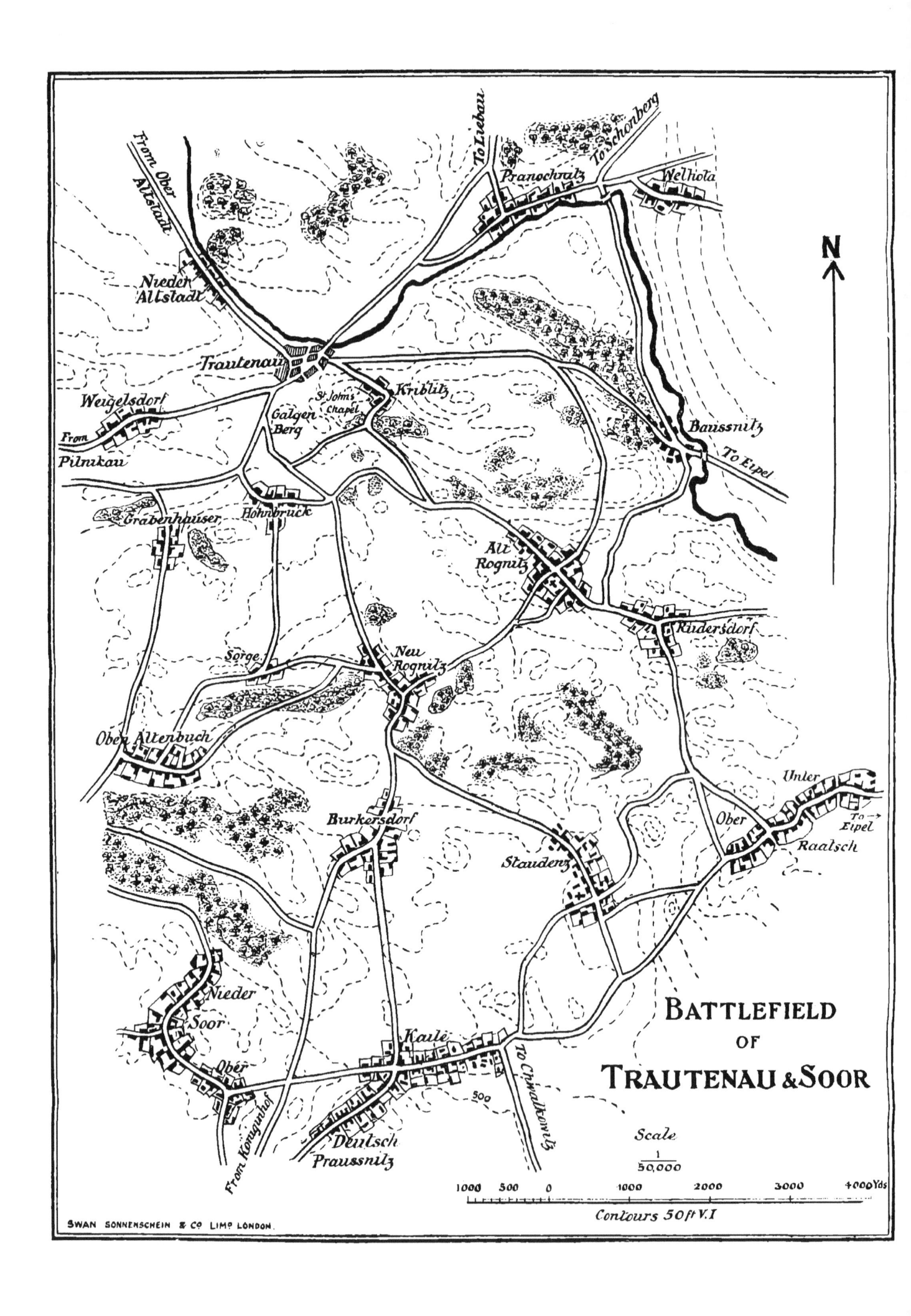

BATTLEFIELD OF TRAUTENAU & SOOR

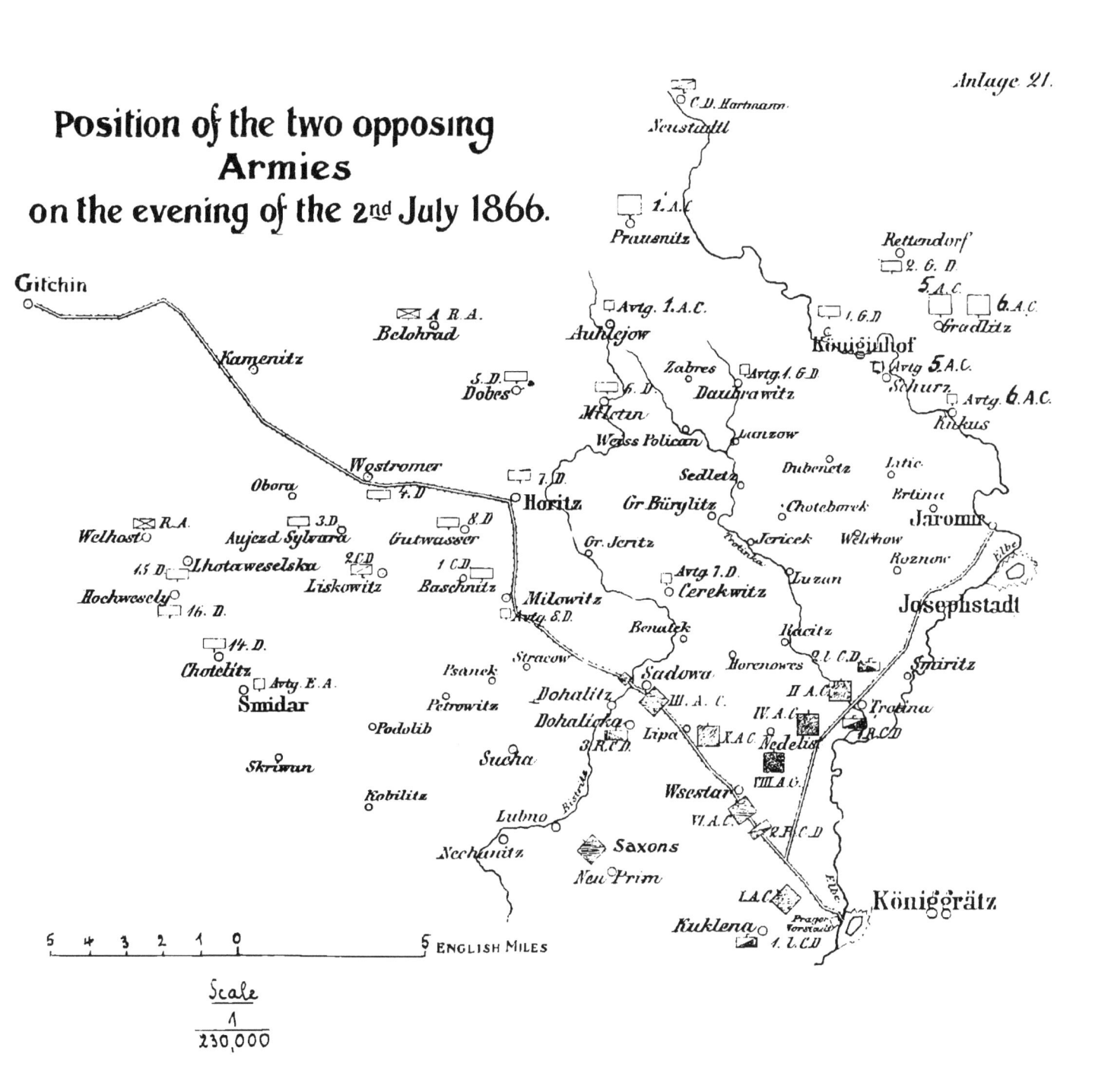

Position of the two opposing Armies on the evening of the 2nd July 1866.

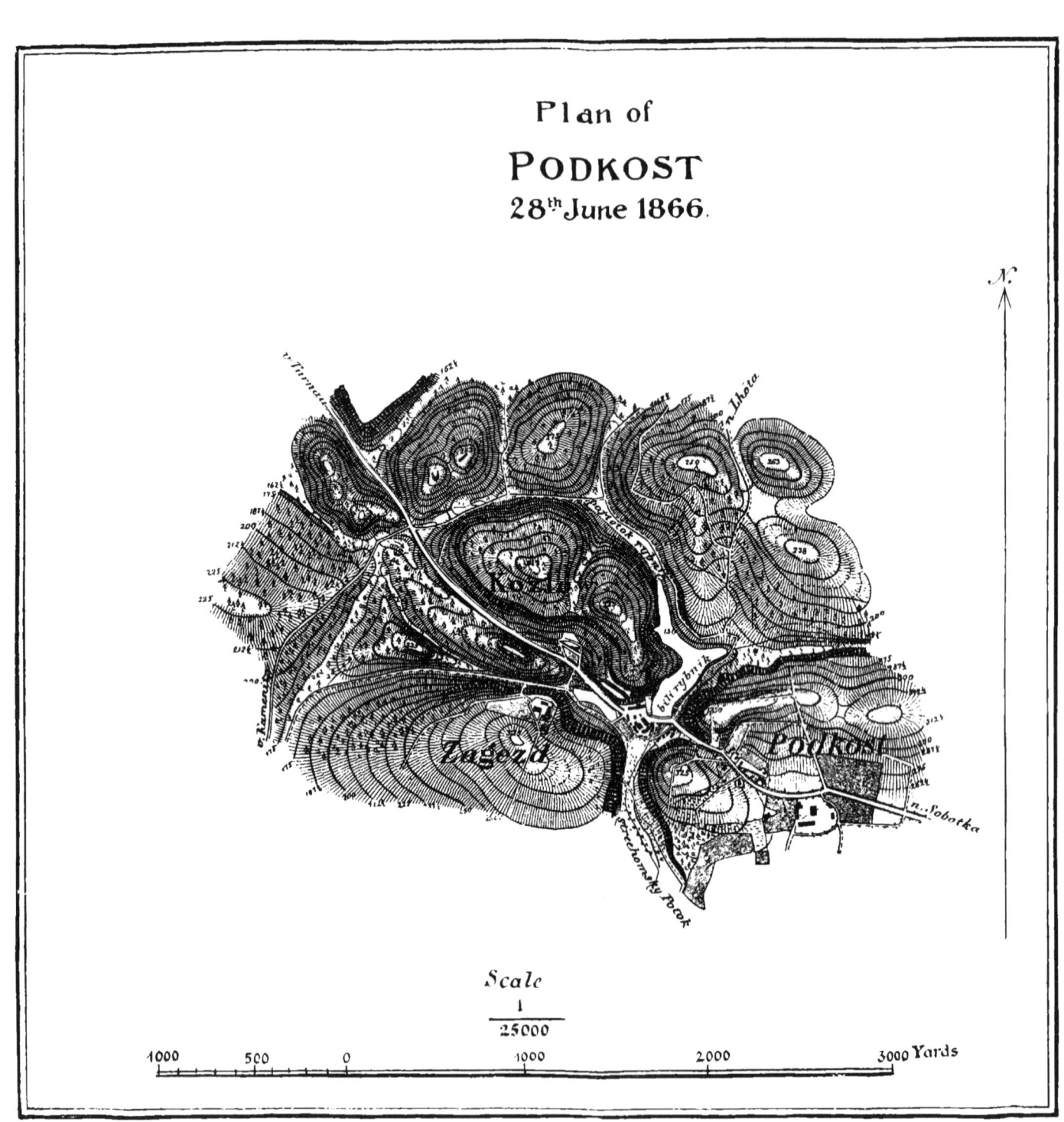

Plan of
PODKOST
28th June 1866.

Scale
1
25000

1000 500 0 1000 2000 3000 Yards

Swan Sonnenschein & Co Limd London